DØ811474

Women and Politics in Latin America

Nikki Craske

Rutgers University Press
New Brunswick, New Jersey

First published in Great Britain 1999
by Polity Press in association with Blackwell Publishers Ltd.

First published in the United States 1999
by Rutgers University Press, New Brunswick, New Jersey

Copyright © Nikki Craske 1999

Library of Congress Cataloging-in-Publication Data and British Library
Cataloguing-in-Publication Data are available upon request.

ISBN 0-8135-2692-2 (cloth)
ISBN 0-8135-2693-0 (pbk)

Printed in Great Britain

Contents

List of Tables

Acknowledgements

Firstly I wish to thank the British Academy for funding my field-work trip to Argentina and Chile in 1995. In Argentina special thanks go to Andrea Conde, of the British Council in Buenos Aires, who provided many invaluable contacts, practical help and friend-ship. I also wish to acknowledge the friendship of María Luisa Livingstone, who made my stay in Buenos Aires particularly enjoyable. While in Argentina I enjoyed the institutional support of CEDES (Centro de Estudios de Estado y Sociedad) and wish to thank, in particular, Silvina Ramos and Mónica Gogna for their kindness. In Chile the help, advice and friendship of María Luisa Rojas at SERNAM (Servicio Nacional de la Mujer) proved indis-pensable. Thanks must also be given to all those I interviewed during the research in both countries.

The incalculable help of friends in developing ideas over the years must be acknowledged: particular gratitude to Fiona Macaulay, whose research trip to Chile coincided with mine, making it much more enjoyable and productive thanks to her gen-erosity; to Alejandra Massolo, whose friendship over many years has been inspirational; to Mariela Méndez, whose kindness in Argentina and support throughout the writing of the text is greatly appreciated; and to Paul Cammack, who gave me sound advice when embarking on the research, filled many gaps in my knowledge of Latin American politics, and made many helpful comments on the manuscript. Thanks also to Mark Jones for responding promptly to queries and advising me on errors. Special acknowledgement must go to Adrian Leftwich, who gave insight-ful criticisms and encouragement in the final stages. Particular gratitude to Jim Martin for the enlightening discussions and for the

patient reading of certain sections of the text. Thanks also to Liam
O'Hagan for compiling the tables in Chapter 3. During my
research trips my family has always provided much practical
support, as well as a quiet corner in which to work when needed:
in this regard special thanks must go to Pippa Craske and Val
Hodges.

The writing of the book took place in the Department of Politics
at Queen's University, Belfast. I wish to thank my Head of
Department, Bob Eccleshall, and colleagues for providing a positive environment in which to complete the task. The staff at Polity
were always helpful and supportive, and I particularly wish to
thank Caroline Richmond for her excellent editorial work. Many
friends and colleagues read all or part of the text and made valuable comments which helped improve it: Vittorio Bufacchi, Judith
Clifton, Richard English, Alice Feldman, Moya Lloyd, Kate Lynch
and Maggie McBride. Any errors, of course, remain mine.

                                                    Nikki Craske

Acronyms

Argentina

APDH:	Asamblea Permanente de Derechos Humanos
	Permanent Assembly for Human Rights
CGT:	Confederación General de Trabajadores
	General Confederation of Workers
CNM:	Consejo Nacional de la Mujer
	National Women's Council
FREPASO:	Frente País Solidario
	Country Solidarity Front
PJ:	Partido Justicialista
	Justicialist Party (Peronists)
PPF:	Partido Peronista Femenino
	Women's Peronist Party
UCR:	Unión Cívica Radical
	Radical Civic Union

Bolivia

MNR:	Movimiento Nacional Revolucionario
	National Revolutionary Movement

Brazil

CNDM:	Conselho Nacional dos Direitos da Mulher
	National Council for Women's Rights
PT:	Partido dos Trabalhadores
	Workers' Party

Chile

EPF:	El Poder Femenino
	Women's Power
PD:	Partido por la Democracia
	Democracy Party
PS:	Partido Socialista
	Socialist Party
SERNAM:	Servicio Nacional de la Mujer
	National Women's Service

Costa Rica

PLN:	Partido de Liberación Nacional
	National Liberation Party

Cuba

CCP:	Cuban Communist Party
CDR:	Comités de Defensa de la Revolución
	Committees for the Defence of the Revolution
FMC:	Federación de Mujeres Cubanas
	Federation of Cuban Women

Mexico

DIF:	Desarrollo Integral de la Familia
	Integral Family Development
EZLN:	Ejército Zapatista de Liberación Nacional
	Zapatista Army of National Liberation
PAN:	Partido de Acción Nacional
	National Action Party
PRD:	Partido de la Revolución Democrática
	Party of the Democratic Revolution
PRI:	Partido Revolucionario Institucional
	Institutional Revolutionary Party

Nicaragua

AMNLAE:	Luisa Amanda Espinosa Nicaraguan Women's Association

AMPRONAC: Nicaraguan Association of Women Confronting National Problems
APMN: Alianza Patriótica de Mujeres Nicaragüenses
Patriotic Alliance of Nicaraguan Women
FSLN: Frente Sandinista de Liberación Nacional
Sandinista Front for National Liberation
OMDN: Organización de Mujeres Democráticas de Nicaragua
Nicaraguan Organization of Democratic Women

Peru

APRA: Alianza Popular Revolucionaria Americana
American Popular Revolutionary Alliance

General

CEDAW: Convention on the Elimination of all forms of Discrimination Against Women
EAP: economically active population
EPZ: export processing zone
ISI: import substitution industrialization
NAFTA: North American Free Trade Agreement
NSS: National Security States
PGI: practical gender interests
SAP: structural adjustment policy
SGI: strategic gender interests

1
Argument

Women have played a central role in the development of Latin American societies and have had a substantial impact on the political systems which have emerged. This book gives an account of women's political participation in Latin America since the 1940s. As it is used here, the term 'political' includes a wide range of activities in which women have participated and through which they have had an effect on political institutions and practices. A central theme in the book is the relationship between motherhood and citizenship and the extent to which the two are compatible. Further, the book considers the political development of a region which has been dogged by authoritarianism and exclusion. By looking at women, the nature of that exclusion and the challenges to it are brought into greater focus. From such a perspective, then, it is also a book about the increasing democratization of Latin America.

In the remainder of this chapter I shall lay out the basic arguments that inform the separate chapters of the book.

Why women?

I start from the premise that women's participation in all aspects of any democratic society is crucial to the quality of democracy itself. Fundamentally, this includes their participation in political institutions. For a political system to be representative, members from all sections of society need to be brought into the decision-making community. Women's participation, therefore, is important for the interests of democracy. This does not imply that there is something inherently unique about women that allows them a greater claim in the political sphere. Yet in many democratic societies women have specific experiences which are systematically excluded from the usual practice of politics. These experiences tend to be associated with 'private' and 'domestic' issues and as such conform to a public–private divide which, as the following chapter argues, is an arbitrary but powerful categorization. As a result, many women have come to organize and resist the constraints on their representation. Often this resistance begins from within the very same conditions of subordination: this is a key feature of women's participation in Latin America.

Politicized mothers

Not all women are mothers; nevertheless, many identify with a notion of womanhood which emphasizes nurturing and caring as 'natural' female characteristics. Women's engagement with caring can add important dimensions to the development of political institutions, and the focus on caring has certainly been a catalyst for many potent political movements in Latin America. If this aspect of life is to be valorized adequately, women have an interest in a democratic practice which ensures that 'their interests' are represented. By including women's concerns, the practice of politics and citizenship can be more sensitive to issues of difference. Yet it is important that these differences should not imply hierarchies. By examining women's increased political participation, we are made aware of how citizenship is a continually developing and dynamic concept.

The focus on women also highlights the diversity of women's experiences. In the past there has been a tendency to see women as a unitary category with specifically 'women's interests'. As a subordinate group women may have some interests in common, but, like men, they have numerous facets to their identities which can lead to a variety of different political agendas. In many cases, identities other than those of gender are at the centre of political mobilization. As Jean Franco suggests, there are moments when 'women's emancipation is bound up with the fate of the larger community' (in Molyneux, 1998: 227).

A common identity among Latin American women is that of motherhood. In Chapter 2, I discuss how motherhood is central to women's identities and cuts across class, ethnicity and nationality. It has significant cultural and political currency and as such lends legitimacy to demands made within this rubric. Thus women often make it a strategically useful mobilizing point. Given this connection between political action and a mothering role, there has been a tendency to view women's collective action as part of the social rather than the political sphere. Latterly, however, the increased involvement of women activists in various arenas and the new research uncovering hidden histories of participation have shown that the stereotype of women's apolitical character has not always been reflected in reality. These developments have challenged some of the paradigms we use to understand political action.

As we shall see in the rest of this book, there is a growing tension between the identities that women have employed in order to gain a foothold in the political arena and the diversity of experiences that characterize their lives in society.

Political exclusion

Women's growing participation has to be understood in the context of a generalized exclusion which has characterized the region's political systems and the long-term struggle for democracy challenging this exclusion. Although political exclusion has been generalized, women have been absent from political participation to a greater degree than men. A number of factors explain these conditions: i) Latin American political systems have been largely authoritarian and have discouraged popular participation except for moments of populism; ii) gender construction in the region has decreed that politics is part of a man's world and an inappropriate activity for women; iii) this in turn has resulted in women's political involvement being ignored, since it has been interpreted as social rather than political. Yet, despite the many constraints which limit their participation in the region, women have succeeded in claiming and colonizing political spaces during the course of the century.

The predominance of authoritarianism and political corruption has had two important consequences for the development of opposition movements. One is the emphasis on autonomy and distance from the institutional political arena: it is often difficult to strike a balance between autonomy and co-optation. The other consequence, particularly for women, is the stress on moral superiority of opposition organizations. For women this becomes linked to motherhood by reinforcing ideas of self-abnegation and rejection of self-interest, thus reflecting an idealized motherhood where women are encouraged to deny their own interests and concentrate on the needs of their children. This suffering for others is often interpreted as women being more able to 'feel' the needs of the community. Both of these factors, however, can act to constrain political activity, not only by limiting tactics and strategies, but also by restricting the possibilities for negotiation, which is an intrinsic part of the political process.

Institutional empowerment

It is my contention that contemporary political, economic and social structures have the potential to aid the empowerment of citizens by conferring and acknowledging rights, providing transparent procedures for the exercise of those rights, and providing support in demanding and claiming rights. Such structures, however, tend towards inertia and are resistant to change; pressure is consequently required to effect and maintain the momentum for change. Given women's participation in all aspects of national development, this is necessary from many sectors: feminist organizations, social movements, workplace organizations, within bureaucracies and from political parties. In my view it is important that the pressure is multifaceted to ensure against a single interpretation of women's interests.

The shifting terrain

Although the region's political systems have tended towards exclusion, there have been important, positive developments linked to women's political participation. There is a dialectical relationship between political change and women's participation, as one reinforces the other. The most salient moments are: i) the democratization struggles which dominated the region in the 1970s and 1980s and which presented new opportunities for women through their involvement in social movements; ii) the re-evaluation of political participation to include previously hidden 'women's issues'; and iii) the development of feminist debates which have an impact on political discourses. This has encouraged a more inclusive notion of citizenship in the new democracies and has stimulated women to claim more rights. This is not to say, however, that the majority of women embrace feminism.

In the following chapters I analyse different areas of social, economic and political life and the impact of women's participation in them. I demonstrate that different arenas present both opportunities and constraints for women's political participation and have different consequences for the development of women's political identities. Since women do not form a homogeneous category, it follows that the impact of parties, work and feminism will vary depending on class, ethnicity, age, access to education and other variables. Women use the resources available to them to further their aims: they conform to social norms in some moments and subvert them in others. The military governments of the 1970s closed traditional political spaces and created the catalyst for new forms of political activity where women were key participants. The transition to democracy was an important moment for making gains while the political process was more fluid. The process of consolidation, however, has resulted in the demobilization of these 'new' actors, and the continuing economic difficulties have reinforced the narrowing of political activity to electoral participation. Consequently, while important gains have been made, particularly for women, for many political participation has declined as social movements have been side-lined by political parties. Furthermore, governments continue to focus on economic restructuring rather than social provision, which was the focus of social movements.

Mothers, women, citizens: tensions

Despite the increased political participation of women over the past few decades and the development of a more inclusionary notion of both citizenship and politics, there are new challenges. I argue that there remains a gender division of labour within institutional politics. Women and men both participate to defend and promote their 'interests', and, in so doing, construct their interests in particular ways. These interests reflect gender construction in society which, for women, still privileges the identity of motherhood. Although motherhood is a key element in gender construction, women have other identities which may challenge motherhood ideals. The emphasis on motherhood has resulted, however, in women focusing more on social and domestic issues when engaging in political activity, as I demonstrate throughout the book. Although motherhood may underpin certain forms of women's political action, there is no direct relationship between

motherhood and particular political agendas, actions and ideologies: motherhood does not determine women's interests
within traditional political discourses such as left–right or progressive–reactionary. Furthermore, parties and regimes of all political
hues have embraced the idealization of motherhood. This idealization tends to essentialize the mothering experience, seeing it as
'destiny' for women, and reinforces the links between womanhood
and social reproduction.

This book also discusses democratization and the development
of citizenship in the region. Most Latin American governments
today endorse liberal democratic values and, consequently, a
liberal concept of citizenship. If citizenship is to be meaningful and
open to all adults, it cannot be predicated on an exclusionary identity. For this reason, among others, motherhood cannot be the basis
of citizenship, but some of the characteristics currently associated
with motherhood, such as caring and life preservation, can inform
and expand an understanding of citizenship. Mothering is a personal experience which gives rise to particularistic demands
among women: citizens' rights must have universal application.

Although women have been able to forge their own spaces,
organizations and agendas, there are still many limitations and
constraints on their political participation. Many women still insist
on an apolitical identity which removes them from long-term participation in the institutional political arena. As such, they are
choosing to reject political participation. This, perhaps, is not surprising given the nature of many political regimes in the region,
which have depended upon coercion and corruption to maintain
control. In these circumstances, it is not unexpected that politics
should remain tainted by these practices and that women should
choose to distance themselves from the political arena. Other limitations and constraints reflect a number of issues: i) that old
vested interests (particularly, in this case, those such as the
Catholic Church, which wishes to preserve traditional gender constructions) are capable of regrouping and reasserting themselves
anew; ii) that the energy needed for ongoing mobilization is great
and that 'mobilization fatigue' sets in; and iii) continued economic
difficulties both generate political demands and limit government
options. Despite women's increased participation, particularly in
social movements, it is the institutional arenas in which the longer-
term consequences are likely to be felt, particularly since social
movements have been on the wane following the return to elected
governments in the 1980s.

Organization of the book

The discussion of women and politics in this book examines different arenas of politics in which women have participated: namely, institutional politics, the workplace, social movements, revolutionary movements and feminism. The institutional political sphere is important as the major decision-making arena and where citizens rights are conferred and defended. Women's legal rights have been established and parties and governments are quick to use women-friendly rhetoric, but they are less keen to promote women representatives. The workplace is a potential area of empowerment since financial independence has helped many women negotiate shifting gender relations. For men paid work remains a principal identity, while for women it is secondary at best. This has implications for workplace struggles and deciding which issues are seen as workers' concerns. Despite women's engagement in wage labour, to date, mainstream unions are not very attractive to women; however, women workers are having an impact in certain professions, most notably teaching. There are also interesting examples of a more holistic approach to union activity, one which does not try to separate rigidly public and private issues and one which is more appealing to women. These may have lessons for the labour movement generally in an era of deregulation.

A discussion of social movements is essential given their important contribution to the development of citizenship and democratization in the region. This is all the more necessary since women have been major protagonists in the rise of social movements. Chapter 6 demonstrates that women are successfully mobilized when their interests, however they define them, are at the centre of campaigns. Women's political education through these movements has had broad implications for the post-authoritarian settlement, but it has been difficult for women to maintain the pressure on government when economic conditions are governments' main concern.

The region has experienced a number of revolutions and armed struggles over the years, and the advancement of women has often been caught up in these struggles. In the case of Cuba and Nicaragua, the new states addressed women's concerns directly. Consequently no discussion of women and politics in the region would be complete without an analysis of revolutions. Chapter 7 shows how resilient gender discourses are, and how revolutionary regimes mobilize women around the same motherist ideals prevalent in other political systems. Revolutionary states have provided some important opportunities and structures for improving the lot of women, but many 'women's issues' remain side issues and have been sacrificed in difficult times.

Despite the antagonism towards feminism from all types of political actors and institutions, feminist thought and activities have had an impact on political development in Latin America. The discussion on feminisms in Chapter 8 demonstrates the dynamism of women's activism at all levels. There is much tension between different women's organizations in the region, which reflects the many feminist theories that abound as well as the conflicts between 'womanist' and 'feminist' perspectives. Although the majority of women do not identify with feminism, it has had an undeniable effect on political discourses and participation by bringing new debates into the arena.

However, before we look at women's substantive, material participation, chapters 2 and 3 will review the context in which that activity occurs. Chapter 2 discusses the development of gender construction in the region. Gender relations are constantly being renegotiated at the personal level, but ideal types are much more resistant to change and are reflected in public discourses across the political spectrum. Chapter 3 surveys the social, political and economic context, as well as looking at the 'average' Latin American woman through a discussion of demographic characteristics.

Conclusions

The underlying claim of this book is that it is important to note the many changes women have effected in the development of citizenship and political structures without denying the continued problems and challenges. These challenges continue in a time when, increasingly, the Latin American political arena is narrowly focused on the electoral stage. The political arena is itself constrained by stringent economic limitations, given the costly restructuring which is ongoing in the region: these issues pose particular problems for women. I would suggest that the 1990s represents a period of consolidation and political quiescence after the years of struggle against authoritarianism. Even in the heyday of political activism, only a minority of women were involved. The gains made through women's participation can be enormous for individuals, but on the broader canvas they can be small and, regrettably, often reversible.

2
Women and Political Identity in Latin America

Introduction

In this chapter I focus on the development of gender construction in Latin America and how this is reflected in the political identity of women. It is important to examine the different cultural constraints and opportunities which dictate 'appropriate' behaviour for women and how these constructions are continually challenged by them. Over the course of the century women have become greater players in the politics of the region. Women's exclusion from the power arenas must be understood in the context of highly authoritarian and exclusionary systems (discussed in the following chapter), but systems have been gendered in a way which leaves women in a weaker position than men. Clearly, there are other constraints, such as ethnicity, class, geography and age, but the main focus here is on the constraints gender construction places on women.

Despite the difficulties, women have achieved a greater voice and presence in the region's politics, and consequently they have had an impact on the development of citizenship. For the majority their political identity remains tightly linked to the mothering role. Motherhood offers a particular entry into politics and has significant cultural value which allows a power base for women, but it brings with it certain constraints. The discussion of gender constructions here includes an analysis of machismo and *marianismo*. This is followed by an examination of the role of motherhood within political identities, which draws on Kaplan's (1982) notion of 'female consciousness' and Alvarez's (1990) formulation of 'militant motherhood'. Defence of motherhood roles has led to the emergence of new rights, which have been incorporated into discourses around citizenship and which, in turn, have become more sensitive to 'gender interests': to understand this, I analyse the development of gender interests and citizenship.

Constructing gender relations

Gender construction is a cultural phenomenon, inasmuch as the content and significance of being a woman (or a man) is not constant across different countries or indeed necessarily within one country. It is clear that being a twenty-year-old working-class woman in Buenos Aires is very different from being an elderly peasant woman in the Bolivian Andes or a professional in Mexico. So while there are biological distinctions between women and men, the most obvious being the ability to bear children, these do not explain the gendered power relations that exist. Nevertheless, there are trends underpinning gender relations in many societies which give rise to biological explanations for the subordinate position of women. The role of motherhood is a biological function but its value is culturally given.[1]

In Latin American societies, as in many others, motherhood is seen as the primary role for women, although fatherhood is not seen as the overriding role for men. Emphasis is placed on the complementary nature of the roles of women and men in society but with the authority of the male (Martin, 1990), which can disguise subordination. Many factors influence the development of gender relations: Latin America has many ethnicities and races, including indigenous peoples, colonizers predominantly from the Iberian peninsula, entrepreneurs (especially from Britain in the nineteenth century), slaves from Africa, and, latterly, immigrants from southern Europe (particularly Italians in Argentina). All these peoples brought with them social formations which included particular gender relations, but the dominant form was set by the colonizers and reinforced by the Catholic Church.[2] Gender relations both shape and are shaped by political structures in society; consequently there is a dialectical relationship between gender relations and political change. Changes in one lead to changes in the other, with a constant set of (re)negotiations.

Socio-political structures have been predicated upon a separation of public and private spheres. Within this model men were actors in the public, powerful world of politics and the economy, while women have been dominant in the private world of domestic organization and responsible for reproduction. This separation represented an idealized type mediated by class and ethnicity, and corresponded more to the lives of the rich. Safa (1995) suggests that the distinction is greater in Latin America than in industrial Western societies. Here, poorer and subordinate ethnic groups crossed the divide particularly in relation to work, stigmatizing wage-earning women given the strong associations with these subordinate groups (ibid.). Most aspired to conform to the ideal of woman as home-maker and man as breadwinner, so the home became women's priority, regardless of other responsibilities. Since the public and private dichotomy is not a description of lived realities of the majority, it frequently contributes to making women invisible or undervalued by, for example, depicting them as 'unproductive housewives' when they are involved in income-generation activities (see Chapter 5).

The importance of the divide for this analysis is its influence in constructing the ideal of a non-working woman whose main role is mother and housewife, and the degree to which women identify with this regardless of personal circumstances. Although women cross the public–private divide to work and involve themselves in community activities, these are often perceived as secondary or complementary to their home-making activities. The distinction helps reinforce exaggerated gender stereotypes of machismo and *marianismo*, to which we now turn.

Machismo and *marianismo*

The term 'macho' has inveigled its way into the English language to mean sexist attitudes and behaviour coupled with masculine bravado. Stevens (1973: 90) describes it as 'the cult of virility [whose] chief characteristics are exaggerated aggressiveness and intransigence in male-to-male relationships and arrogance and sexual aggression in male-to-female relationships'. It incorporates a notion of fearlessness and honour which gives men certain rights over women, perhaps best reflected in the laws which, in certain circumstances, allowed men to kill with impunity adulterous wives,[3] and granted them control over children (*patria potestad*). In addition there are cultural norms which reflect machismo, including excessive drinking, domestic violence, insistence on a large family to indicate virility, and the demand that a wife stay at home to concentrate on family life and be a 'good woman'.[4]

The notion of honour is important to these constructions of both femininity and masculinity. Within this model it is accepted that men enjoy sex and have relationships outside marriage while women do not. Women are classified as good women ('pure' women: mothers, sisters and wives) or whores (effectively the rest). Obviously, these characteristics do not reflect the attitudes of all Latin American men, but they do indicate certain parameters of acceptable behaviour and the lack of sanctions for behaviour which is prejudicial to women's welfare.

The female corollary is *marianismo*, where the ideal of womanhood is self-abnegating motherhood. This is very much reinforced by the iconography of the Virgin Mary that is central to Catholicism. The key to understanding the cult of the Virgin is that it is an impossible role model to follow: a virgin mother. Evelyn Stevens (1973) points out that the cult of motherhood can be traced back to pre-Christian times and has certain parallels in the pre-Hispanic Americas: the apparition of the Virgin of Guadalupe in the early years of conquest was on the site of worship of a mother goddess (Stevens, 1973: 94). Although her essay may seem dated and gives exaggerated examples of appropriate female behaviour, the basic underpinnings of the construction of womanhood, and thus gender relations, hold true. The key aspects are moral superiority and spiritual strength combined with a submissiveness towards men. But latent in this submissiveness is the conviction that men are like children who need to be humoured. These characteristics are seen throughout this book as lying behind official discourses on women, public pronouncements by politicians of all political shades, and women's views of themselves. As Stevens acknowledges, women have rarely conformed to this ideal type; however, like machismo for men, *marianismo* does influence women's views and activities and sets parameters for 'appropriate' female behaviour.

Like women everywhere, however, Latin American women are taking on new roles in all areas, involving both costs and benefits at the personal level, but 'decent' women have to be wary of moving too far beyond the idealized types. Despite the changes, it remains unusual for women to live alone outside the grand metropolis; many women, if they are financially able, give up work on marriage or when they have children; and men are still expected to pay for women on dates: these hold true to varying degrees depending on the country. I would suggest that at present there are frequently clashes between what women expect as of right, resulting from recent struggles, and what they think due to them as a result of more traditional gender constructions.[5] To put it bluntly, they want the best of both worlds, understandably maybe.

Marianismo *and politics*

The persistence of *marianismo* with particular emphasis on mother-hood is seen in women's involvement in Latin American politics. Politics is viewed as part of the male arena and tainted by corruption. Consequently, it is not the place for 'decent' women unless (as is demonstrated in chapters 4 and 6) extreme circumstances prevail or their participation reflects 'social issues'. Martin (1990) suggests, in the Mexican case, that the use of the image of the Virgin of Guadalupe in crisis moments in the nation's history underlines the association of women and exceptional politics. In the political arena there is still a strong association between woman, mother and social reproduction, which is reflected in the areas in which women participate. In her work on 'supermadres', Chaney (1973) demonstrates how women have entered the political arena as an extension of their domestic role and use the language of the home. She also shows how women were often set apart from the 'serious' side of politics in women's sections that dealt with 'appropriate' feminine concerns of welfare: there was a concern that women would find politics too seamy – 'the wife might hear something not nice for her ears' (in Chaney, 1973: 117).

Although these views are changing, the perception of the moral superiority of women, especially if they are mothers, still permeates ideas regarding their role in politics. This occurs both in the formal sphere of institutions and the informal arena of social movements (Martin, 1990). The populist discourse of the 1940s placed particular emphasis on marianist ideals of motherhood and submissiveness, which is exemplified by Eva Perón's speeches. Furthermore, people on both the left and the right emphasize the superior moral qualities of women, whom they see first and foremost as mothers.[6] In the 1990s there are indications that there is a new breed of female politician emerging who has broken away from identifying too strongly with these stereotypes: it is difficult to imagine Argentina's Julia Alsogoray or Mexico's Beatriz Paredes conforming to these norms. But change is slow, and one of the region's most high-profile politicians, Garciela Fernández Meijide, commented that many male politicians still saw her as 'Mrs Mop', there to clean up politics. Furthermore, as Molyneux

(1998: 222 fn 7) notes, women have made inroads into traditional male preserves, but 'this has not implied an erosion of gender roles as such; rather it has required a redefinition of women's place within society as a whole, one which has added on to, rather than eliminated, their traditional gender responsibilities, while leaving men's largely untransformed.'

Motherhood and paid work

The centrality of the motherhood role has withstood the transformations brought about by changing work patterns. Despite the increased participation of women in paid labour, a recent study on working mothers in Mexico indicated how motherhood remained their prime identity. Furthermore, this was changing slightly only for the few women who were engaged in 'the professions': 'many women from different social classes still consider motherhood as their source of identity and only a very educated and privileged group speaks with ambivalence regarding their mother's role' (García and de Oliveira, 1997: 382). In this study, however, the authors comment 'that the ideology of motherhood hardly touches upon the real content of mothering, its contradictions, its conflicts and the heavy burden that it entails' (ibid.: 370). Biology may not be destiny but it does overshadow women's lives, and motherhood seems to be remarkably resistant as a cultural identity. Changes in work patterns may be quite marked, but the commitment to the reproductive arena generally takes precedence over work and careers.

The more extreme elements of *marianismo* have waned,[7] but there remains a construction of womanhood which emphasizes mothering and nurturing as the natural destiny for women. The maintenance of the good moral characteristics of women has been predicated on excluding them from key areas of power. Consequently, women's freedom of movement is more constrained than men's: they cannot come and go with the same ease, and this has an impact on their political participation. Women (or more particularly girls) are still occasionally discouraged from pursuing education; are sometimes forbidden, or strongly discouraged, from working outside the home, particularly after having children (yet women's income generation remains vital to the survival of many families); and cannot go out with friends easily in the evening. While these constraints may be more prevalent in Latin America, they can still be found alive and well in many 'progressive' northern countries as well. Nevertheless, although motherhood remains central to women's lives, reflecting many marianist ideals, what it signifies does not remain static. It may constrain women and limit their choices but it has also given them certain rights in the public domain in defence of nurturing roles (see particularly Chapter 6). Below we discuss female consciousness and militant motherhood as politicized versions of *marianismo*.

Conceptualizing women's political participation

Given its cultural importance, it is not surprising that motherhood should be central to the political identity of many women. This sometimes leads to what Alvarez (1990) terms 'militant motherhood' or politicized motherhood (see also Bouvard, 1994; Perelli, 1994; Craske, 1993). Throughout this book it is clear that the mothering role specifically has pushed many women into political action. Temma Kaplan's (1982) work on female consciousness has focused on this type of political action and has been used in the literature on Latin America. She identified it when examining the activities of women strikers in Barcelona in 1919–20. She maintains that there is something unique about women's view of the world which gives them a particular attitude to political activity that is closely allied to protecting life: 'the bedrock of women's consciousness is the need to preserve life' (Kaplan, 1982: 546). This resonates with Catholic teaching on women: a woman 'cannot find herself except by giving love to others'.[8]

Female consciousness

When examining women's collective action, Kaplan uses the language of life preservation in a broad way which generally corresponds to daily reproduction. In her analysis, women's defence of the gender division of labour is central; that is, the action does not challenge dominant gender constructions. Kaplan's concept is particularly useful in focusing on women from the popular classes and how they mobilize in defence of their interests, and it brings the domestic arena into the political picture. Generally these issues conform to Molyneux's (1985) concept of practical gender interests (see below).

That there are ideas central to the world view of women and which, if under attack, become the basis for collective action is evident in Latin America. The rise of social movements in the 1970s and 1980s which focused on human rights and family welfare illustrate women's defence of nurturing roles (see Chapter 6). While female consciousness tends to reinforce the distinction between public and private spheres of action by defending the gender division of labour and the domestic world of women, it supersedes the distinction when the conditions are extreme and public action needs to be taken. The concept, I suggest, is more useful for understanding women's motives when they are mobilizing in 'women's groups'[9] than when they participate in more 'conventional' political organizations, such as parties. It is a rather static concept which may explain the reasons why some women *begin* to organize collectively, but it doesn't really allow for growth as new issues and perspectives are introduced. Indeed, as Kaplan acknowledges, it is a concept of conservative political behaviour.

The idea that these activities 'preserve life' may be the case in extreme circumstances, such as human rights and communal survival organization. In the Latin American context, however, the issues raised within the rubric of what might be called female consciousness also include projects which improve family welfare. The language of life preservation seems overly emotional and can overemphasize gender differences: good caring women/bad uncaring men. Furthermore, the concept of female consciousness tends towards a monolithic reading of womanhood which positions the protection of life at the centre and thus places women's political activity within certain confines. So while this vision of womanhood may explain a significant amount of political action, particularly for those women who identify with the nurturing role created for them in *marianismo*, not all women can be said to conform to it. The idea that women have a 'unique' consciousness could lead to the reversing of a hierarchy which has privileged men's political activity in the past. Are we to assume that women who display another set of motivations for political activity are deviant? One is led to think of classic cases such as Margaret Thatcher, Indira Gandhi or Golda Meir, but also Eva Perón, who may have used the language of motherhood, but whose interest in power was not in defence of the gender division of labour.

Female consciousness may be a politicized version of *marianismo* and can add to our analysis of women's political participation, but as it stands it is too steeped in essentialism. It is more useful if we see female consciousness as something learned through identification with certain gender constructions that centre upon nurturing, rather than focusing on the emotive language of life preservation. Thus while more women than men come to politics through issues associated with nurturing, this may shift as gender constructions shift. If Kaplan's reading of 'life preservation' is broad enough to include daily reproduction, it could also include many activities in which men habitually engage: trade union activity is concerned with job security and wages, which have an impact on life preservation in the same broad fashion. The concept, nevertheless, was important for highlighting the connection between motherhood and political action through the politicization of 'networks of everyday life' (Kaplan, 1982: 545). Furthermore, it shows how potent motherhood can be as a political identity.

Militant motherhood

Militant motherhood is a more useful conceptual tool for Latin America. Alvarez (1990) sees this in the development of social movements in Brazil during the military government (1964–85). The politicization of daily life was heightened by the extreme conditions of the military National Security States (NSS) coupled with the severe economic crisis from the mid-1970s. The NSS closed off the usual channels of political participation and ignored women's collective action because the military didn't understand it as political. Women's usually social, reproductive role became the centre of a new political identity and militant motherhood became a force to be reckoned with (see Chapter 6). Both female consciousness and militant motherhood indicate that issues previously seen as apolitical and/or social concerns are readily politicized in certain circumstances. Furthermore, mother as political actor subverts marianist notions of motherhood and has great symbolic power. There are many, such as the Argentinian Madres de la Plaza de Mayo, who see motherhood as 'above' politics and who engage with marianist ideals of women's moral superiority. Their claim on the political arena responds to a higher moral claim. Martin (1990) suggests that women's role of suffering for their children allows them to 'feel' the problems of the community more keenly. Despite this emphasis on 'extraordinary' politics, chapters 4 and 5 demonstrate that women, like their male counterparts, also become involved in activities which have little direct bearing on their domestic identities. The focus on motherhood can overshadow women's other interests and demands.

Alvarez sees the process of politicization in a more dynamic way than is implied in female consciousness: 'motherhood, not citizenship, provided the principal *mobilizing referent* for women's participation in urban social movements' (1990: 50; emphasis in the original).[10] Motherhood is the starting point for mobilization but can change over time. Alvarez stresses that gender discourses are 'constantly modified in response to changing vertical and horizontal strategic linkages and transformations in the structure of political opportunity' (1990: 264). That is, women's participation has to be understood within multiple political processes which offer ever-changing opportunities and constraints: in the 1970s and 1980s the backdrop to women's increased political participation was the struggle for democracy; by the 1990s that context has changed.

It is important to see political participation as constantly evolving and to acknowledge that some women move beyond narrow identification with the family as their new experiences lead to new horizons and options. Although 'motherhood' contextualizes the lives of women generally, many of their activities challenge the constraints this implies. Consequently, women have fought in revolutionary movements, demanded equal rights and continue the struggles in contemporary feminism. This indicates that women's interests, to which I now turn, are more diverse than might be implied by female consciousness.

Gender interests

The notion of women's interests tends to evoke ideas of child-care, flexible working hours and, particularly in the case of Latin America, service provision. There is an alternative reading, however, that focuses on other non-domestic demands around equality of treatment and opportunity (some of which are discussed in Chapter 4). This dualism has led to assumptions about feminist and non-feminist (or feminine) issues (a debate that is explored further in Chapter 8). For the present, I focus on understanding women's gender interests and what they tell us about motivation for participation. In what is a seminal article, Maxine Molyneux (1985) considered gender interests in the context of the Nicaraguan revolutionary state. Although women may seem to have interests in common, Molyneux noted that there was no consensus on what these might be. She divided gender interests into two categories: strategic gender interests (SGI) and practical gender interests (PGI). Women's SGI are derived in the first instance deductively, that is, from the analysis of women's subordination and from the formulation of an alternative, more satisfactory set of arrangements to those which exist ... The demands that are formulated on this basis are usually termed 'feminist' as is the level of consciousness required to struggle effectively for them. (Molyneux, 1985: 232–3)

As such, struggling for SGI tends to challenge dominant gender constructions. PGI, on the other hand, are

given inductively and arise from the concrete conditions of women's positioning within the gender division of labour. In contrast to strategic gender interests, these are formulated by the women who are themselves within these positions rather than through external interventions. (Molyneux, 1985: 233)

Mobilizations around PGI tend to defend dominant gender constructions: Molyneux suggests that PGI 'cannot be assumed to be innocent of class effects ... [and] do not in themselves challenge prevailing forms of gender subordination, even though they arise directly out of them' (ibid.). Strategic interests, as Molyneux suggests, have sometimes been considered feminist: she later emphasizes the 'transformative potential' of strategic interests (Molyneux, 1998: 232). Practical interests, conversely, have been viewed as feminine (see, for example, Alvarez, 1990, and Singer, in Chuchryk, 1994). Molyneux points out that there are frequently tensions in pursuing SGI, since this may result in short-term costs in PGI. As such, the two types of interest are frequently seen in opposition to one another, which is not necessarily the case. Although dichotomies are conceptual tools which help us to understand the world, they are generally too simplistic and rigid.[11] Consequently, considering practical and strategic gender interests as poles of a continuum, or seeing a dialectical relationship between the two, may be more helpful.

Strategic and practical interaction

There are of course many issues which have dual characteristics: the struggle for adequate contraception might be a practical issue for a woman with concerns to maintain standards of living for an existing family, but it may also have strategic implications regarding a woman's right to choose and have autonomy over her own body. Although women may begin mobilization for practical reasons, the strategic implications can have a more lasting effect on them and their future participation. In her later article, Molyneux (1998) highlights the ways in which practical and strategic are interrelated. She states, 'the political *links* between practical and strategic interests are ones which can only emerge through dialogue, praxis and discussion' (1998: 236; emphasis in the original).

Although PGI tend to be regarded as less controversial, given their defence of dominant gender constructions, it is the SGI which have found the new institutional terrain easier to negotiate, which may reflect the actors' greater political experience and expertise. Consequently feminist groups have maintained greater pressure on governments than other social movements which have been in decline (Waylen, 1993). In relation to this, Molyneux analysed the responses to women's demands of Nicaragua's revolutionary state. She concluded that the needs of the state remain paramount: 'It is a question therefore not just of *what* interests are represented in the state, but ultimately and critically of *how* they are represented' (Molyneux, 1985: 251; emphasis in the original). The most successful groups are those which adjust their strategies and tactics to reflect the context in which they participate. Throughout Latin America it is clear that practical interests are not necessarily the easiest for governments to respond to, since they frequently require material resources which are not always forthcoming. Responding to demands for legal equality may therefore be easier for governments to tackle (this point is developed in Chapter 4), although they may be challenging culturally.

Molyneux's divide highlights and helps explain some of the tensions between different women's groups, and undermines any idea of universal interests. The divide, however, can be interpreted too rigidly and can imply an exclusivity which could deny the links between the two. Interests are always given in a particular context and are therefore contingent. It is important not to essentialize women's interests, no matter whether they are considered practical or strategic. In Chapter 8, the exchange between 'feminists' and other women activists shows the sometimes tense dialogue can also result in broadening of the perspective of both groups of women.

These conceptual tools and their application to Latin America demonstrate that motherhood and the domestic sphere do play an important role in women's political activity. Furthermore, it appears to be easier for most women, and I would suggest men as well, to engage in political activity when it is in defence of dominant political identities, rather than when it challenges them. Nevertheless, sometimes in defending these identities the actors' perspectives change, and challenging them becomes the best way to further the wider goals. It is important to note that the political process is one of continual change: goals shift, identities are renegotiated and political terrains mutate as boundaries are challenged. These movements and changes are not unilinear and progressive, but are subject to advance and retreat and sideways moves. Political participation is dynamic and the vested interests which generally try to rebut challenges are also strong and able to regroup. Whether or not women mobilize around practical or strategic interests, it is clear that increased political actions and the debates around women's rights have had an impact on the emerging democracies and the development of citizenship.

Developing citizenship

Much of this book is concerned with the development of meaningful citizenship and political subjectivity in the struggle for democracy. Central to the notion of democracy is 'rule by the people' through representatives who make laws and policies and are, through elections, publicly accountable. Accordingly, citizenship is fundamentally about inviolable rights, which also entail responsibilities, across a polity: each citizen has the same rights which are legally recognized. Over time citizenship has expanded – to include women, for example – but also new rights have been incorporated which have tended to focus on welfare and quality of life issues, such as access to housing, education and work. Although the term 'citizen' is ostensibly gender neutral, there are those who argue that it is substantively masculine, since it assumes a public individual with characteristics normally associated with men (see Dietz, 1989). It is suggested today that, while women have the same legal rights as men in liberal democracies, there are still serious problems of access which make the exercise of these rights more difficult for women (ibid.). This is reflected in the generalized weaker position of women in society regarding wages, participation in key decision-making arenas, hours worked and access to education.

It is not clear, however, that citizenship in practice does embody the rights of a gender-neutral individual, since in many countries there is protective legislation affecting women. Furthermore, not all responsibilities are gender neutral, since only men are required to bear arms and die for their country (although women can choose to be soldiers). The responsibility of women is to bear children for the state.[12] Bearing arms and bearing children have been equated as the citizenship duty of men and women respectively by politicians and activists in many diverse situations, as will be demonstrated (see Pateman, 1992). These differing citizenship duties reflect the public–private distinction central to liberal citizenship.

The public and private divide

As women have struggled for citizenship, the distinction between public and private spheres has been challenged. Women's increased political participation has demonstrated the fluid nature of the boundary between public and private spheres and emphasized that there is not a clear border between them. It is preferable to follow Tiano's (1984) example and see the public and private as two poles of a continuum where most actors and issues are drawn to the centre. By doing this, there is less likelihood of ignoring women's contribution to the public world by miscasting it as ineluctably private. A less rigid conceptualization of public and private is borne out by the analyses presented in the various chapters below, particularly the discussion on work (Chapter 5) and social movements (Chapter 6). As I suggested above, the divide has never been a realistic description of peoples' lives but an idealized account of social and gender relations which gave markers for appropriate behaviour. As women claim citizenship, not merely in a constitutional but also in a material manner, the distinction becomes less meaningful as a gendered divide. I return to this point in the concluding chapter.

In Latin America, authoritarian political structures have made the practice of citizenship difficult for all, as political rights have been denied by the military or undermined by clientelism. The fact that contemporary Latin American countries are liberal democracies of sorts (with the exception of Cuba) partly reflects citizens' struggles to claim and defend their rights. The collective action which has established citizenship rights in the region has had to challenge the personalized nature of clientelism and has been an important part of the region's democratization over the past three decades.[13] The actors involved assume a political subjectivity, that is, a sense of self and identity in political terms, which is important in a region where people have frequently been objects of the political process with little influence. A critical part of this is the making of strategic and political choices which 'are only rarely individual because their defining quality is their social and relational content' (Foweraker, 1989: 251 fn 5). So while the practice of citizenship is typically individual, the demand making and the claiming of rights intrinsic to it are often a result of collective action, particularly through social movements (cf. Foweraker, 1997). Given the heavy involvement of women in these movements, the political subject is not just the masculine citizen of traditional Western liberalism. Rather, it also includes 'feminine' characteristics because women's demands have made it successfully on to the political agenda through collective action.[14] But a word of caution: the impact of collective action is varied, sometimes forcing radical change at both the individual and the national level, while at other times it may be a localized affair which does little to challenge political structures or mindsets (cf. Perelli, 1994).

Empowerment

One of the important elements in the development of an effective citizenship is empowerment. Empowerment is a complex process which includes both shifts in identity and political structures. Empowerment in a formal sense includes the provision of opportunities such as the vote, open access to legal systems and access to adequate information. This, however, is not sufficient in itself: it also requires change in the personal perception of the empowered subject. Bystydzienski (1992: 3) sees empowerment as the 'process by which oppressed persons gain some control over their lives by taking part *with others* in development of activities and structures that allow people increased involvement in matters which affect them directly. In its course, people become enabled to govern themselves effectively' (my emphasis). The struggles for effective citizenship for Latin American women and their empowerment have developed together, and collective action has been central.

Empowerment clearly involves power itself and thus is a political process, but it is 'power to' (control one's own life) rather than 'power over' (others in a coercive sense) (Bystydzienski, 1992). In many of the movements and campaigns outlined in this book, a process of personal empowerment emerges through an acknowledgement that women have the same rights as men and that their views are just as important. This is not to say that they do not perceive and accept areas of competence which are gendered, but those who have been involved in campaigns generally gain a sense of political efficacy which is not gendered: women have become politically visible. Bystydzienski uses the literacy campaign, pioneered by the Brazilian educationalist Paulo Freire, as a good example of the process of empowerment: the strategies used by Freire were mirrored in many social movements in the region.[15] Clearly, not all autonomous collective action leads to empowerment, partly 'because informal power structures can operate "tyrannically" in the absence of formal limits or procedural rules governing the exercise of power; and secondly because autonomy can in some contexts mean marginalization and a reduced political effectiveness' (Molyneux, 1998: 228).

Obviously not all women participate in political activity, no matter how broadly defined. Consequently the empowerment process can be achieved through shifts in discourses which result in non-activist women also acknowledging their rights (and responsibilities). In some of the literature, and particularly in the programmes of aid agencies, there is an implicit idea that one person can empower another. This is something with which I would take issue. The formal liberties which provide opportunities are part of the empowerment process and can be granted without a struggle – the extension of the Ecuadorian franchise in 1929 might be a good example – but individuals are not empowered unless they identify with these rights.

Thus I would suggest that empowerment is, crucially, a personal process which can be gained in many ways, but there is no formula for mass empowerment. Furthermore, governments and other political actors in a hierarchy will do much to limit empowerment and channel the process through certain avenues, such as the electoral system, and will act to disempower groups which mount strong challenges based on radical socio-economic reform. Cammack (1994) points to some of the tensions among citizenship, capitalism and democracy in the newly democratized Latin America. He concludes that 'it has taken the "skilful political crafting" of political leaders in Latin America to engineer, with the enthusiastic endorsement of today's empirical theorists, a new phenomenon: democracy without citizenship' (1994: 193). While this may be an overly negative assessment, the use of co-optation and clientelism, which have underpinned Latin American political systems in the past, continue in current attempts to disempower the region's population. A struggle for any state is the balance between the desire for a quiescent population and the need for enough genuine interest and support to be legitimately in control. Women's empowerment is evident in the shifting gender relations and the challenge to the public and private spheres through the claiming of rights. Empowerment has helped make women more politically visible, but there are challenges whereby women (and men) suffer disempowerment through changes in labour regulation and the withdrawal of state-sponsored welfare programmes. This is exacerbated by the narrowing of political debate and the emphasis on concensus at the expense of open discussion.

Conclusions

The aim of this chapter has been to give pointers for reading this book. I have highlighted the challenges which women face in their struggle for political equality and how their different strategies and tactics have resulted in changes in Latin American political systems. The changes that have occurred over the past years have resulted in women challenging boundaries, both conceptual and material, which have served to constrain their political participation. New political identities have emerged which affect not only women but more generally the Latin American citizen of the 1990s: women's demands have become citizens' rights.

Women's political identity has changed over time, although the centrality of motherhood seems more resistant to change. There are, however, still problems. Women may have made significant inroads into male bastions of power, but they are still heavily under represented in the major power arenas, they remain underpaid and overworked in relation to men, and many of the costs resulting from the neoliberal state's socio-economic adjustment falls on their shoulders. The changing political environment requires new tactics and strategies for furthering women's political participation. At present women's political involvement is less obvious than it was at the height of social movement activity, and this reflects the general demobilization of recent years.

3
Setting the Scene

Introduction

Through an analysis of political, economic and social structures, this chapter presents the context in which Latin American women's political participation has developed. It also gives a 'picture' of Latin American women. It is, of course, difficult to discuss 'Latin American women' given the diversity of women's experiences between countries and the ethnic, race and class cleavages within them. Nevertheless, it is possible to demonstrate generalized trends and to indicate where there have been significant changes – in educational attainment, for example – and where shifts have been slower – such as gains in socio-economic equality. Clearly, many of the changes indicated here are also seen in other regions of the world.

It is essential to examine the political, social and economic structures which contextualize women's lives, since these structures can be used to aid empowerment of citizens (by establishing equal opportunity laws or providing labour opportunities, for example). They can, however, also act as serious constraints to people's development and autonomy. In the case of Latin America, these structures have, for the majority, presented constraints more often than opportunities, and these have been gendered in their effect: for most it is a region of political, economic and social exclusion. This exclusion has been challenged over the decades, and in the following chapters the ways in which women have overcome the obstacles presented to them are discussed.

It is evident from the analysis below that the region's exclusionary social, economic and political structures have resulted in highly stratified societies headed by a small and powerful elite. This exclusion reflects issues of class, gender and ethnicity, which leaves Indian peasants, particularly women, at the bottom of the pile. It is important to stress, however, that women are not simply passive victims reacting to shifts in their external circumstances, but actors who help shape those structures and who are adept at capitalizing on opportunities when available. There have been many gains made, but there are still deficiencies in terms of gender equality and social justice which prejudice women's lives.

It is also important to note that shifts in social, economic and political structures generally have both positive and negative impacts, and affect people in different ways depending on age, geographic location, marital status, etc. In the discussion on 'Latin American women' the differences between and within countries is highlighted through an examination of education, social welfare and work opportunities. In the course of the book it is evident that structures and institutions can be used to help promote empowerment, and in this chapter the material changes to women's lives as these structures have changed is assessed. It is, of course, impossible to give a clear picture of all the differences and nuances among the region's women, but it is important to remember that 'development' in any arena is an ambivalent experience full of complexities which offers people both opportunities and constraints.

The chapter is organized as follows: a brief discussion of the main political characteristics of the region, followed by an assessment of the shifting economic and social conditions. The bulk of the chapter is dedicated to the examination of women's lives. The increased globalization of culture and economies has meant that certain characteristics are found in other regions, but there are, of course, some issues more particular to Latin America.

Latin American political systems in the twentieth century[1]

Latin American political systems have been characterized by their authoritarianism. This has been extreme, in the cases of highly repressive states, or more covert, evident in state corporatism. Authoritarianism has allowed little access for the majority to the decision-making arena, which has made women's struggle for political subjectivity all the more difficult. The legacy of colonialism has been a highly stratified society with hierarchies of class, race and gender. A social elite of *'gente decente'* emerged, who act as the role models for poorer people and non-Iberian communities. This legacy gave the region a number of characteristics which have reinforced political exclusion: *caudillismo* (strongman politics), personalism, clientelism and centralism. The struggle for democracy and political inclusion has been evident in the revolutions, guerrilla warfare and popular protests which have occurred in many Latin American countries. Military intervention in politics has been a particularly salient characteristic in Argentina, Bolivia, Brazil and Peru throughout the twentieth century. The politics of exclusion reached their height with the National Security States of the 1960s and 1970s and affected countries with democratic histories such as Chile and Uruguay.[2] Currently, Latin America is experiencing the longest period of stable, civilian rule the region has witnessed, with all countries, with the exception of Cuba, holding regular, multi-party elections.[3]

Corporatism and populism

Corporatism has dominated political relations in many countries and is particularly associated with Argentina, Brazil, Mexico and Peru. Corporatism has its roots in the fascist regimes of southern Europe of the early twentieth century, particularly that of Mussolini in Italy. In corporatist systems, popular participation is contained and controlled through state-sanctioned, non-competitive sectors. These are generally clearly delineated to foster a system of 'divide and rule'. The sectors tend to reflect work identities (peasants, industrial workers, the military) rather than geographic or ethnic groups, although there are sections for women and youth.[4] The sectors are 'vertical' structures where the boundaries between each are rigidly defined. This contrasts with class movements which are 'horizontal', linking together people of similar socio-economic circumstances. Peasants, for example, are encouraged to identify with the rural sector, and thus with landowners, rather than consider themselves allies of industrial workers. Although women can obviously be peasants, workers and young, the use of women's sectors in corporatism reflects a rather one-dimensional view of women, closely linked to social reproduction.

Populism, a dominant political form in the 1940s, was mediated by these corporatist structures: 'For "classical" theorists, populism in Latin America is a loosely organized multiclass movement united by a charismatic leader behind an ideology and programme of social justice' (Roxborough, 1987: 119). Populism has generally emerged in moments of rapid change, resulting in social disloca- tion; consequently most populist projects include reform pro- grammes but are not revolutionary. The charismatic leaders aim to establish a direct link with 'the people', emphasizing the natural ordering of society which made some people leaders and others followers: the rhetoric of the Peróns reflects this (see chapters 4 and 8). Populism encouraged an 'organic' understanding of the world, one which mobilizes ideas of destiny: this has particular implica- tions for gender construction, with the role of motherhood being reified. With the focus of populism centred on the charismatic indi- vidual, there is the reinforcement of *caudillismo* and centralism as power is concentrated in one person. The legacy of populism remains evident in Latin America today, with some presidents seeking to bypass congress to speak 'directly' to the people.[5] Indeed congresses are often blamed by presidents for stalling the political process. This has been particularly evident in the lan- guage of President Collor (1990–92) in Brazil and President Fujimori (1990–) in Peru.

Corporatism, populist or otherwise, encouraged political stabi- lity through a mixture of state control of political mobilization (which separated potential allies), reform packages (which co- opted some opposition), and strong emotional, generally national- ist, rhetoric. Nevertheless, the regimes remained authoritarian and continued to use coercion against serious opposition. Clientelism has also been a factor in the maintenance of political stability. This is a patron–client relationship based on favour-trading between unequal partners, leading to an asymmetrical power relationship. It is an obstacle to the development of citizenship, and con- sequently democracy, since the individual's ability to obtain goods and services from the state (or other organizations) depends on their ability to trade something, especially votes, in return. The patron–client relationship has eroded the establishment of defens- ible rights and has contributed to the arbitrariness of the political process which has underpinned authoritarianism. Given that the opportunities for establishing client–patron relations is based on access to people more powerful than yourself – local politicians, officialist trade union leaders[6] and business leaders, for example – women have fewer opportunities to develop such relationships. They are less likely to be unionized (see Chapter 5) and they par- ticipate less in political parties and government (see Chapter 4), so

their main opportunity for establishing such ties is through neighbourhood and community organizations, reinforcing their
domestic identity (see Chapter 6). While the political systems in
Latin America do not necessarily aim specifically to exclude
women, the structures have been biased against them.

Party systems

Despite the prevalence of corporatism, there have been some
examples of liberal democracies in the region: Chile, Costa Rica,
Uruguay and Venezuela have been the best examples. Nevertheless, the predominance of civil and military authoritarianism
has affected the development of parties, leaving them generally
weak and subject to personalism and factionalism.[7] Mexico, Peru
and Argentina also have well-developed parties, but, without participating in systems with free and fair elections, these have frequently contributed to the countries' authoritarianism.

Party identities in the region are generally underdeveloped and
politicians are frequently seen as self-serving and corrupt. In the
first administration after the restoration of civilian rule in Brazil in
1985, a third of representatives changed parties while members of
congress, indicating the low levels of party identification and
loyalty. There is general public antipathy and scepticism towards
party politics, and recently independent candidates have been successful in presidential competition in two countries.[8] This antipathy towards parties, which reflects the weakness and corruption
evident in party politics, has been gendered, with women generally being less enthusiastic about the role of parties; however, there
are indications that this is changing (see Chapter 4).

The current phase of political stability is based on liberal democratic government, but the competing parties often have remarkably similar policies, particularly regarding the economy. The
emergence of civilian governments owes much to social movements where women were particularly active, as Chapter 6 demonstrates. Many of these movements focused on socio-economic
exclusion and demanded that the state take responsibility for citizens' rights. Despite the return to civilian government, for the
many there remain problems of access to the major decision-
making arenas and serious difficulties resulting from socio-
economic inequalities. But autonomous political organizing is
easier in the current systems, and parties increasingly acknowledge the demands emanating from society. Continued political

stability, however, should not be taken for granted, since the economy continues to pose problems.

Revolutions and military states

Alongside these more traditional political systems, Latin America has also experienced political violence resulting in very different state types. In the 1960s and 1970s the region suffered a number of military take-overs, which left virtually all South American countries with military governments of one sort or another. These governments were highly repressive and brooked no or little opposition. In Argentina, Brazil, Chile and Uruguay the take-overs were distinct from previous interventions in that the military did not represent a 'transition' government. On the contrary, they were there to stay for the foreseeable future: indeed, they lasted twenty-one years in Brazil and sixteen years in Chile. They were also different in that they aimed to restructure society. In the event, they succeeded in repressing the populations mainly through terror, and helped make the already precarious economic situation worse in most countries. The levels of repression and the policies executed helped fuel opposition movements outside the usual political institutions, as discussed in Chapter 6. These movements helped politicize women.

Highly repressive personalized dictatorships were also overthrown through revolutionary struggle. There have been four major revolutions in Latin America: in Mexico (1910), Bolivia (1952), Cuba (1959) and Nicaragua (1979). The first two led to a redistribution of power, although Bolivia soon experienced another military coup. In the case of Cuba and Nicaragua, the restructuring was more radical and they became internationally renowned. In these two cases, the role of women in society was considered and many policies directed at improving women's lives were developed: they are discussed in more detail in Chapter 7.

All these political systems reinforce gender constructions which rely on women's identification with motherhood. The struggle of women for a greater political voice has to overcome this narrow vision of womanhood. It must also challenge the authoritarianism which excludes large sections of the population on grounds other than gender, such as ethnicity, age, class and geographic location. Consequently, the battle for effective citizenship for women has to be waged on several fronts for a more inclusive polity generally.

Economic developments

Import substitution industrialization

Political developments have been tied to economic issues, which also feed into, and are affected by, gender constructions. Most of Latin America followed, to some degree, import substitution industrialization (ISI), which focused on the internal market as a response to the severe crisis following the 1929 Wall Street Crash. This had demonstrated the problems of dependency on the primary product export model, which was the norm until the 1930s. Although it was intended to substitute imports with domestically produced goods, a bottle-neck occurred when countries failed to produce expensive capital goods – the final stage to self-sufficient production (although not all countries reached this stage). ISI also led to tariff barriers, overvalued currencies, bloated bureaucracies and generally inefficient production.

Despite the aims of government, demand for imported goods remained high and domestically produced goods were seen as inferior by many. Notwithstanding these problems, Latin American economies grew rapidly, particularly in the 1960s, although not always in keeping with population growth. States played a key role in economic development under ISI and funded much of the investment. The model, however, could not adjust to changing global economic conditions, and both a fiscal deficit and a balance of payments deficit ensued. The degree of state penetration into the economy had oiled the wheels of clientelism; consequently, in some countries, the economic restructuring has aided democratization by removing the potential for kickbacks and by introducing more transparency into government economic policy: it must be stressed, however, that there are no causal links between economic and political models.[9]

Structural adjustment

In the early 1970s the economies of Latin America began to stagnate, with negative growth, hyperinflation and rapidly increasing debts to international agencies. The 1973 oil crisis exacerbated the problems, as the global recession affected the region. Governments responded to the crisis with a shift towards an externally oriented economy and a radical readjustment which centred on the reduction of the state's role in the economy. Structural adjustment policies (SAPs) were introduced, with all the economic hardship this implies, particularly for the more vulnerable in society. These were also gendered in their impact (Daines and Seddon, 1994; Gabriel and Macdonald, 1994; Sparr, 1994a; IDB, 1995).

There are four main components of SAPs: i) a currency devaluation to curb imports and make exports more competitive; ii) a reduction in government spending, particularly through a reduction in subsidies (often in basic foodstuffs and basic services), public welfare provision and making public employees redundant; iii) the removal of any restrictions on interest rates to discourage borrowing, curb inflation and help stop capital flight; and iv) the abolition of price controls and the introduction in some cases of wage restraints (Sparr, 1994b: 7). There is also the removal of tariff barriers as part of the 'opening-up' of the economy.

Reduction in public spending and the removal of government subsidies has a direct impact on the lives of women as carers. It also creates an insecure working environment, which has particular effects on male unemployment, forcing more women into income-generation activities (see below). The economies were already contracting with the economic crisis, and this was heightened, in the short term at least, by the effects of the SAPs. To counteract the loss of work, the informal sector grew along with small-scale production which took place in the community. This work is insecure and accounts for much female labour (see below). Structural adjustment is ongoing, and many countries continue to feel severe economic challenges; furthermore, these policies interact with pre-existing inequalities (cf. Gabriel and Macdonald, 1994). The economic problems resulting from Latin America's disadvantaged position in the global economy continue to limit governments' choices in domestic politics, and economic hardship fuels the demands of the electorate. There have been some positive outcomes from SAPs, but the benefits have not been evenly distributed.

Political implications of economic reform

Socio-economic inequality is perhaps the greatest threat to political stability in the region at present: it also limits the ability of many women to participate fully in politics, as more time is spent in income generation (see Craske, 1998). The changing economic models and the 'crises' which have affected the region have a major impact on the lives of women and, as Chapter 6

Table 3.1 Urban income distribution

	circa 1980			circa 1992		
	Gini[a] coefficient	Share of the gini coefficient for the poorest 40%	Share of the gini coefficient for the wealthiest 10%	Gini coefficient	Share of the gini coefficient for the poorest 40%	Share of the gini coefficient for the wealthiest 10%
Argentina[b]	0.365	18	29.8	0.408	15.2	31.6
Bolivia	N/A	N/A	N/A	0.478	13	40
Brazil	0.493	11.7	39.1	0.535	9.6	41.7
Chile	N/A	N/A	N/A	0.452	14.6	38.2
Colombia[c]	0.518	11	41.3	0.454	12.9	34.5
Costa Rica	0.328	18.9	23.2	0.363	17	27
Cuba	N/A	N/A	N/A	N/A	N/A	N/A
Dominican Republic	N/A	N/A	N/A	N/A	N/A	N/A
Ecuador	N/A	N/A	N/A	N/A	N/A	N/A
El Salvador	N/A	N/A	N/A	N/A	N/A	N/A
Guatemala	N/A	N/A	N/A	0.479	12.1	37.9
Honduras	N/A	N/A	N/A	0.461	13.2	35.4
Mexico	N/A	N/A	N/A	0.414	16.5	34.7
Nicaragua	N/A	N/A	N/A	N/A	N/A	N/A
Panama	0.399	15.5	29.1	0.448	13.3	34.2
Paraguay[d]	N/A	N/A	N/A	0.391	16.2	29.2
Peru	N/A	N/A	N/A	N/A	N/A	N/A
Uruguay	0.379	17.7	31.2	0.301	21.9	25.9
Venezuela	0.306	20.2	21.8	0.387	16.3	28.9

[a] The Gini Index is a global measure of inequality in income distribution. It varies from 0 for egalitarian distribution to 1 for total inequality.
[b] Argentina figures taken from Greater Buenos Aires area.
[c] Colombia figures taken from the eight largest cities.
[d] Paraguay figures taken from Asuncion.
Source: Valdés and Gomáriz (1995: 32)

demonstrates, has introduced them to new forms of political organization as they have tried to mitigate the worst excesses of these changes. The economic conditions are affected by and, in their turn, have an impact on social structures. Although the economic situation in the region has frequently been difficult, the developments have also provided opportunities for women and men. Frequently it is need which pushes women deeper into income-generation activities, as we see below, but the impact can be positive in terms of empowerment (see Chapter 5).

For the most part, however, the benefits of economic development have reached only a few and there has been little real attempt at income distribution. Over the past two decades of structural adjustment income distribution has become more skewed (see table 3.1 for urban income distribution), and women suffer to a greater degree than men since they are concentrated in lower income groups, especially in rural areas (IDB, 1995). Despite the richness of the region's resources, its economic history has not been a happy one. The role of dependent economies mixed with highly skewed societies has helped reinforce political authoritarianism.

Social structures

The changes in social and cultural conditions this century have been considerable for all regions of the world. In Latin America there has been a major shift in populations as predominantly rural countries have become increasingly urbanized. Population growth has slowed, but it has still resulted in large populations and megacities in most countries. Similarly, family sizes have decreased but remain larger than those in Europe. Access to education has improved, with benefits for women, reflected in changing job opportunities. Before examining the changes in women's lives over the past decades, a discussion of more general trends is required.

Urbanization and population growth

Latin American countries are predominantly urban, but there are clear distinctions between countries such as Uruguay and Venezuela, which register over 90 per cent urban populations, and Bolivia and Paraguay and Central American countries, which have

Table 3.2 Life expectancy and population distribution (rural/urban)

	Life expectancy, 1970–75		Life expectancy, 1990–95		Population distribution (%), 1995	
	Women	Men	Women	Men	Urban	Rural
Argentina	71	64	75	68	87	13
Bolivia	49	45	64	59	54	46
Brazil	62	58	69	64	79	21
Chile	67	60	76	69	86	14
Colombia	63	60	72	66	73	27
Costa Rica	70	66	79	74	50	50
Cuba	73	69	78	74	76	24
Dominican Republic	62	58	70	65	65	35
Ecuador	60	57	69	65	61	39
El Salvador	61	57	69	64	47	53
Guatemala	55	53	67	62	41	59
Honduras	56	52	68	64	48	52
Mexico	65	61	74	67	75	25
Nicaragua	57	54	69	65	63	37
Panama	68	65	75	71	55	45
Paraguay	68	64	70	65	51	49
Peru	57	54	67	63	72	28
Uruguay	72	66	76	69	90	10
Venezuela	69	64	74	67	93	7
Western Europe/ other developed	75	69	79	73		
Africa	51	48	60	57		
Asia and Pacific	59	56	68	64		

Sources: IDB (1995: 199), UN (1995: 60–64, 66–67)

around 50 per cent rural populations (see table 3.2). The degree of urbanization has an impact on access to social welfare provision such as schools and health-care centres, and, with the commercialization of agriculture, work opportunities are limited and under increasing pressure. In countries such as Bolivia, Ecuador, Guatemala and Peru the rural populations include significant Indian populations (see table 3.3), who may be further excluded on account of their different languages or social customs. Unlike the case in other developing regions, notably Sub-Saharan Africa, rural women are more likely to migrate to the cities in search of work while men stay behind to farm (table 3.4) (UN: 42). The population growth combined with the migration to the cities has added to the pressures on governments in their attempts to provide adequate services. Problems with service provision, which have been exacerbated by the economic conditions, have fuelled social movements (discussed in Chapter 6).

The numbers of children born to women have decreased dramatically within one or two generations (see table 3.5). This in part reflects improved health care, which means that children are no longer needed as insurance for old age and that more children are surviving, so there are fewer pregnancies. It also reflects greater access to contraception and a change in attitudes towards the cultural significance of large families. The reduction in family size is mediated by class and geographic location: middle-class and urban families tend to be smaller. Despite the decline in population growth and the reduction in family size, Latin American populations are very young; 38.5 per cent of the region's population in 1995 was under fifteen years of age (see table 3.3). The more urbanized the country, the more equally the population is distributed in different age groups. Men slightly outnumber women in the lower age groups, and this trend is reversed for those over fifty (Valdés and Gomáriz, 1995: 40).

Household structures are also changing, reflecting shifting opportunities and constraints. New work opportunities for women result in greater possibilities for independent living, so there has been a growth in female-headed households. The economic crisis has acted as a catalyst for an increase in extended families living in the same household, with several income-generators contributing to the family income. In such circumstances older women often provide unpaid services to the family.

Table 3.3 Indigenous population in 1990 and percentage of the population under 15 years of age (both sexes)

	% of population under 15 years of age in 1995	% of population under 15 years of age in 2010 (projected)	Indigenous population in 1990	Indigenous population as % of total population in 1990
Argentina	28	26	350,000	1
Bolivia	40	36	4,900,000	71
Brazil	32	25	300,000	0.2
Chile	30	26	1,000,000	8
Colombia	33	27	600,000	2
Costa Rica	35	29	30,000	1
Cuba	23	21		
Dominican Republic	36	29		
Ecuador	37	30	3,800,000	38
El Salvador	41	35	400,000	7
Guatemala	44	39	5,300,000	66
Honduras	43	36	700,000	15
Mexico	36	29	12,000,000	14
Nicaragua	46	38	160,000	5
Panama	33	27	140,000	6
Paraguay	40	35	100,000	3
Peru	35	30	9,300,000	47
Uruguay	24	23		
Venezuela	35	28	140,562	0.9
United Kingdom	20	19		
United States	22	20		

Sources: UN (1995: 23–5, Table 1); Valdés and Gomáriz (1995: 51)

Table 3.4 Females per 100 males in urban and rural areas, 1995

	Females per 100 males in **urban** areas	Females per 100 males in **rural** areas
Latin America	106	90
Caribbean	109	94
Northern Africa	97	98
Sub-Saharan Africa	95	106
East Asia	95	94
South-East Asia	99	101
Southern Asia	88	97
Western Asia	90	96
Western Europe and other developed countries	106	96

Source: UN (1995: 42)

Global culture?

The shift to the cities has a number of cultural consequences. Local indigenous customs and languages are lost or diluted as people migrate and interact with others. Cities offer greater contact with 'global culture', especially through the entertainment industry and fast-food outlets, which particularly brings US influence. Globalization is reinforced by rapid transformations in communications and technology and the hegemony of free-trade-based economies with global factories. This does not mean, however, that culture has homogenized to the point that there are no regional and country differences. Rather, there is a cross-fertilization of cultures which reflect the traditional and the new, and they are always mutating. The interaction of different feminisms discussed in Chapter 8 demonstrates the ways in which global and local discourses and experiences interact to produce a dynamic agenda for change.

There has also been a change in religious identification. Latin America has traditionally been a region of Catholic countries; recently, however, there has been a shift towards Protestantism. This has been particularly marked in Brazil, Central America and southern Mexico, and has had an impact on gender construction, with less emphasis being placed on the iconography of the Virgin Mary. Nevertheless, the majority of Latin Americans, 84 per cent,

Table 3.5 Average household size; use of contraception among married women of reproductive age; birth rates for women aged 15–19; and percentage of births attended by a trained attendant

	Average household size, 1970	Average household size, 1990	Total fertility rates, 1970–75	Total fertility rates, 1990–95	Contraceptive use (%) among married women of reproductive age, 1990	Births per 1000 women, (%), aged 15–19, 1990–95	% births attended by trained attendant, 1986–90
Argentina	3.8	3.9[a]	3.1	2.8	74	66	92
Bolivia	N/A	4.6	6.5	4.6	30	83	29
Brazil	5.1	4.2	4.7	2.7	66	41	73
Chile	5.2	4.5[a]	3.6	2.7	N/A	66	98
Colombia	5.9	5.2	4.7	2.7	66	71	51
Costa Rica	5.6	4.3	4.3	3.1	70	93	97
Cuba	4.5	4.0	3.5	1.9	70	82	100
Dominican Republic	5.3	4.5	5.6	3.3	56	70	44
Ecuador	N/A	4.8	6.1	3.6	53	77	26
El Salvador	5.4	5.0[b]	6.1	4.0	47	131	66
Guatemala	5.2	5.2[a]	6.5	5.4	23	123	23
Honduras	5.7	5.4	7.4	4.9	41	100	63
Mexico	4.9	5.0	6.4	3.2	53	88	45
Nicaragua	N/A	N/A	6.8	5.0	49	153	42
Panama	4.9	4.4	4.9	2.9	58[a]	83	85
Paraguay	5.4	4.7	5.7	4.3	48	76	30
Peru	4.8	5.9	6.0	3.6	59	68	78
Uruguay	N/A	3.3	3.0	2.3	N/A	60	100
Venezuela	5.8	4.8	5.0	3.1	49[b]	71	82
Latin American (av.)	5.1	4.6	5.3	3.5			
United Kingdom	2.9	2.5[c]	2.0	1.9	81[d]	34	98
United States	3.1	2.6	2.0	2.1	74	58	99

[a] Figures refer to a year between 1980 and 1984. Also, figures for contraceptive use for Panama exclude abstinence, douche and folk methods.
[b] Figure refers to a year between 1975 and 1979.
[c] England and Wales only.
[d] Excluding Northern Ireland.

Source: UN (1995: 5, Chart 1.7; 28–32, Table 2; 84–8, Table 6)

identify themselves as Catholic, although this does not mean that all are practising.[10]

The shifts within the Catholic Church have had an impact on the social and political developments in the region. The Second Vatican Council was a profound restructuring which famously endorsed 'the option for the poor'. This gave the church a more overtly political role, and one not necessarily in support of the elite. Many lay clergy and priests, in keeping with this new teaching, have become involved in social movements. Women, especially, have found the support of the church of great value in their struggle for social justice (see Chapter 6). Many clergy, however, went further than the intention of Vatican II and engaged in liberation theology, particularly popular in Brazil. The old guard of the church have now reasserted themselves, and Pope John Paul II has been critical of liberation theologians, frequently censuring clergy who are deemed to have acted outside their remit. In the Latin American case the role of clergy has been of great positive benefit to the struggle for social justice, but, as discussed in Chapter 6, the impact on women activists associated with church groups has been mixed. The ongoing importance in the region of the Catholic Church, and religion more generally, distinguishes Latin American from European norms, and its Catholicism distinguishes it from the USA.[11]

These changes in social and economic structures are 'universal' inasmuch as similar changes can be seen in other countries: a young woman in Mexico City is likely to listen to the same music and go to see the same films, and may even work for the same company, as her 'sisters' north of the border. Indeed, she may have more in common with her peers in the USA than in Chiapas. Equally, Argentinians and Uruguayans pride themselves on their Europeanness. Clearly there are significant differences within countries and between countries. No matter how 'European' or 'American' the countries may seem, they are still Latin America with their own stories.

Latin American women: a glance at the statistics

This section is devoted to a discussion on the empirical data available in an attempt to give an indication of 'typical' Latin American women. The indicators examined below provide broad brushstrokes.

Education and health

At the beginning of the century only the richest in most countries had open access to education. As provision improved, girls were often ignored in favour of boys. Gradually the situation became equitable, with girls matching boys firstly at primary school, then at secondary school and finally in tertiary education. Women are currently outnumbering men in some university subjects. Education is not the panacea for all development problems, but the impact of improved educational attainment is significant. Influencing job opportunities, and consequently income, family size, and attitudes to marriage, it changes expectations about what life has to offer.

By 1990 female/male differences as regards basic literacy in the region were minimal, with the exception of Bolivia and Peru: in both these cases it is rural women who have been left behind, and almost half are unable to read and write (see table 3.6). Highly urbanized societies register high literacy rates with little gender difference, but poorer and more rural countries encounter more problems, and many teachers do not want to work in isolated communities. The large number of indigenous languages in the Andean highlands and in Central America can act as a barrier to gaining access to education. In these communities women are more likely to be monolingual non-Spanish speakers. As table 3.6 indicates, the change in the education of women is not confined to basic literacy; they are also taking their studies much further. In the region as a whole women make up 48 per cent of university enrolments, with seven countries registering 50 per cent or more (Valdés and Gomáriz, 1995: 108). In most countries women are represented in greater numbers in humanities and social sciences, but there are increasing numbers in 'male' subjects such as engin-eering and transport and communications (ibid.: 109). These changes in education have occurred very rapidly: in 1970 the majority of rural women in seven countries were illiterate; by 1990 the majority in all countries were literate.

There have been similarly radical changes in health care. This is reflected in greater life expectancy and in the reduction of infant and maternal mortality. Improved access to health-care facilities is of particular importance to women, since they are the ones who generally have to wait in medical centres and attend to sick family members. Government spending on health has never been great as

Table 3.6 Illiteracy rates and education, 1990

	Percentage of illiterate women			Percentage of illiterate men			Ratio of female to male enrolment (× 100)	
	Total	Urban	Rural	Total	Urban	Rural	Second level[b]	Third level[c]
Argentina	4.9	N/A	N/A	4.5	N/A	N/A	107	88
Bolivia	27.7	15.5	49.9	11.8	3.8	23.1	85	N/A
Brazil[a]	18.6	13.6	34.7	18.4	11.5	37.5	116	110
Chile	6.1	4.4	17.5	5.7	3.6	16.3	106	80
Colombia	14.1	N/A	N/A	12.5	N/A	N/A	116	107
Costa Rica	6.9	N/A	N/A	7.4	N/A	N/A	101	N/A
Cuba	7	N/A	N/A	5	N/A	N/A	108	136
Dominican Republic	17.9	10.8	31.4	17.5	8.7	29.7	122	N/A
Ecuador	13.5	6.5	25.1	9.1	3.6	15.5	101	64
El Salvador	30	N/A	N/A	23.8	N/A	N/A	102	49
Guatemala	47.8	27	60	34.2	16.5	45.6	90	N/A
Honduras	29.4	N/A	N/A	24.5	N/A	N/A	122	75
Mexico	15	13.5	38.7	9.6	N/A	N/A	99	75
Nicaragua	24.1	N/A	N/A	23.2	9.6	39.1	137	122
Panama	11.1	N/A	N/A	10.3	N/A	N/A	105	139
Paraguay	11.9	N/A	N/A	7.9	N/A	N/A	101	86
Peru	17.4	6.3	45.6	4.1	2.2	10.4	88	54
Uruguay	4.1	N/A	N/A	3.4	N/A	N/A	112	140
Venezuela	9.9	N/A	N/A	8.7	N/A	N/A	133	89

[a] Figures for illiteracy rates for Brazil are taken from 1988.

[b] Second-level enrolment figures for Brazil and Uruguay refer to a year between 1980 and 1984, and for the Dominican Republic to general secondary education only.

[c] Third-level enrolment figures for Argentina, Ecuador, Mexico and Paraguay refer to universities and equivilant degree-granting institutions only. Figures for Peru refer to a year between 1980 and 1984. Figures for Honduras and Uruguay refer to the university/universities only.

Sources: Valdés and Gomáriz (1995: 99), IDB (1995: 201)

a percentage of GDP, and during the years of economic crisis spending decreased (see table 3.7). Life expectancy is higher for women than men in every category, but again there are major differences, with highly urbanized societies registering much higher life expectancy rates (see table 3.2). The seven countries in which women's life expectancy is less than 70 years all have large rural populations: Bolivia (64), Guatemala (67), Peru (67), Nicaragua (69), Ecuador (69), Brazil (69) and El Salvador (69).[12] Even in these countries there have been vast improvements on the life expectancy figures of twenty years ago.

Table 3.5 covers issues concerning reproductive health. While contraceptive use is not universal, it is clear that the majority of women have chosen to control their fertility: this is also reflected in fertility rates.[13] More young Latin American women (15–19 years old) have children than European women, but family size, as we see below, has decreased. The average number of children per woman in the region is 3.1, compared with 5.9 between 1950 and 1955. Guatemalan women have the greatest number of children (5.4) and Cuban the least (1.9) (Valdés and Gomáriz, 1995: 44). Table 3.5 also shows the clear differences between women's access to trained attendants at birth, with, again, rural women having the lowest access. It must be noted, however, that many indigenous and rural communities have untrained local midwives who are versed in traditional health-care methods who meet most women's needs: 'modern' medicine is not the only option. The problem is obviously when there are complications: then access to well-equipped health-care centres is important.

Changes in reproductive health are reflected in smaller family size, but, given the concentration of young people in most populations, overall population growth will continue to put serious pressures on governments' abilities to provide social welfare services. Abortion is still illegal in most circumstances in most countries: Cuba is the only country to have abortion on demand, a fact that is possibly reflected in the smaller family sizes there. Given that abortions are carried out clandestinely, it is difficult to obtain statistics: in the case of Argentina, the gynaecologist Dr Margarita Moreno cited unofficial statistics where abortion accounts for a third of deaths of women of fertile age and suggested that, in the capital, Buenos Aires, there are 1.2 abortions for every live birth.[14] It is perhaps ironic that Latin American women cannot have access to legal abortions, but the state encourages and occasionally coerces women to have sterilizations. Sterilizations are common in

Table 3.7 Public spending on health care

	Public spending on health care as a percentage of the GDP			Per capita spending in 1980 US$		
	1970	1980	1990	1970	1980	1990
Argentina	0.3	0.5	0.3	11	21	10
Bolivia	0.9	1.7	0.3	6	13	2
Brazil	1.3	1.3	2.9	14	26	55
Chile	1.7	2.1	1.8	35	48	45
Colombia	N/A	4.8	3.6	N/A	59	52
Costa Rica	0.4	0.9	1.3	5	14	19
Cuba	N/A	N/A	N/A	N/A	N/A	N/A
Dominican Republic	N/A	2	1.1	N/A	23	12
Ecuador	0.5	1.8	1.6	4	26	22
El Salvador	1.3	1.5	0.8	9	12	5
Guatemala	N/A	1.2	1.2	N/A	14	11
Honduras	1.5	2.2	2.4	8	16	16
Mexico	N/A	0.4	0.3	N/A	10	7
Nicaragua	0.7	4.4	5.8	7	33	28
Panama	1.8	1.6	2	25	29	31
Paraguay	2	0.4	0.4	15	5	5
Peru	0.9	0.8	0.6	10	10	5
Uruguay	N/A	1	1.2	N/A	23	27
Venezuela	1.7	1.3	1.1	82	53	37

Figures for 1990 are circa 1990.

Source: Valdés and Gomáriz (1995: 31)

Brazil, Mexico and Peru. In the last case, the government has been criticized for its handling of 'population programmes', where poor Indian women in the highland areas have been sterilized without adequate emotional or medical care, leaving them unable to cope.

Household structure

Changes in household structures relate to family size and the number of generations living in one household. The nuclear household has become more common but is by no means typical. In many countries consensual unions, rather than formal marriages, are more common, and female-headed households have increased, reflecting changing cultural norms and work opportunities. Rural–urban migration has had an impact on household structures as extended families have fragmented and new ones emerge in the cities. Economic crisis has also played its part, forcing some people to pool resources, and different family members live under one roof.[15] As regards marital status, Central American and Caribbean countries register higher rates of consensual unions, with marriage being more popular in other countries (see table 3.8). Divorce/separation rates are low, but this is possibly because people engage in new relations and do not remain single, and therefore register as married or in consensual relations. Nevertheless, divorce rates are increasing, albeit more slowly than in many European countries. Cuba and the Dominican Republic register very high divorce rates at just over a third of marriages, but the rate has been consistent since the 1980s (Valdés and Gomáriz, 1995: 59). Women establish unions at a younger age than men and are more likely to be divorced, separated or widowed; men are more likely to be single (Valdés and Gomáriz, 1995: 55).

Female-headed households have increased over the years but have not reached the proportions that some were suggesting a few years ago (Varley, 1996). For urban Latin America as a whole, about 22.7 per cent of households are headed by women: in both Nicaragua and Cuba rates are around 35 per cent (Valdés and Gomáriz, 1995: 61). Some households grow with the incorporation of widowed women to look after grandchildren while mothers work outside the home. Despite the changes over the years, the majority of Latin American women marry and have children, and they tend to do this when they are slightly younger than their European counterparts. Change is most noticeable in the increase in divorce and the increase in female-headed households. While

Table 3.8 Marital status (as a percentage)

	Age group considered (years of age)	Year from which figures are derived	Married	Single	Consensual union	Separated/ divorced	Widowed
Argentina	14 and over	1980	51.6	28.1	6.7	2.6	11
Bolivia	12 and over	1988	35	57.6	N/A	2	5.1
Brazil	12 and over	1989	56	31.1	N/A	3.4	8
Chile	12 and over	1985	48.5	37.3	2.2	3.2	8.8
Colombia	10 and over	1984	31.3	43.4	12.8	4.7	6.3
Costa Rica	10 and over	1984	45.6	35.1	9.6	4.6	5.1
Cuba	14 and over	1981	22	43.3	20.9	6.8	7
Dominican Republic	15 and over	1981	24.5	32	28.2	9.4	5
Ecuador	12 and over	1982	37.7	36.3	14.2	3.1	5.2
Mexico	12 and over	1990	45.5	37.9	7.5	2.8	5.6
Nicaragua	15 and over	1985	26.6	22	27.1	16.1	8.1
Panama	15 and over	1990	27.7	27.9	27.9	11	5.3
Paraguay	12 and over	1982	39.4	43.9	10.1	1.5	4.2
Peru	15 and over	1981	38.5	39.4	12.4	2.3	6.7
Uruguay	10 and over	1985	37.7	43.6	4.5	4.5	9.7
Venezuela	12 and over	1990	34.7	33.3	17	5.1	8.7

Source: Valdés and Gomáriz (1995: 54)

these experiences do not reflect those of the majority, they do bear out those of a significant minority, and one which is growing.

Much emphasis has been placed on female-headed households in the development literature, and this can help 'invisibilize' the majority, particularly in Latin America (Varley, 1996). Nevertheless, there are indications that women prefer not to re-establish a union, since they enjoy the independence that comes with remaining single and changing work opportunities offer them more possibilities. One worker commented,

> Men are machista. They think that if the woman works she will rule too much, because that's the way it is here in Santo Domingo – that when a woman works she is liberal, a little too liberal, that they can't mistreat or abuse her. . . . When the woman isn't working, she has to wait, to have a bad time, to put up with many things from a man, but when the woman is working things change, because we are both working. (in Safa, 1995: 42–3)

This quotation amply illustrates the shifting attitudes of women (and men) in response to changing circumstances.

Changing work trends

Women have participated in economic activity to a much greater degree than was previously recognized, but much of their labour has been hidden and considered 'domestic tasks' rather than work. In Chapter 5, I discuss how work affects political activity and women's political identity; for the moment it is important to examine the changes in women's work patterns. The changing economic conditions, as well as their improved educational attainment, have an impact on the types of work carried out by women. The shift towards the neoliberal economic model has resulted in the closure of traditionally 'male' industries such as autos, cements, petroleum and mining, to more 'female' employment with assembly plants and tertiary sector employment, much of it in the informal sector. The combination of economic crisis and structural adjustment has resulted in women playing a greater and more direct role in income generation, frequently in deteriorating working conditions (Mitter, 1994). The work available to women is dependent on a number of issues: educational attainment, age and civil status and geographic location, as well the jobs themselves. Women tend to change jobs more often than men and are frequently engaged in more than one activity: it is generally accepted that women complete the bulk of the world's working hours.[16] Within the formal labour sector women's involvement has been significantly less than that of men, and there are differences between countries in the degree of women's insertion into the labour market. Women have long taken advantage of the informal sector since it allows for greater flexibility – particularly useful to women with their greater domestic responsibilities.

In most Latin American countries at least a quarter of women are economically active (both employed and unemployed), and in some countries economically active women make up over a third of the total number of working-age women. At the regional level, the percentage of women participating in the economically active population (EAP) has increased over the past forty years, from 23.1 per cent in 1950 to 27.2 in 1990, with a dip in the 1960s and 1970s (Valdés and Gomáriz, 1995: 67). Their participation peaks between the ages of twenty-five and twenty-nine and decreases slowly thereafter (ibid.: 76). Smaller percentages of women aged under twenty and over fifty worked in the 1980s, however, compared with the 1950s: this trend contrasts with that in developed countries, where there is a dip in the participation of women in their thirties (Psacharopoulos and Tzannatos, 1992: 14–15). This would indicate that fewer women in Latin America stop working when they have children.

Other data indicate that the numbers of economically active women have more than tripled in the period 1960–1990, while the numbers of men have not even doubled (Valdés and Gomáriz, 1995: 63). Countries with large rural sectors tend to have lower female participation rates, especially Central America and Ecuador; the lowest recorded rate is in Guatemala, at 15.6 per cent, although it is difficult to know how much of women's work is invisible due to narrow definitions of work. The highest participation rates are found in Uruguay (39.5 per cent) and Cuba (34.8 per cent) (see table 3.9); the average rate for the region is 27.2 per cent. The percentage of women working has increased from 18.1 per cent in 1960, while men have registered a decrease, from 77.5 per cent in 1960 to 70.3 per cent in 1990 (Valdés and Gomáriz, 1995: 66–7). In their peak working years (from the age of twenty-five to forty-nine) between a third and a half of women in most countries have jobs; in Uruguay over 60 per cent of women in this age group are employed (Psacharopoulos and Tzannatos, 1992: 66–7). Similarly, women's share of the EAP has risen from 19.1 per cent in 1960 to 28.1 per cent in 1990. By the 1990s only in Honduras do

Table 3.9 Employed female population by sector of economic activity (%); and economically active female population, 1990 (%)

	Year	Agriculture	Manufacturing	Services	% of women working, 1990
Argentina aged 14 and over	1980	2.2	23.9	73.9	
	1990	1	17.4	81.6	26.1
Bolivia aged 7 and over	1976	27.2	18.5	54.3	
	1992	43.9	9.4	46.7	28.5
Brazil aged 10 and over	1981	19.8	13	67.2	
	1988	14.7	12.7	72.6	30.3
Chile	1980	2.8	16.3	80.6	
	1989	5.9	15.7	78.4	27
Colombia aged 12 and over	1982	0.4	24.3	75.3	
	1989	0.6	24	75.4	31.6
Costa Rica	1983	5.1	21.7	73.2	
	1992	5.5	25	69.5	21.3
Cuba	1980	10.6	21.6	67.8	
	1990	N/A	N/A	N/A	34.8
Dominican Republic	1981	6.4	14.6	79.1	
	1991	6	14.1	79.9	30.3
Ecuador	1982	13	17.1	69.9	
	1990	15.8	15.7	68.5	19.4
El Salvador aged 10 and over	1980	N/A	N/A	N/A	
	1990	2.7	22.4	74.9	24
Guatemala	1980	12.9	28.3	58.8	
	1989	16	22.8	61.2	15.6
Honduras aged 10 and over	1980	N/A	N/A	N/A	
	1990	5.7	22.9	71.4	21

Mexico	1980	N/A	N/A	N/A	29.2
aged 12 and over	1990	0.3	21	78.7	
Nicaragua	1980	N/A	N/A	N/A	32.8
	1990	N/A	N/A	N/A	
Panama	1982	5.6	11.8	82.6	26.3
aged 15 and over	1989	4.7	12	83.3	
Paraguay	1982	12	23.4	64.6	25.6
aged 12 and over	1990	0.8	14.8	84.4	
Peru	1981	26.1	12.9	61	27.5
	1990	N/A	N/A	N/A	
Uruguay	1981	3	23	74	39.5
aged 12 and over	1985	4.4	19.8	75.8	
Venezuela	1976	4.9	18.6	76.5	26.9
	1990	2.5	15.8	81.7	
Western Europe/other					
developed areas	1994	7	20	73	
Northern Africa	1994	25	29	46	
Sub-Saharan Africa	1994	75	5	20	
East Asia	1994	35	29	36	
South-East Asia	1994	42	16	42	
Southern Asia	1994	55	25	20	
Central Asia	1994	33	20	47	
Western Asia	1994	23	15	61	

Figures for El Salvador and Mexico are taken from urban areas. Figures from Argentina are taken from Greater Buenos Aires. Figures from Colombia are taken from seven major cities. All other figures are nationwide figures.

Sources: Valdés and Gomáriz (1995: 67, 79), UN (1995: 113)

women constitute less than 20 per cent of the EAP (17.8 per cent), and in many countries they make up more than 30 per cent (Bolivia, Colombia, Cuba, Nicaragua and Uruguay) (ibid.: 64, 69).

Table 3.9 also shows the sectors in which women predominate. Women are much more likely to participate in the service sector, followed by the industrial sector: the exceptions are Bolivia and Peru, where women engage in the agricultural sector in much larger numbers. It must be remembered that women who participate in the agricultural sector often go unreported, since their contribution is seen as domestic rather than 'work', and many are seasonal workers easily overlooked in the data. The decline in traditional industries has had a greater impact on male than on female unemployment, and the development of export processing zones (EPZs), particularly in Central America and Mexico, has favoured women. The service sector is heterogeneous and incorporates many different working practices: at the upper end the work is professional and well paid, but for many it is insecure work with poor conditions. In all countries women are underrepresented in managerial positions (IDB, 1995: 205). Although this may change as the effects of improved education filter through, experiences from other regions suggest that most women professionals encounter a 'glass ceiling'.

There are changes in work patterns over the course of a woman's life reflecting both the impact of having children and economic developments. Generally the arrival of children changes the nature of work, and more women turn to the informal sector for income generation or combine domestic labour with surplus household production for sale. The economic crisis of the 1980s has changed the work patterns inasmuch as more women are available for work and define themselves as unemployed rather than inactive. However, women are finding it more difficult to get work and are experiencing higher unemployment rates than their male counterparts (Psacharopoulos and Tzannatos, 1992). There is evidence that the impact of economic crisis on household formation pushes young (those under fifteen) and older women into family management roles to allow adult women to engage in further income-generation activities (Chant, 1993; 1991). The innovative ways in which women have engaged in income generation at all ages is a good indicator of their resourcefulness, but the work undertaken is often extremely low paid, has no security and is irregular.

Single women have found it easier to be employed in those salaried jobs available, such as teaching and clerical work, and in the *maquilas*.[17] This reflects both employers' preferences and the attitudes of husbands; many men disapprove of wives working outside the home, complaining that it will lessen their commitment to the family. Again there are great regional disparities; in some countries, particularly in Argentina, Chile and Uruguay, working women are more accepted, although what they do is not seen as important as men's work. Furthermore, with increasing education, more women are entering the labour force and developing careers.[18]

It must be remembered, however, that political conditions have an impact on women's economic participation. Under the repressive military regimes women were forced to engage in income generation on being left heads of household when their partners 'disappeared'. The fall-out of disappearances was exacerbated by the harsh economic conditions resulting from the policies of the military. Women's greater participation in work cannot be divorced from political conditions. For those women for whom working outside the home is difficult, home-based production is an important option (Craske, 1993). Wilson (1993) suggests that, with the economic crisis, women who have left employment on marriage or having children are returning to work, but more often in the informal workshops which are closer to home-based production. Chant (1994) finds adult women moving into the labour force in Costa Rica and Mexico, where they represent the largest section of new workers responding to the economic crisis. Similarly McClenaghan (1997) found that, in the Dominican Republic, employers preferred married women as employees.

Although women are re-entering the workforce, this is still viewed as secondary and exceptional; consequently it reinforces the notion that men are the primary breadwinners and women earn money for their own extra (and implicitly non-essential) expenses. This in turn helps to keep their wage rates significantly lower than men's, and, ironically, it is also helping to keep men's wages lower as more women move into the labour force providing wage competition. On average the region's women earn 71.6 per cent of men's wages (Valdés and Gomáriz, 1995: 93). The *maquiladoras* have deliberately employed women because of the lower costs of wages among other reasons, with most men being employed as supervisors (Peña, 1987; Pearson, 1991, cf. Safa, 1995). The economic crisis may have eroded some of the unease felt about women working outside the home, but many, both women and men, think of the ideal as a woman staying at home concentrating on domestic tasks. Another result of the interaction of family gender relations and paid labour is that many women underplay their own financial contribution to the family income in order not to embarrass or undermine their husbands (Craske, 1993).

Most women have engaged in income-generation activities, although it has frequently been underreported. Education, economic crisis and changing discourses on the role of women in society have all had an impact on women's work choices and opportunities. Work is an ambivalent experience for women: for the majority it adds to their burdens, but it can also offer opportunities for independent living which is partially reflected in the increased numbers of female-headed households. In Chapter 5 I discuss the political implications of work in terms of developing collective action and political identity, and the impact on women's sense of empowerment and gender relations.

Conclusions

This chapter has demonstrated the ways in which the lives of Latin Americans have changed over the past decades by focusing on social, economic and political structures. These structures have been exclusionary, benefiting, for the most part, a narrow band of elite and, more specifically, white men. Change has been slow and resisted at almost every stage, frequently accompanied by social, economic and political repression. The transformations in women's lives particularly reflect socio-economic developments. In many ways their lives have improved, materially at least, over the past years, but there are still serious deficiencies, both in terms of gender equality and social justice, and the trends are not always favourable. Their changing experiences have an impact on what women expect from life, including their political involvement, as the remainder of the book demonstrates.

The socio-economic developments and changes in women's life experiences have taken place against a backdrop of political authoritarianism. The political systems in which the majority of Latin Americans live have not been open to the demands and aspirations of the people. Socio-economic developments create their own political agendas, resulting in campaigns and political struggles in which women have engaged. Women have succeeded in altering the conditions in which they live and in creating new citizens' rights, but they have also had to confront significant constraints which limit their autonomy. They have to balance their different identities within the political terrain. As we have seen from the discussion above, women are disadvantaged in many arenas, but this is changing. The struggles which have resulted in change are analysed in the various chapters. In the next chapter, women's participation in the formal structures and institutions of politics is analysed: as is the case in social and economic developments, women have become more visible in the political world as well. The gradual changes resulting from increased access to education, different work opportunities and fluctuating economic and political conditions all have an impact on women. Over time, the opportunities and constraints discussed have led women to demand a greater political voice in the many arenas discussed in the following chapters.

4

Formal Political Representation: Governments, Parties and Bureaucracies

My aim is to help gain access to power for groups that have traditionally been locked out. I don't have any illusion that I'm going to change the whole system, but I can make small gains ...

Benedita da Silva (in Benjamin and Mendonça, 1997: 69)

Introduction

In Chapter 1 I argued that political institutions were potentially structures for empowerment and therefore could be useful tools for the advancement of women. I also suggested, however, that such institutions tend to be conservative and defend the status quo and therefore need constant pressure from outside. Given the rather conservative characteristics of political institutions, most women who have broken into them have found it easier to conform to dominant gender relations. Consequently there is a gender division of labour within political institutions where women tend to be concentrated in tasks associated with reproduction: this is the case in government, in parties and in bureaucracies. Political institutions have supported gender constructions which have seen women as mothers and responsible for social reproduction more generally. Despite this conservatism, there have been advances in terms of levels of representation and the passing of laws which supported women's equality. Furthermore, some changes have made political structures tools for empowerment: quota laws, women's ministries, and initially the extension of franchise.

Although women in institutional politics have more often conformed to gender stereotypes than challenged them, there are exceptions, and, as more women become involved in political institutions, they move beyond narrow identification with the reproductive sphere. Clearly there have always been women who have not conformed to the stereotypes – women who have not married and become mothers but who have dedicated themselves to politics full time, such as Beatriz Paredes in Mexico and Julia Alsogoray in Argentina. Like their male counterparts, women who have succeeded in 'high' politics have tended to come from the elite, and their reproductive 'duties' have been considerably lightened by paid assistance: it is extremely difficult for poor women, especially poor women of colour, to break into the decision-making arenas. Women who became politically active in social movements in the 1970s and 1980s have generally not moved into the institutional political arena. The consolidation of democracy of the 1980s and 1990s has demonstrated that the hopes for more inclusionary political systems in the post-authoritarian period have, for the most part, not been realized.

This chapter is divided into four main sections: an examination of women's participation in governments and congresses; an analysis of the strengths and weaknesses of the Argentine quota law and the region's women's ministries; a discussion of the attitudes of political parties towards women's representation; and a survey of the integration of women into state bureaucracies. I argue that during the transition from authoritarianism to democracy there were greater opportunities for women (and others) to press their claims, as the political arena was more fluid. Consequently there are more women representatives in congresses and a number of key laws for women were passed: in short, women became more visible politically. But during the consolidation phase institutions have 'bedded down' and there has been a return to exclusionary political practices in some countries, such as negotiated settlements, clientelism and corruption, despite the challenges emanating from the grassroots. These practices are reinforced by the economic constraints, discussed in Chapter 3, under which Latin American governments labour.

The struggle for formal citizenship

Latin American women gained the vote between 1929 (Ecuador) and 1961 (Paraguay). The circumstances of attaining this basic citizen's right, however, varied in different countries, and there is little correlation between levels of development and 'modernity' and the granting of the female vote. In some cases, particularly that of Argentina, Brazil, Cuba and Mexico, women militated to demand the vote, while in others governments, quite often conservative ones (notably that of Ecuador and the personalized dictatorships of Trujillo in the Dominican Republic and Stroessner in Paraguay), enfranchised women in the expectation that they would support them and bolster their position.

The case of revolutionary Mexico is illustrative of the problems women faced in achieving citizenship. The 1917 Mexican constitution gave *citizens* the right to vote, yet, despite the deployment of this ostensibly gender-neutral term, the vote was not extended to women on the grounds that they were subjects of the domestic arena and the family, and thus would not develop a political consciousness (Fernández Poncela, 1995: 38). The first post-revolutionary governments were reluctant to extend the vote, arguing that it would jeopardize revolutionary gains, particularly in the field of education, which had been secularized in the 1930s. It was not until 1953 that this right was granted by Adolfo Ruíz Cortines, a more conservative president than his predecessors, by which time only Colombia, Honduras, Peru, Nicaragua and Paraguay had yet to introduce universal suffrage (see table 4.1). Cuba, on the other hand, had already realized some advanced legislation in relation to women, including the extension of franchise, long before the revolution (Stubbs, 1994). The majority of Latin American women were enfranchised in the 1940s and 1950s (see table 4.1).

The struggle for the vote led to the establishment of a number of women's parties and pressure groups. Perhaps the most famous is the Partido Peronista Femenino (Women's Peronist Party: PPF) in Argentina, which Eva Perón, President Juan Perón's charismatic second wife, founded to support her husband.[1] Many credit Eva Perón with winning the vote for women in Argentina, but it must be remembered that there was a long struggle for the vote by feminists before she became a prominent political figure, and she was only one influence among others. The lack of the vote had implications for a woman's right to practise law in certain countries or to hold other positions of responsibility.

Soon after enfranchisement women began to run for office, although there were one or two cases of women holding official positions while not full citizens. In Nicaragua, for example, women were appointed as judges; in Peru, however, in 1951, when women

Table 4.1 Dates of women's enfranchisement in Latin America

Ecuador	1929
Brazil	1932
Uruguay	1932
Cuba	1934
El Salvador	1939
Dominican Republic	1942
Panama	1945
Guatemala	1945
Costa Rica	1945
Venezuela	1947
Argentina	1947
Chile	1949
Bolivia	1952
Mexico	1953
Honduras	1955
Nicaragua	1955
Peru	1955
Colombia	1957
Paraguay	1961

Source: Miller (1991: 96)

were still not enfranchised, the Supreme Court vetoed them from sitting as secretaries or court reporters (Valdés and Gomáriz, 1995: 167). While women gained the vote after men, there is another important distinction to be remembered. In most countries there was a literacy clause which effectively silenced women from indigenous communities for much longer, for some until the 1980s (ibid.: 160). Given the tendency for men to outnumber women as voters in most countries, there have been assumptions about women's apolitical nature. As Randall (1987: 53) shows, however, the lesser interest of women in voting is not inherent 'but, contingent and transient', depending particularly on degrees of urbanization and education. Furthermore, this tendency appears to be changing (see below).

Women's legislative representation and office holding

Although women have had the vote for several decades, there is still only limited representation of women at all levels of government and within state bureaucracies. The problems that women have faced in developing their political identity has been compounded by the nature of the political arena in the region. As indicated in Chapter 3, democratic rule has been intermittent in many countries and political participation in authoritarian systems was constrained for all. But even in countries with continuous electoral politics for the past forty years or more (Colombia, Costa Rica, Mexico, Paraguay, Venezuela)[2] women's involvement as political representatives in the institutional arena has been limited. Chile, long considered one of the most European countries, demonstrating competitive party rule until the advent of Pinochet in 1973, has few women in congress, the cabinet, or local and regional levels of government. In equally 'European' Uruguay, women have been similarly underrepresented in government and congress. I examine below the participation of women in the executive positions of the presidency, cabinet and regional and municipal heads. This is followed by a discussion of women's role in legislative politics at national, regional and local levels.

Executive positions

The highly centralized nature of most Latin American political systems means that the focus of electoral competition has been at the national and particularly the presidential level. There have been only three women presidents in Latin America: Estela de Perón, Juan Perón's third wife, was president of Argentina from the latter's death in 1974 until 1976; Lidia Gueiler was briefly president of Bolivia from November 1979 to July 1980; and Violeta de Chamorro (the only one to be elected) was president in Nicaragua between 1990 and 1996. Both Perón and Gueiler were overthrown by military coups. Although there are only these three, they illustrate the importance of personal relationships, since two of them were the widows of important political figures in their countries (Chamorro and Perón): only Gueiler had a history of political activism as a member of the Movimiento Nacional Revolucionario (MNR) from the 1950s (Ardaya Salinas, 1994).

Family connections were underlined further by Chamorro, who emphasized her role as mother and widow by always wearing white and talking of her husband, who was killed by the Somoza regime. The discourse of mothering was particularly important, and she spoke of Nicaragua as a family. As Kampwith (1996: 69) argues, 'Doña Violeta presented herself not only as an exemplary wife and widow, but also an exemplary mother who managed to keep her children united against the odds.' Chamorro herself commented, 'I am not a feminist nor do I wish to be one. I am a woman dedicated to my home, as Pedro taught me' (ibid.). Women have become vice-presidents in Costa Rica and Honduras, although it must be noted that in both cases there is more than one vice-president (Valdés and Gomáriz, 1995: 161).[3]

The first woman cabinet minister (without portfolio) was appointed in 1948 in Cuba, and Chile followed in 1952 with the appointment of a woman as minister of justice; Argentina and Paraguay, however, did not have female ministers until 1989. The highly centralized and personalized political systems found in many countries does mean that networking is key to gaining high office. Furthermore, it is evident from the data that there is a gender division of labour within cabinet positions, with women being found mainly in 'caring' ministries such as education and welfare. This hasn't changed much since Elsa Chaney identified the 'supermadre' syndrome in the early 1970s. Furthermore, Chaney noted that women felt they had to attend to their private responsibilities with more commitment than other women if they wished to be involved in political life. Consequently, to legitimize their political involvement further, they tend to choose interests compatible with 'women's interests', such as health, education and social welfare, taking *marianismo* into the political environment (Chaney, 1973). While this has continued there are signs that it is changing: in 1998 there were two female foreign ministers – Rosario Green in Mexico and María Emma Mejía Velez (who went on to become vice-presidential candidate for the Liberal Party in 1998) in Colombia.

Four Latin American states (Argentina, Brazil, Mexico and Venezuela) have federal constitutions with important regional legislatures (states or provinces). Argentina, Brazil, Colombia, Mexico, Paraguay and Venezuela also have elected governors, and Uruguay's mayors are the functional equivalent of governors. Again there is the familiar pattern of few women achieving these positions. Recent data show that in most federal countries women make up less than 10 per cent of governors. Only three countries have more than 20 per cent: the Dominican Republic with 28 per cent, Panama with 22.2 per cent and Costa Rica with a staggering 71.4 per cent – that is, five out of the seven *appointed* governors. There is more openness at the local level, with women mayors in many entities, but it is not always possible to compare across countries; Mexico and Brazil have several thousand municipalities each while Uruguay has only nineteen. Uruguay has the greatest number of women mayors, with 15.8 per cent of the total (1992), while, ironically, Costa Rica has none. In fifteen countries the numbers of women mayors does not reach 10 per cent (Valdés and Gomáriz, 1995: 163).

What appears to be a common pattern is that women are more strongly represented in smaller municipal governments; it is hard to compare a town of 10,000 with places such as Mexico City or São Paulo with several million inhabitants. Luiza Erundina was elected mayor of São Paulo in 1988, which represented a major shift for women's political representation: as an immigrant from one of the poorest areas of the country, she is all the more remarkable (Tabak 1994: 132; see also Macaulay, 1996). It is difficult to come to any firm conclusions about the role of women in local government since, as Pinto (1993) points out, many countries are undergoing municipal reform with an emphasis on decentralization; consequently trends are difficult to detect. Others note that women engage in similar commissions at the local level as they do at the national, namely the 'feminine' social issues: health, social assistance, housing, human rights (Bruera and González, 1993).[4] It is sobering to note, when considering the democratic process, that there were more female municipal heads appointed under Pinochet than are currently elected in Chile.

The role of first ladies

'First ladies' and wives of office holders often have certain symbolic responsibilities, and some have used their positions to establish their own power bases – the most obvious example being Eva Perón. Ironically, though, it was her successor as Perón's wife, Estela Martínez, who succeeded in becoming the country's vice-president, which eventually led to her taking the highest office when Perón died. Evita's legacy is reflected in a particular popular construction of women political actors linked to the party system, but not with a specific gender perspective.[5]

In other countries the president's wife is expected to head social welfare programmes, such as the Desarrollo Integral de la Familia (DIF) in Mexico;[6] this is repeated at the regional level, with governors' wives heading the state-level DIFs. Again, in Costa Rica the women's branch of the Partido de Liberación Nacional (PLN) was run by the wife of the president or presidential candidate. This paternalist pattern of female political power undermines women who want to compete on the same terms as men by giving them a political space which is highly controlled and dependent on male political prowess, and which also institutionalizes their domestic role. It does, however, allow them some political space which has potential for further development. Certainly Evita's charitable foundation allowed her a key power base, although she always emphasized her subordination to Perón (Navarro, 1982). The obvious problem is that these spaces only function within the existing political system, and radical change, particularly regarding shifts in gender relations, will be difficult to effect from there.

Congresses

There are both unicameral and bicameral congresses in Latin America. In two-chamber systems women's representation tends to be higher in the lower house (see table 4.2). With only three exceptions, average female representation has not exceeded 10 per cent in national congresses.[7] In the majority of countries women attained their highest levels of representation during the 1980s, although Argentina is a marked exception and partly reflects the activities of Eva Perón and the Partido Femenino in the 1950s. Latterly the country's *ley de cupo* (quota law), passed in 1991, has dramatically increased the presence of women in congress, from 5 per cent in 1991 to 16.3 per cent in 1993, 21.8 per cent in 1995 and 27.6 per cent in 1997. Chile currently has only thirteen women deputies (10.8 per cent of the total), despite its well-developed women's movements, the existence of the Servicio Nacional de la Mujer (SERNAM – the women's ministry) and good relations between the two. Brazil has similarly disappointing levels of female representatives, despite the high degree of interaction between popular movements and political parties, particularly after the formation of the Workers' Party (Partido dos Trabalhadores: PT) in 1979. Uruguay, perhaps, demonstrates the most discouraging scenario: no women were elected to the first post-military chamber of deputies in 1984, despite their participation in opposition politics, which had helped oust the military.

Table 4.2 Women's representation in Latin American chambers of deputies, 1998

Country	Years	Av. repr. (%)	Term	Highest (%)	Current repr. (%)	World ranking	Comments
Argentina	1952–97	7	3 years	21.6 (1955)	27.6 (1997)	8	15.5% 1952
Bolivia[a]	1979–93	5	4 years	6.9 (1993)	6.9 (1993)	N/A	
Brazil	1945–94	1.44	4 years	6.6 (1994)	6.6 (1994)	72	1945 no deps
Chile[b]	1945–97	4.13	4 years	10.8 (1997)	10.8 (1997)	47	8% in 1965
Colombia[c]	1994	11	4 years		11 (1994)	39	Only other datum 1970: 5.7%
Costa Rica	1949–98	5.8	5 years	19.3 (1998)	19.3 (1998)	21	No deps 1949
Cuba	1976–98	24.5	5 years (approx.)	33.8 (1986)	27.6 (1998)	8	
Dominican Republic[d]	1970–94	7.8	4 years	7.6 (1982)	11.7 (1994)	43	No data 1974 & 1978
Ecuador	1979–96	2.7	4 years	5.2 (1994)	3.7 (1996)	89	
El Salvador	1982–97	8.5	3 years	16.7 (1997)	16.7 (1997)	27	No data for 1988
Guatemala	1954–95	2.8	4 years	12.5 (1995)	12.5 (1995)	35	No data for 1961
Honduras	1981–97	7.1	4 years	11.7 (1989)	9.4 (1997)	55	
Mexico	1955–97	10	3 years	17.4 (1994)	17.4 (1997)	26	12.4 % (1988–91)
Nicaragua	1979–96	17.5	6 years	21.6 (1979)	10.8 (1996)	47	Appointed at different times in 1979
Panama	1946–94	4	4 years	9.7 (1994)	9.7 (1994)	47	
Paraguay[e]	1968–93	2.96	5 years	5.5 (1989)	2.5 (1993)	97	
Peru	1980–95	5.5	5 years	5.5[f]	10.8 (1995)	47	Congress suspended 1992
Uruguay	1946–94	5.7	5 years	8 (1954)	7.1 (1994)	63	Incl. substitutes
Venezuela	1948–93	5.24	5 years	9.9 (1988)	5.9 (1993)	76	No dep 1968
Mean		6.9		11.18	12		

[a] No elections 1973–90.

[b] Elections March 1998: no data available. These results apply to 1993.

[c] Elections 1997 but not disaggregated for gender: these results apply to 1994.

[d] Elections May 1998: no data available. These results apply to 1994.

[e] Elections May 1998: no data available. These results apply to 1993.

[f] Highest achieved before suspension of congress in 1992.

Source: Compiled by the author using data from the Inter-Parliamentary Union

Mexico currently has its highest female representation (1997–2000), at 17.4 per cent, and women's representation has been growing since the 54th legislature (1988–91), the first in which the dominant Partido Revolucionario Institucional (PRI: Institutional Revolutionary Party) did not win two-thirds majority. The Mexican case highlights a worrying point, however: in 1991 the highest number of women candidates to date stood for election, although fewer were elected than in 1988. This would suggest that the failure of women candidates to be elected in part stems from the fact that they stand in seats where their party is weak and only 17.4 per cent are in the first five names on candidate lists (Fernández Poncela, 1995: 55). Women's difficulty in being candidates in winnable seats is reflected in the drafting of the Argentinian quota law (detailed below).

In the upper houses (table 4.3) the picture is broadly the same. The average representation of women since the 1950s barely reaches 6 per cent and in no country does it exceed 10 per cent. Indeed, throughout the region women's representation is even lower in the senate than in the chamber of deputies, although in 1997 things looked more hopeful, with women exceeding 10 per cent of senators in two countries (Mexico and Paraguay).[8] The highest numbers of female representatives have occurred over the past ten years – with the exception of Argentina, which again had large numbers of women senators in the 1950s. Women have also been speakers of parliament in a number of Latin American countries. The first was in Argentina in 1973. Since then women have achieved this position in a further eight countries (Bolivia, Costa Rica, El Salvador, Mexico, Nicaragua, Panama, Peru and Venezuela), six of them since 1990. At one point in Mexico women were speakers in both houses. In 1998, however, only Venezuela had a woman speaker (Inter-Parliamentary Union, 1997).

Although women are making inroads into representational politics, progress is painfully slow and subject to setbacks. Furthermore, women are still highly marginal to the process, with levels of representation generally under 15 per cent – far below the 30 per cent usually suggested for quotas (although most Northern liberal democracies fare no better). A common feature of countries in the region is that few of the women active in popular protest have secured entry into institutional politics. Even in Argentina, which has seen a massive increase in the number of congresswomen due to the quota law, only one, Graciela Fernández Meijide, was involved in collective action (as a human rights

Table 4.3 Women's representation in Latin American senates, 1998

Country	Years	Av. repr. (%)	Term	Highest (%)	Current repr. (%)	Comments
Argentina	1952–95	5.7	6 years	17.6 (1952)	5.6 (1995)	No reps 1958–62
Bolivia	1980–97	5.6	4 years	7.4 (1991)	3.7 (1997)	No women before 1980
Brazil	1945–94	N/A	4 years	7.4 (1994)	7.4 (1994)	Senators only 1978 & 1990
Chile[a]	1945–93	3.05	4 years	6.5 (1993)	6.5 (1993)	
Colombia	1994	6.9	4 years		6.9 (1994)	Only other datum 1970: 3.3
Dominican Republic	1970–90	9.8	4 years	14.5 (1970)	No data	No data 1974, 1978 & 1990
Mexico	1964–97	8.5	6 years	15.6 (1988)	14.8 (1997)	12.7% 1994 and 4.7% 1991
Paraguay	1968–93	5	5 years	11.1 (1993)	11.1 (1993)	
Peru	1980–90	5	5 years	6.7 (1990)	Suspended[b]	
Uruguay	1946–94	4.1	4 years	10 (1950)	6.5 (1994)	No data 1971 & 1984
Venezuela	1948–93	2.7	5 years	8.9 (1993)	8.2 (1993)	No women 1953, 1958, 1963, 1974, 1983
Mean		6.5		10.8	7.6	

[a] No elections 1973–90.
[b] Since 1995 Peru has had a unicameral system.

Source: Compiled by the author using data from the Inter-Parliamentary Union

campaigner after the disappearance of her son) prior to her election. Given the weakening of social movements, it is unlikely that more will come through along this route to institutional politics. Fernández Meijide comments that social movements have lost strength since the return to electoral rule: 'While the human rights movement was very strong here during the dictatorship, and pushed the issues in the post-dictatorship politics, it no longer has the same strength. You cannot even say that feminist movements in Argentina are strong. There are no great social movements here' (in *NACLA: Report on the Americas*, 31/1, 1997: 9).

In Mexico parties have attempted to establish links between themselves and grassroots organizations, notably the leftist Partido de la Revolución Democrática (PRD) and the PRI, but since women are generally the backbone rather than the head of these movements, it is often the men who reap the rewards of earlier participation when candidacies are negotiated.[9] In Brazil the link between grassroots organization and parties is aided by the activities of the PT, which grew out of social movements, particularly the labour movement, in the late 1970s; the first black woman senator, Benedita da Silva, was elected for the PT. Generally, however, women's formal political representation in Brazil is low. As Benedita da Silva comments: 'Our society is so divided between rich and poor, black and white. But the fact that I'm a black woman from a poor background allows me to break a lot of stereotypes' (Benjamin and Mendonça, 1997: 81). She also notes that she had to learn to deal with sexism in her own team as well as within the political system generally. It is a struggle to confront racism and sexism daily: 'I know how critical it is to constantly fight against discrimination. People call me ugly and a monkey. They tell me to go pick bananas and to go back to the kitchen. I receive racist and sexist letters written on toilet paper. And now that I'm more vocal about these issues and more well-known, I'm attacked more than ever' (ibid.: 61).

What can be deduced from this discussion is that women are increasingly active in institutional politics at all levels, but that there are certain pessimistic conclusions to be drawn. First, it is the status of the position that is gendered, with women in greater numbers in the least influential positions; Camp points to large numbers of women in the judiciary in many countries, which he explains as due either to lower financial rewards or to the fact that the posts require fewer political skills (Camp, 1995: 157). Secondly, although women have been very active in community politics, it has been difficult for them to break through into electoral politics, even at the local level. This reflects the return of parties as the major political actors at this level, along with a particular political agenda, and suggests a greater division between social and political action than was apparent in the 1980s. Thirdly, the re-emergence of electoral politics has brought with it the traditional political discourses of left–right, social–political and public–private. Although women continue to be active in social movements, the issues do not fit neatly into the divides presented to them and often undermine their strength.

A vicious circle emerges whereby women feel excluded from political parties and prefer to participate in social movements, which allows parties to continue marginalizing them and the issues which interest them. A gender division of labour does permeate procedural politics, with women being overrepresented in bodies which deal with social issues and underrepresented in those dealing with the economy or foreign affairs, often seen as 'hard subjects'.[10] This gender division of labour, although weakening, is a problem at all levels of government. It is important to note that, contrary to traditional notions of women being uninterested in politics, in many cases women outnumber men as party members but are still not being selected as candidates and/or elected (see below): it is significant, therefore, that María Emma Mejía Velez was vice-presidential candidate for the Liberal Party in Colombia (1998) and that Fernández Meijide is likely to be the presidential candidate in Argentina (1999) for the Frente País Solidario (FREPASO).

There are ongoing difficulties for women who have succeeded in politics. Many comment on the tension of 'double militancy', that is, balancing the gender agenda with party loyalties.[11] Secondly, as Jutta Marx comments (1994), the characteristics of good parliamentary practice remain male: long, unsociable work hours, aggressiveness in debate and a tendency to dominate. In these circumstances she argues, women are pushed in contradictory directions: they are expected to adapt to 'male' characteristics without losing their 'femininity'. She goes on, 'in this way they are required to act as bi- or asexed [*bi- o asexuados*] beings' (Marx, 1994: 127). In talking to women engaged in representational politics, a recurrent theme appears: there has to be a cultural change which erodes the idea that the domestic world is women's sole responsibility – something with which many in Northern liberal democracies would agree.

Government impact on women's political participation

I suggested above that political institutions had the potential to be structures of empowerment. Government policies can facilitate such empowerment (as well as acting as constraints at times). In the first years after the return to civilian rule, countries such as Argentina and Chile passed many laws which had particular benefits for women: relegalizing contraceptives, changing the divorce laws, giving women as well as men the rights of *patria potestad*,[12] to name but a few. There are also a number of policies specifically directed towards women, including the establishment of women's ministries, gender-sensitive programmes in social welfare projects, and the promotion of quotas to encourage women's participation. All policies, however, have gendered outcomes, frequently not to the advantage of women.

I have argued elsewhere that neoliberal economics has a negative impact on women's *political* participation, principally through the bureaucratization of demand making, which had fuelled the women-dominated social movements in the 1970s and 1980s (Craske, 1998). Structural adjustment policies also rely on women to continue to provide social reproduction services at little cost to the state as the latter withdraws from many areas of social welfare provision. As Brodie (1994) suggests, the neoliberal project is gender blind but is effectively masculine and ignores women's unpaid labour. This places time constraints on women which has a negative impact on the possibilities for their political involvement. Given that governments are prioritizing economics over politics, there seems to be little hope that this will change in the near future.

Nevertheless, there have been positive changes reflecting a number of issues: firstly, in many countries the moment of transition was auspicious for promoting new agendas. Linked to this, the important contribution to the struggle for democracy of women had made them more politically visible and a constituency to be targeted. There had also been a number of external catalysts, such as the UN Decade for Women: all Latin American countries are signatories to the UN Convention on the Elimination of all forms of Discrimination Against Women (CEDAW). Returning exiles and local activists were also exchanging ideas around the role of women in society, and their key contribution to national development was thus better understood. These different elements came together to place pressure on political organizations to be more aware of women's political contribution. In the 1990s, however, the political arena has narrowed and the economic conditions are not auspicious for making more advances, especially for women engaged in grassroots political participation, and further legislative gains look unlikely at present. The areas which were repeatedly mentioned as pending during my fieldwork were legalization of abortion; more work on domestic violence (particularly in enforcing current laws); more sensitivity around prosecution of rape cases and acknowledgement of rape within marriage as a crime; and greater access to contraceptives, with more information to avoid the stark choices of state-sponsored sterilizations and back-street abortions. In Argentina nearly all the interviewees mentioned the increased influence of the conservative Catholic Church and the consequent reinforcement of the 'backlash'. In the first years of civilian government the church was quiet, having been implicated in the regime, but it is now refocusing its effort on 'family values'.[13]

It would, of course, be impossible to analyse all government policies and the gender implications, so I limit myself to a discussion of women's ministries and the Argentine quota law. Both have been important in elevating and institutionalizing the more public role of women, but neither should be seen as anything more than a useful tool in promoting women's status. They both have limitations, and are especially vulnerable to accusations of co-optation and the corporatization of women's political participation.

The Argentine quota law

There are examples of quota systems in Latin America designed to increase the number of women holding political office within parties. Argentina, however, pioneered the integration of quota systems into the electoral code. Indeed Argentina was the first country in the world to introduce such a law.[14] The law was proposed by a Radical Party senator but would probably have failed without the backing of the Peronist president Carlos Menem. It was passed in 1991, and as a result the numbers of female Argentinian deputies have increased dramatically, almost reaching 30 per cent in congress. Nélida Archenti suggests the struggle for the quota law is notable in that it demonstrates a shift in tactics of many Argentine feminists as they fought for their place in the decision-making process, rather than rejecting power and politics as male arenas.[15]

The Argentinian law is clear in its aims: women have to constitute 30 per cent of candidates on all lists; it is a 'transitional' measure to even the gender gap in representational politics; and it is designed 'to humanize political culture' by introducing social and domestic perspectives on policy development.[16] Although the number of women representatives has increased dramatically, there are obvious problems with using quotas. A major criticism is that the 30 per cent becomes a 'ceiling' instead of a 'floor', and there are indications that 30 per cent is still too few women to be more than tokenistic. It is suggested that there needs to be a minimum of 40 per cent, particularly if the goal is for a change in political culture.[17]

In other countries where quota laws apply it is generally through internal party rules, and parties of the left are more likely to use this device to increase women's political participation. In a study of Chile, Riet Delsing discovered the attitudes among party leaders were very mixed, with some completely against any quotas and others suggesting 40 per cent. Certainly other governments in the region (and beyond) are anxious to see the long-term consequences of the Argentine example. For many, quotas represent a return to the bad old days of state corporatism, where vertical structures gave different groups in society their place (see Chapter 3). They are considered anti-democratic since they stifle autonomous political expression and identity, something which has particular resonance for Argentina. The lawyer and activist Haydée Birgin was particularly critical of the use of laws to change the levels of representation She argues that in Argentina the party system is not sufficiently well developed for a quota system to benefit women. She suggests that the parties include a wide range of views so it is difficult to know what a woman is fighting for within the broader agenda: the focus of the struggle should be for parties to democratize and include women rather than to have a national law.[18]

The increased number of congresswomen is not automatically translated into policy development. In the case of many countries, including Argentina, ministers are not necessarily chosen from the ranks of congress; therefore the importance of congress is lessened and ministers are not accountable to the electorate. Consequently, in Argentina we have the case of one of the highest levels of female representation in a national parliament (currently seventh in the world (Inter-Parliamentary Union, 1997), but only one female secretary of state (Susan Decibe was appointed minister of education in 1996) and few under-secretaries. Women are being encouraged into one of the less powerful areas of government, but are finding that entry into key power arenas remains difficult.

Furthermore, women who gain representation through quotas cannot be assumed to be any more committed to improving women's lives than anyone else. As the socialist councillor Clori Yelicic comments, famous rather than capable women have been chosen as candidates, a point echoed by María Eugenia Estenssoro, who considers that female deputies have generally been a bad advertisement.[19] Jutta Marx suggests that women know that a strong pro-women stance will limit their chances of being chosen as a candidate.[20] A further difficulty which the quota law has not resolved is that men still control the drawing up of the party lists of candidates.

In Argentina the quota law has been extended to the regional level, with twenty-one of the twenty-four provinces having quota laws for their legislatures, and there are plans to extend it further to municipal level, to the senate and to the country's trade unions.[21] A major problem has been to ensure that parties adhere to the law: two of the principal parties, the Radicals and the Peronists, have had women candidates contest their lists (see Jones, 1996: 79, for details). In 1994 there was an important change to the law which allowed cases against parties to be brought by individuals other than the woman concerned. The act of prosecuting a party had resulted in great personal cost to some women, and could deter many if they were perceived to be disloyal to their party. The National Women's Council (Consejo Nacional de la Mujer: CNM) is also now allowed to challenge parties' non-compliance with the law on the woman candidate's behalf, which reduces confrontation for the candidate herself.

It is worth pausing to consider why quotas for women were established at this juncture. The prevalence of women in the popular protest organizations highlighted women as political actors and also the new political demands they were making, not all of which could be addressed by governments. I would suggest that quotas are a relatively easy way of demonstrating commitment to women's issues and acknowledging women as political actors without devolving power or shifting political priorities greatly. Jutta Marx argues that it also demonstrates Argentina's 'modernity', not its response to demands from organized groups.[22]

Although having greater numbers of women deputies is an advantage, in itself it changes little for women generally if these women are not organized and agreed on a workable agenda: quotas can empower women only if they take advantage of them at both personal and collective levels. The government has demonstrated its support of women as political actors through the quota law, but does not appear to be addressing a 'women's agenda'. Finally, the women who enter parliament through quotas can be non/anti-feminist and may vote against measures which they perceive as challenging women's traditional domestic roles. Congresswomen may defend *marianismo*, reflecting their female consciousness, rather than choose to champion women's rights and be identified with feminism in a country that has little sympathy for it.

Despite these limitations, I believe it is important to have more women in political institutions, whatever their political agenda. Greater participation from a range of women helps erode the equation that sees women equalling mothers – which equals responsibility for reproduction in its broadest sense. Furthermore, as argued by Clori Yelicic, the presenting of the quota law may not be positive in terms of increasing the number and quality of representatives, but it has raised the debate within political parties and society at large.[23]

Women's ministries[24]

All Latin American countries have women's ministries of one kind or another. The first such department was set up in 1960 in Cuba; however, it was over twenty years before another such organization was established, in Guatemala in 1981. The majority of such ministries have been established since the demise of authoritarian governments and, to some extent, are designed to demonstrate these countries' new democratic credentials. Brazil's women's council, the Conselho Nacional dos Direitos da Mulher (CNDM) was established by the new democratic government in 1985. It was a bottom-up initiative and strongly shaped by activists from the women's movement. Its successes and failure influenced the development of other ministries in the region. Its strength has waned, however, since the late 1980s, and it has never achieved ministerial status.[25]

The ministerial affiliation of women's departments is worth noting as a reflection of whether the government considers the issue central to government policy, or whether women are a 'minority' interest. The Federación de Mujeres Cubanas (Federation of Cuban Women: FMC) answers to the Ministry of Culture, Youth and Sports! In many Latin American countries women's ministries are part of the office of the president. In four countries (Costa Rica, El Salvador, Peru and Uruguay) women's advancement is overtly linked to their reproductive role by the combination of a ministry for women with that for children or the family.

Bolivia is an interesting exception, with a sub-secretariat for *gender* (within the Ministry of Human Development): in other countries, however, there have been heated discussions regarding the meaning of the concept 'gender', particularly in advance of the UN Beijing Conference in 1995. In Argentina, for instance, the term was banned in the Ministry of Education, leading to resignations, including that of the feminist Gloria Bonder. Argentina is unusual in having a Gabinete de Consejeras Presidenciales (a female 'shadow cabinet') to advise the president; however, this has no binding role. Similarly, the country's Consejo Nacional de la Mujer does not have ministerial status, unlike its predecessor, which was disbanded in 1989.[26] On a positive note, the CNM was staffed through open competition to avoid a pro-Peronist/Menem institution, which was innovative for executive positions where heads were usually appointed. Its current head, Susana Sanz, believes that the CNM, despite its lack of ministerial status, has an important role in initiating and defending the new political spaces open to women. It is also trying to gather more information on women's lives.[27]

The advantages of such a ministry are that it can co-ordinate activities aimed at improving the status of women in a given country and can act as a bridge between women's groups and the government. It has been seen, in the case of Chile in particular, that there is often room within such organizations for women who have previously been active in the women's movement. The women's ministry in Chile, SERNAM, commissions reports, co-ordinates activities between the government and voluntary sector and brings the issue of gender to the attention of other ministries. The sub-director, Paulina Veloso, argued that there has been an important change in the categorization of women's issues: a shift away from *asistencialismo* (welfarism) to projects for citizens. Similarly, SERNAM has persuaded the health ministry to change the title '*materno-infantil*' to '*mujeres*' to stress that women are not only mothers. According to Veloso, the aim is to have women's issues discussed at all levels of government through specialist workers, which she referred to as 'Trojan horses'.[28]

While most governments have laws against domestic violence, for example, the ministries can add legitimacy and pressure in the allocation of resources. It must be remembered, however, that these are state bodies and that the ministers and other top positions are generally appointed by the incumbent party/parties. In 1995 the top two appointees at SERNAM, Josefina Bilbao and Paulina Veloso, were women with little previous experience of women's issues and for whom the appointment, taking a mainstream career into account, was not necessarily perceived as a promotion.[29] Although women's ministries can be an important resource, in particular for co-ordinating projects, the presence of a 'women's minister' is not always reflected in resources and status. As in the case of quota laws, it may give the appearance of action rather than proof of such. Its success will vary depending on the commitment of key figures in charge, its budget, how integrated it is within the government more generally, and whether it has the support of key members within government, particularly the president. The efficacy of attempts at 'state feminism' through such ministries has been debated in Stetson and Mazur's edited collection (1995a; see also Chapter 8).

To date, in Latin America, it appears that it has not been easy for women to develop allies in other areas of the state, and there have been casualties; in May 1995 the director of Argentina's CNM resigned after a strong disagreement with the government on abortion; it was some months before a successor was appointed. The impact of a women's ministry depends on who is appointed to run it, and it is clear that it will not necessarily be a woman (or man) with an interest in gender issues. The institutionalization of interest groups (in this case, women) can reflect a corporatization of that constituency which serves to contain its demands. The criticism of corporatization in Latin America is important since such structures have often served to co-opt and silence demands of the popular classes and other subordinate groups, such as women. Stubbs (1994) points out, however, that corporatism is a two-way structure and does allow influence, and points to the important gains that Cuban women made through the FMC.[30]

Women's ministries can be very important tools for advancing women's status, but pressure from outside women's organizations is important to maintain momentum, and also to ensure that women's ministries do not become too mired in bureaucratic concerns which can sap their campaigning edge. Even when they are under constant pressure, as a part of government they tend to be cautious and non-confrontational in most circumstances. Since their existence depends on the state, their approach will generally be reformist rather than radical. Nevertheless, they are useful to feminists and other women's organizations if they are open to outside organizations. Given the current economic constraints which weigh heavily on all Latin American governments, any activities which need high levels of state funding will be difficult to promote, and women's ministries are competing with others for limited resources.

The governments of Latin America have all undergone structural adjustment (see Chapter 3) over the past ten years or more, and long-term economic stability is a priority. This is reflected in the policies and programmes promoted by women's ministries in the region. Many of their projects are linked to income-generation schemes aimed at women in the community. There are also health and education projects which combine emphasis on improving economic efficiency with women's traditional caring roles. Domestic violence is another issue which has received prominence over the past few years and, as a consequence, has made the issue more public, with state campaigns for 'zero tolerance'. A common theme in women's ministries, and both public and private women-oriented programmes generally, is empowerment and the development of women's autonomy and opportunities. This empowerment has focused on localized, decision making within the projects themselves or on encouraging economic independence by providing women with regular sources of income. This focus does not, to date, appear to encourage women to engage in representative politics.

Despite equal opportunity laws in many countries throughout the globe, there are few (if any) of those countries which could boast 'real equality' between men and women. In Costa Rica this gap has been highlighted by the campaign for real equality, and campaigners have demonstrated that there is still a long way to go before women and men enjoy the same opportunities and benefits (González Suárez, 1994). Few governments extend the concept to some kind of standing committee on gender whereby the women's ministry has representatives in other ministries to conduct gender audits on key policy initiatives. Most ministries remain insulated from considering the gendered implications of their policies. With regard to women participants themselves, it appears that, as the consolidation of democracy has progressed, it is those women who are engaged in strategic, rather than practical, gender interests (see Chapter 2) who have succeeded in maintaining a political profile (Waylen, 1993). This would indicate that class issues have an impact on political access, since women from the popular classes tend to be concentrated in social movements which promote practical interests.

Political parties

There is a received wisdom or 'a generalisation that is by now almost a cliché ... that women are politically more conservative than men' (Randall, 1987: 70), and this cliché pertains as much to Latin America as to other regions. But, as with most clichés, the truth is more complex, and disaggregated figures show that women's voting patterns vary across generations and are dependent on the issues. Indeed, evidence suggests that support for the far right is the preserve of men and that possibly women are more in favour of the status quo (Randall, 1987). In the 1980s and 1990s the traditional differences between left and right parties in most countries have diminished, with most parties accepting the neoliberal orthodoxy; this is particularly the case in Latin America. Despite the perception of women as conservative, generally it is those parties perceived as leftist which have more women-friendly policies such as quotas, women's sections and statements of action. Corporatist parties such as the Institutional Revolutionary Party (the PRI) in Mexico and the Justicialist Party (Partido Justicialista: PJ – the Peronists) in Argentina also have a tradition of focusing on women as a 'sector', and both established women's branches decades ago. Where statistics are available, women are members in greater numbers of conservative parties, but there is evidence of their generally increased participation in all parties: in Argentina 47.7 per cent of party affiliates are women (Jones, 1996: 77) and the PRI maintains that 58 per cent of the party membership is made up of women (in Rodríguez et al., 1995: 44).[31] In Buenos Aires women are increasingly active in parties generally, and, according to the socialist councillor Clori Yelicic, in the city women outnumber men in all the main parties.[32]

There is evidence to indicate that women do better in terms of reaching high office within parties which are small (Valdés and Gomáriz, 1995). Despite there being a few examples of women's parties, most women choose to participate in mainstream political parties. It must be remembered, however, that there is a significant difference in being a member of a party, a party activist and a potential party representative or executive member. The gender division of labour within parties must be assessed when examining the interaction between women and parties. Notwithstanding higher numbers of women members, parties on the right have a weaker record regarding women's participation as candidates and executive members. An ex-deputy for the Unión Cívica Radical (UCR) in Argentina, Angela Sureda, argues that parties generally have failed to train and prepare their potential deputies, and that this applies to both women and men.[33]

In terms of congressional representatives, it is leftist parties which have greater female participation. In Mexico the PRD had the highest proportion of women deputies in the 1994–7 legislature, with 21.4 per cent; 14.8 per cent of PRI deputies and only 7.6 per cent of those in the rightist Partido de Acción Nacional (PAN) were women.[34] This could indicate that conservative parties do not encourage (or maybe even discourage) women to stand for elective office. In terms of the representation of women on party executive committees, many parties have made a concerted effort to expand numbers; the Salvadoran National Democratic Union has 40 per cent women on the executive and the Colombian Liberal Party comes in second with 33.3 per cent (Valdés and Gomáriz, 1995).

In attempts to encourage women voters to support them, many parties in the region set up internal party quotas for party positions – though not parliamentary candidates – particularly at the national level. Many parties also have women's branches or sectors to encourage women's support. The PLN in Costa Rica, a country with a long history of democratic government, has had a number of programmes on women since the 1960s. In the party restructuring in 1979, a women's movement was established which has had significant impact both within the party and at a national level when the party has been in office (González Suárez, 1994). The Alianza Popular Revolucionaria Americana (APRA) in Peru has a tradition of family activism which has incorporated women, but with second-class status (Scott, 1994). Mariana Aylwin, a deputy of Chile's Christian Democrats, was asked to investigate the position of women in the party: despite its long history of contact through the Mothers' Centres, this had welfarist overtones.[35] Through the study, she came to acknowledge that women's issues fit into many other areas of debate within politics at the moment.

In Brazil women candidates who were also members of the women's movement attended a national conference in 1986. This resulted in a Women's Charter focusing on a number of issues around discrimination, child-care and the recognition of motherhood as a 'social responsibility', which they pledged to pursue if elected (Tabak, 1994). Although the larger parties in Brazil have had the highest *number* of women representatives, it has been the parties of the left which have had the highest *levels* of female representation. The Workers' Party (PT) has the most impressive record: it had the highest percentage of female candidates; it supported Maria Luiza Fontenele, the first female mayor of a state capital (Forteleza state); and in 1988 Luiza Erundina was elected PT mayor of São Paulo, one of the world's largest cities. The black politician Benedita da Silva became politically involved through neighbourhood organizations and has represented the PT in both houses (Tabak, 1994). María Angélica Ibáñez of the Chilean Socialist Party, however, noted that women politicians are still politicians and are generally pragmatic. She is a feminist, but she decided that she wasn't going to fight with men all the time through promoting women's issues.[36]

Despite the increase in women's political activity and the positive responses of many involved in institutional politics, there is still a great deal of resistance to any kind of 'positive discrimination'. María Antonieta Saa, a deputy of Chile's Democracy Party (Partido por la Democracy: PD) asserts that 'parties have no interest in having more women: to have more women would mean losing men ... In this country, parties are bastions of machismo.'[37] She goes on to comment that, for women, the struggle for power is now naked (*desnuda*); before the struggle was against Pinochet. Since those parties which are less keen on quotas – those on the right – have most support from women, there is no reason to expect a change in their attitude towards women. Even in the Chilean Socialist Party, however, more men voted in favour of quotas![38] In Uruguay, Fisher (1993) argues that, although parties did begin to include policies for women, it was an electoral strategy rather than a fundamental rethinking of their programmes. As in other areas of public life, women seem to gravitate (or are pushed, according to ex-Deputy Sureda) towards issues which reflect their domestic lives. This indicates that there is a gender division of labour within parties which is then mapped onto government should the party be victorious. So, what of women's parties?

Women's parties: the case of the Partido Peronista Femenino

Despite the limited presence of women in national congresses, there have been moments when women have played important roles in the region's politics. Deutsch (1997) demonstrates that parties on the right in the 1930s and 1940s made deliberate attempts to recruit women, although as parties they had limited impact. Chilean feminists established a women's party, Partido Femenino Chileno, between 1946 and 1953 and succeeded in electing a deputy and senator, but the more famous and successful example was the Argentinian Partido Peronista Femenino (PPF), established by Eva Perón in 1949. In 1951 Argentina had the highest number of women deputies in the western hemisphere as a result of the PPF (Deutsch, 1991).[39] Despite having the title 'party', it functioned as a branch of the Peronist party, and the women candidates were placed on the PJ lists. Like PJ members, the bulk of the women active in the PPF were working class. The context in which the PPF developed is worth considering. Argentina was unusual in Latin America, with a tradition of high educational attainment of women, women's involvement in paid labour outside the home and smaller families. By 1947 women registered the lowest participation in the job market, but the occupations in which they were engaged increasingly demonstrated the attainment of qualifications and a professionalization of women's work (Bianchi, 1993).

The Peróns encouraged women's activities outside the home and developed policies in support of this, such as day-care for children, but there was also great rhetorical emphasis on motherhood, families and, coming from Eva, the subordination of women to Juan Perón. In the words of Juan Perón, women were to think of their patriotic duty and

> [accept the] obligation of bearing healthy children and of forming virtuous men who know how to sacrifice themselves and fight for the true interests of the nation. Each woman should consider that her obligations have increased, because the state, on granting rights, also has the need to demand that every mother be a true teacher to her children ... who will intervene in public life to defend this sacred cell of society which is the home.
>
> Bianchi (1993: 702–3; author's translation)

Similarly Eva declared:

> The first objective of a feminine movement which wants to do good for women, which doesn't aspire to change them into men, must be the home. (ibid.)

As Bianchi states, Peronism transformed motherhood into a political function imposed by the state (cf. Chapter 2). The rhetoric of Eva emphasized her role as mother of the nation (though she did not, in her short life, have children of her own) and stressed her subordination to Juan; by example, this exhorted women to subjugate themselves to their husbands (Deutsch, 1991). Eva also distinguished between political and social activity, placing them in male and female arenas respectively (ibid.), but challenged these boundaries by her own actions and through the PPF's representatives – which she chose and nobody questioned (Bianchi, 1993: 704). The PPF reflected the Peróns' strategy in incorporating the working classes, and much of the rhetoric was hostile to middle-class values and lifestyles. Women were paid special attention since they were a new constituency, but it was not just any woman but the Peronist woman defined as 'the real woman who lives with the people' (ibid.). The majority of women who participated in both the PPF and the Eva Perón Foundation[40] were young, single, without family responsibilities and with no previous political experience (ibid.).[41]

The mixture of the traditional and the radical was extremely successful in mobilizing women behind Perón, and they voted for him in great numbers. The strength of the PPF dissipated after Eva's death in 1952 and the party was a casualty of the coup which ousted Perón in 1955: when he returned to power in 1973 it was without the PPF but with his third wife as vice-president. The great success of the PPF was obviously a reflection of Eva's own personal charisma and commitment, both to supporting Perón and to giving women a voice, albeit within the confines of the needs of Peronism. Her relationship, however, was strong not just with women but also with workers generally. She took over, largely on an informal basis, the running of the labour secretariat which Perón had developed before becoming president: it has remained a bastion of Peronist support. Her importance nationally is demonstrated in the title 'Spiritual Leader of the Nation', which congress granted her a few weeks before her death (Navarro, 1982).

The history of the PPF also demonstrates how motherist rhetoric can become a powerful political identity and can be incorporated into the centre of politics. A problem remains, however, if a fixed perception of motherhood is the only political option open to women. Although Eva Perón challenged *marianismo* in her lifestyle, she used its symbolism to generate support, and her rhetoric reflects both *marianismo* and political action based on female consciousness. The political role of women in Peronism challenged few gender constructions directly, but, simply by being there, they demonstrated that women could be politicians. Although many parties have engaged with women's issues and made concerted efforts to recruit women, the Peróns succeeded in mobilizing women in ways which no other party has yet matched. It is ironic, then, that in 1983 'women voted overwhelmingly for Alfonsín while their husbands and sons voted for the Peronist candidate, Italo Luder' (Feijoó, 1994: 67). Despite this Peronist history, Zita Montes de Oca, who headed the Sub-Secretariat for Women under Alfonsín, suggests contemporary parties offer equally uninspiring agendas for women: although there has been a history of women's activism, the challenge for the state today is still how to bring these women into political institutions.[42]

Women as a challenge to parties

Although it has often been assumed that conservative parties want to keep women in the home and therefore must be against women's long-term emancipation, the development of multiple feminisms has meant that there can no longer be assumptions made about left–right 'malestream politics' and the interaction with women's issues. Women's issues are not a discrete group of concerns which can be decided a priori, but result from women's needs and wants in a given context, thus reflecting their experiences. Many of these issues have been depoliticized in the past by being labelled apolitical by definition, since they focused on the domestic arena. The issues which were deemed political concentrated on equal rights and 'feminist' issues, and were more in keeping with leftist ideology: in Molyneux's (1985) language, strategic concerns.

With the rise of 'militant motherhood' (see Chapter 2), parties have been quick to court the female vote, which is reflected in the emergence of women's ministries and changes in laws noted above. Parties' responses had to absorb what, at first, appeared to be fairly traditional female discourses of motherhood and nurturing roles but which had radical political implications (Alvarez, 1990). There have been problems in responding to 'motherist' demands: few contest the legitimacy of the issues and indeed they support many of the solutions, but these solutions are costly at a time when governments are trying to curtail public expenditure. The response for many has rested on rhetorical commitments to the role of women as carers, emphasizing their key role in national development, but without increasing social welfare budgets (where most of the demands fit): governments and parties want to maintain support at the lowest possible cost.

The political role of women is ambiguous since women's identities straddle public and private spheres in a way that men's do not.[43] Few parties advocate socialization of reproductive tasks; consequently they largely accept women's role in the domestic sphere, since this contributes to the capital accumulation project at little cost to the state. Parties and governments have a vested interest in maintaining the link between mothering and social reproduction, and this is reinforced by maternal feminism (see Chapter 8). Also many women would not react positively to party policies which undermine their social roles, including motherhood; they have a deep commitment to these socially constructed roles (Alvarez, 1990; Craske, 1993; García and de Oliveira, 1997).

Militant motherhood has challenged assumptions about the politically conservative nature of motherhood. It is hard to deny women's demands when they are couched in terms of the duties and responsibilities of motherhood, since this legitimizes their demands, particularly with the emphasis placed on such activities by politicians. Parties engaged with and supported the demands of women around consumer issues or human rights when they were challenging authoritarian governments, but they have been less willing and/or able to address the issues in government or opposition. Perhaps, as ex-Deputy Sureda suggests, the general disillusion with parties and the political process, as elections are the norm and problems with corruption remain, is a greater threat to women's increased participation.

Bureaucracies

State bureaucracies offer opportunities and constraints for women both as political actors and as clients of the state. It would be difficult either to accept the notion that the state is a masculine construct which offers nothing to women, or to endorse it as the primary terrain in the struggles for the advancement of women. Certainly the state plays an important role in shaping gender relations (Pringle and Watson, 1992), and the discussion above of different branches of the state demonstrates the continual series of negotiations which accompany the development of gender relations and women's struggle for representation. In her study on Africa, Moore (1988) suggested that Third World bureaucracies are more open to women because they are younger and more flexible, unlike Northern democracies. However, little work has been done regarding Latin American countries, which were the first in the developing world to achieve independence (between 1810 and 1899), and consequently have bureaucracies that are more entrenched towards a male bias.

The Chilean deputy María Antonieta Saa argued that it is within bureaucracies rather than within congresses that women need to fight for quotas. It is here that much work can be done without fixating on parliamentary representation (although that is important).[44] Debates on welfare states would suggest that they can offer women a significant arena for furthering their aims, but they can transfer dependency from men as husbands to institutionalized male power. In the case of Latin America the reach of welfare states is limited, but the bureaucratic structure of the state has allowed certain openings for women civil servants which create the potential for developing feminist and/or women-friendly policies.[45] There is no doubt that the newly established women's ministries outlined above create a useful state arena; however, the very existence of such ministries can sometimes serve to institutionalize specific gender roles. Nevertheless, in a study on Mexico, Bourque (1989) showed how committed feminists were able to have an impact on 'neutral' policies by bringing in researchers who analysed the gendered impact of government policies (in this case in the Ministry of Agriculture).[46]

One of the key roles of bureaucracies is in steering and directing policy from a non-partisan perspective. Until the advent of SAPs, the heavily interventionist state in Latin America led to large bureaucracies, but these are now in decline. As in the party political arena, women have been concentrated in the 'caring' ministries and in the lower rungs of the professional ladder. A study on Uruguay demonstrated these clusters and suggests that the lack of women at the top may reflect changing career patterns of women, rather than women failing to be promoted: that is, women of an age to be in the top positions tend not to have continued their careers beyond marriage or motherhood (Da Silveira et al., 1991).[47] Whatever the explanation, however, it is clear that women are not at the centre of these decision-making arenas. It is reasonable to surmise that people with specifically women-oriented agendas are in even fewer numbers. In the same study, women bureaucrats were in the majority in the Public Health Ministry (69.94%) and made up almost half in Foreign Affairs (49.8%), Tourism (48.02%) and Education and Culture (40.97%). Their lowest representation was in Transport and Public Works (13.42%) (ibid.: 84).

State bureaucracies can offer key resources for the advancement of women, although all are operating under severe budgetary constraints at present. These resources, however, can also act to co-opt potential opposition activities, and even with the current limitations there is still the potential for clientelism (Roberts, 1995). The idea of the state as either friend or foe influences women's strategies for the future. The former view is one held by many feminists in Chile while the latter is more commonly found in Argentina. The differing views have a great impact on strategies and tactics. The difference between the two countries possibly reflects their respective histories of relations between civil society and the state. In Chile, before the advent of Pinochet, there was a tradition of interaction between the two, largely mediated through parties. In Argentina, however, the state has been dominated by authoritarianism, with little room for autonomous political organizing on the part of social groups. Even under Perón, where the workers had greater access to the system than in other moments, it was still highly controlled, and women's issues were mediated through the PPF, as I highlighted above. One of the differences during the transition period noted by Haydée Birgin[48] was that the state reached out to feminists, rather than feminists having to look to the state for a political space.

In other countries feminists have chosen to work both within and outside the state apparatus to further their aims. Women's groups generally will choose those methods which will give the best results, though these may change over time and be dependent on the current issue. Given my premise that the institutional political arena is resistant to change, and bureaucracies more so, it is necessary to maintain pressure at all levels to keep up the momentum for change. States will do as little as possible in terms of expenditure and promoting transformations in the status quo, consequently organized lobbying and campaigning is essential for keeping issues on the agenda.

Conclusions

Women's involvement in institutional politics generally remains limited, despite their increased political mobilization over the years. Nevertheless, more women are political representatives at all levels and more parties and governments recognize women's demands as legitimate, political demands. The transition to and consolidation of democracy has provided many opportunities for women to make demands and achieve significant gains in terms of legal-institutional changes (many social welfare legal changes, women's ministries and greater representation in political parties through quotas are but some). But, as with other groups and constituencies, this has also been a time of intense difficulties, as the new civilian regimes have grappled with competing interests and needs and constraints from the global economy. The struggle for democratization has shown that there is always the potential for change and for power relations to be renegotiated. A pessimistic conclusion has to be, however, that after the wide-scale mobilization of women and the challenges to the constraints on their political behaviour, the current social, economic and political climate is not auspicious for women's increased advancement.

Furthermore, as Gloria Bonder comments, there is still a problem that women are entering male space, without men acknowledging or appreciating the benefits of change for themselves.[49] Women's presence in some national congresses is static, and it was sobering to note that the first post-military elections in Uruguay returned no women representatives.

Although women have made an impact on the political arena, their political identity still reflects marianist tendencies, and breaking away from the prioritization of motherhood is not easy: Graciela Fernández Meijide suggests that women still have much to learn regarding power management.[50] She herself was unsure about standing for office, but she says, 'I didn't enter politics not to fight for power' (*Clarín*, 9 March 1997). This comment finds echoes in the views of the Chilean deputy María Antonieta Saa: '... women aren't disposed to make this fight. Women have a certain conception about the quality of life and less a vision about having power for power's sake [to make a difference].'[51]

There has been much written about the public–private dichotomy, and to a lesser extent the public–social distinction, and how this undermines and hides women's political involvement.

Less attention has been paid, however, to how the left–right also threatens progress on women's issues since it pitches women against women as they defend their party identities. There are moments, which Latin America resoundingly demonstrates, when women surmount the many obstacles which surround them, and these are often moments of great flux, such as the period of transition in the 1970s and 1980s. It is also evident, however, that the structures and discourses which contextualize our reading of politics are very resistant to change. Women's struggle for political subjectivity is one subversive element in the challenge to these structures. It appears that the consolidation of democratic rule is 'normalization', which in effect means the return of male-dominated political parties and gendered policies, and mass depoliticization of social movements with particular implications for women: in short, a remasculinization of politics.

A gender division of labour is still very much in evidence in Latin American politics, although it is being eroded. After the dynamism of the 1970s and 1980s many actors, both female and male, are choosing to withdraw from political activity. This withdrawal is sometimes reinforced by difficult economic conditions which constrain socio-political participation as a result of greater concentration on income generation. For many women, their involvement means a triple burden after productive and domestic tasks. In the next chapter we see how a different 'burden', work, has an impact on their political identity.

5

The Impact of Work on Political Identity

So in general the women who are active in unions are single, widowed or divorced or they have husbands who are militants, or who are exceptional. Sadly that's the way it is. The other women are interested, they might help you out on the odd day but they don't want to be committed.

Sonia (in Fisher, 1993: 58)

Introduction

The relationship between work and political identity is unclear. The separation of public and private spheres has meant that work and political activity, both public pursuits, have been seen as related, as well as largely masculine, occupations. In this chapter I argue that work is an ambivalent experience for most Latin American women and has a limited impact on their political identities. Paid labour offers opportunities for empowerment, particularly as regards financial independence, and can have an impact on gender relations, but these opportunities are frequently private and individual. Consequently it is difficult to generalize and develop a model for women's empowerment from these experiences. For many women, work reflects not choice but need, and conditions are frequently oppressive. Accordingly, the opportunities for workplace collective action to further the establishment of citizens' rights and the development of political subjectivity are limited. Furthermore, the identity of women as workers remains secondary to their identity within the family, which limits their workplace collective action. Where women are engaged in wage earning, it is generally seen as part of providing for the family, giving rise to a tension between caring for others and personal need, so the development of individual rights and thus citizenship is constrained. Despite this, women have engaged in collective action, joined unions and participated politically as a result of their work experience.

Where women do mobilize, however, gender interests are not necessarily clearly articulated – something which is echoed in the following chapter on social movements. From the discussion below, it is clear that the most successful unions for women are those which take a holistic approach to demands that does not separate workplace issues from domestic issues. Women are aware of their multiple identities and that sexism places undue burdens on them, but they generally continue to prioritize their domestic roles, and this is fairly consistent across class. While motherhood and social reproduction are so closely entwined, it seems unlikely that an identity as 'worker' will dominate women's views of themselves. This is exacerbated by the fact that work conditions are generally poor and that the current economic situation is making the work experience ever more burdensome: under such circumstances, work is rarely an edifying experience. Despite the problems, however, a more holistic approach has had results and women have been able to exert pressure in key areas and develop their sense of empowerment. Furthermore, I would argue that such an approach is a better way forward than the deeply fragmented male model, where work life is separated from domestic life.

The potential political implications of engagement in paid labour are threefold: i) the development of collective action to make demands and establish workers' rights; ii) the development of empowerment stemming from receipt of an income and/or engagement in collective action which can result in political subjectivity; iii) the restructuring of gender relations in both public and private spheres. Clearly, it cannot be assumed that these positive outcomes are inevitable consequences of paid labour: does work contribute to empowerment by giving greater financial independence and occasionally a more public identity, or does it add to a woman's responsibilities, becoming a double or triple burden? Are gender relations within the factory and the home made more equitable and democratic, or are there further tensions as women are overworked and men feel undermined?

As shall be seen, elements of both are evident in Latin America, and, to date, there is no blueprint for the development of workplace political action which results in improving women's quality

of life. Nor does paid labour necessarily give them a greater political profile in the labour movement or the political arena more
generally. Despite the combination of positive changes in relation
to women within established unions, the rise of independent
unions and the impact of feminism, the identity of women as
workers is still underdeveloped; consequently, it has limited
impact on their political involvement and sense of empowerment.
Under the current economic conditions, most unions are under
pressure and are concentrating on what they perceive to be core
demands (predominantly wage levels and job security), reflecting
the masculine working practices which have informed the labour
movement to date.

This chapter examines different arenas of collective action: mainstream unions, independent organizing and spontaneous action.
This is followed by a discussion of the broader political implications of work around personal empowerment. I begin with an
examination of shifting work experiences.

Changing work experiences

Research from the United States indicates that occupation has an
impact on women's political involvement and sense of efficacy,
and that professional women in particular are more politically
active (Beckwith, 1986). Analysts in Latin America such as María
del Carmen Feijoó have suggested that women need to engage
more in the wage economy as a strategy for empowerment. Feijoó
emphasizes the benefits of financial independence and the development of networks with co-workers which helps form the basis
for the development of political identities.[1] While these observa-
tions may be valid, they assume that women conform to male
work patterns, and do not take into account the multiple ways in
which Latin American women already contribute to family income
generation. Furthermore, they ignore the burdens that such
involvement can place on women, constraining their political
activity rather than encouraging it.

Defining 'work'

It is clear that women are engaged in wage labour, as Chapter 3
demonstrated. There are a number of issues involved when examining women's participation in paid labour and income generation.

Firstly, much of their work has been rendered invisible over the years and ignored because of the location of the work. Sometimes it is difficult to establish clear boundaries between 'private' reproductive work and surplus production for income generation.[2] Research has also shown that most women, particularly among the popular classes, work in addition to their daily reproductive tasks, whether this is remunerated or not. Such activities, however, may not fit into European and North American notions of work, which is generally considered to take place outside the home and which is more easily distinguishable from reproductive tasks. It is now appreciated that women work both inside and outside the home, often blurring all distinctions between domestic and non-domestic consumption/production, and take domestic tasks, such as child-minding, into the workplace. The heavy focus on remuneration can hide women's contribution to family income; in family-owned businesses women have often played a key role which reduces the need for external paid labour, but such activities have been seen as part of women's domestic responsibilities. Linked to this is the involvement of older women in free child-minding, which allows the mothers to engage in income generation, but these activities rarely lead to collective action.

Over recent years, research has demonstrated the key contribution that women make to economic development both at the national and the household level. Despite this, another way of undervaluing women's work, and therefore women themselves, is the persistent way in which it has been seen as secondary and complementary to the 'real' work carried out by men. This is particularly manifested in two ways: there is the notion, firstly, that only single and/or childless women work and that they cease to be involved on marriage/child-birth, and secondly, that women's income is private 'pin' money rather than an integral part of the family income. By reinforcing these images, the myth of the male breadwinner is reinforced and women's identities as workers, with all the symbolism that this entails, are undermined. Women's work is neither secondary nor complementary; rather it is essential and central to the household's well-being. Nevertheless, this image persists despite the fact that women contribute more of their income to family expenditure than do men.

The impact of economic reform

The work opportunities open to women, whether inside or outside the home, are in part conditioned by government policies. Over the past twenty years there has been a generalized shift in Latin America from import substitution strategies to trade liberalization (see Chapter 3). This in turn has shifted the locus of Latin American industry away from traditionally 'male' industries such as autos, cement, petroleum and mining to 'female' industries, particularly textiles, telecommunications and electronics and the service sector: this shift is a global phenomenon. An image which has dominated in analyses of trade liberalization is the rapid increase in *maquiladoras*,[3] particularly along the US–Mexican border, which have employed large numbers of relatively well-educated young women. While this has been an important phenomenon, it is certainly not the most common work experience for women in Mexico, let alone those in other parts of the region.

However, a generalized result of trade liberalization, which all countries have experienced (with, perhaps, the exception of Cuba), is that wage competition is coming from other regions. Asia is a particular threat: here labour costs are frequently lower, economic growth is greater and political stability, albeit frequently of an authoritarian nature, is more secure.[4] This shift to free markets has had an impact not just on the type of industrialization: there are wider and perhaps more important implications for women, in particular, resulting from the changes in government welfare provision. Privatization and reduction in public spending has had repercussions on both the domestic and the income-generation activities of women. The consequences have included women's taking on some of the welfare tasks and engaging in more home-based production to make up for the reduction in food subsidies: as Safa (1995: 33) comments, 'the philosophy behind structural adjustment policies is to shift all responsibility for survival from the state to the individual and the family, forcing families to absorb a greater share of the cost of living by reducing government policies aimed at redistribution.'

The cutbacks, coupled with the ongoing economic strictures, have forced many women to play an even greater and more direct role in income generation, frequently in deteriorating working conditions (Mitter, 1994). At the same time the demand for domestic service employees has decreased, as the middle classes also feel the pinch of economic constraints (Joffre Lazarini and Martínez, 1994). These changes have resulted in an increase in the informal sector, which in turn has had a negative impact on collective action and the possibilities for developing political subjectivity.

The shifts in political economy have a great impact on union development and thus on women's experiences of unions. As Prates indicates (1989: 271), the interaction of economic and macrosocial conditions gives the parameters of possible activity. Increasing competition within the market limits the possibilities to defend rights, as low wages and a quiescent labour force are central to governments' economic policies and political repression constrains the ability to organize. Roldán (1993: 51) remarks, 'fear of unemployment and, in the past, outright repression have played a crucial part in labour control.' The economic crisis which has engulfed the region over the past years has also pushed women deeper into the workforce and it is they who have made the greatest adjustments in their lives to minimize the impact on standards of living.

Gendered disadvantages

Despite the increased participation of women in income generation, they are still disadvantaged in terms of conditions, wages and treatment.[5] This reflects the cultural interpretation of their work as secondary. The different perception of women's and men's work is also marked in attitudes to unemployment. In Argentina, Deputy Graciela Fernández Meijide suggests that, when a man becomes unemployed, people have compassion, and some even try to understand, if not condone, resultant domestic violence. When a woman loses her job, however, a job which may have given her some independence and self-worth, nobody pays much attention, saying that she still has a house to look after.[6] This understanding of women's work feeds into their identity, which, because it does not prioritize their work life, tends to underplay work issues as reasons for engagement in collective action; however, women do participate in great numbers in community organizations.

Participating in unions

Despite their considerable participation in the workforce, women remain underrepresented in labour movements and appear less interested than men in unions. Data on membership is limited, but Valdés and Gomáriz (1995) indicate that women rarely make up more than a third of union members and have even lower representation on executive committees. Given the precarious character of women's work, however, and the attitude of trade unions towards women, both in terms of their occupations and their demands, it is surprising that women participate in unions at all.[7] As Swasti Mitter (1994: 7) writes in her comparative study:

> The lack of interest in unionism among women workers does not result from any inherent characteristic of women as such. The culture of mainstream trade unions, for historical reasons, does not sufficiently address the needs of working women. The issues of child care, sexual harassment, lack of access to capital, and the social subordination of women are rarely central to the concerns of traditional unions; women, as a result, either remain unorganized or mobilize themselves in informal, unregistered associations that are free of daunting bureaucratic procedures.

The discussion below on the Latin American experience reflects many of Mitter's comments. This is partly because of the gendered attitudes of union officials and assumptions about the nature of work, but also because traditionally the strongest unions have been in industries where men have predominated. In the few cases of peasant unions, women's involvement in agricultural labour has often been overlooked and perceived simply as part of their domestic work. Increasingly, however, women peasants are engaged in organized activity (Radcliffe, 1993). Similarly there are independent unions which have emerged over the past two to three decades through workers' initiatives, rather than by state fiat, which have given women greater scope for developing political identities (Amado and Checa, 1990; Carrillo, 1990; Tirado, 1994; Anderfuhren, 1994; Joffre Lazarini and Martínez, 1994; Delgado González, 1994). There is also research indicating that women are involved in non-formal workplace protests which express their opposition to certain labour practices (Peña, 1987).

Collective action in the workplace

As industrialization took hold in Latin America labour movements also developed, but these have always found it difficult to unite all segments of the popular classes, particularly those involved in the small-scale, artisanal production common throughout the region. There is a tradition of union organizing in Latin America but its fate has not always been a happy one. The challenge for unions is to maintain sufficient independence from the institutional arena to be able to represent their members' interests without co-optation, but, simultaneously, to be close enough to exert influence. The

Argentine labour movement has traditionally had close links with Peronism, but this has frequently limited its room for manoeuvre.[8] Similarly, Mexico's official unions are compromised by their close relationship to the government, and are more likely to demand labour quiescence than push for workers' demands. In these and other countries with strong union traditions, unions often formed part of a top-down corporatist system which became enmeshed in the clientelistic relations that have characterized Latin American politics.[9] This has limited their ability to represent all workers and has created labour hierarchies with workers in the 'modern' sector at the top. Such top-down organization strategies were also used in Brazil under Vargas and in Peru under the military between 1968 and 1975.

In other countries such as Venezuela, Uruguay and Chile, unions were not so tightly controlled by the government but were strongly influenced by political parties. Many unions were repressed by the military governments: in Chile, after sixteen years of Pinochet, only 13.8 per cent of the workforce is unionized and only 8 per cent have collective contracts; the rest are on individual contracts, which means that women lose out.[10] Regardless of the existence of established unions and party dominated unions, however, there has always been a degree of spontaneous, grass-roots organization from below: in some countries these are referred to as independent unions. With few exceptions such movements have not fared well. There have been three outcomes: i) they fade on account of organizational problems and failure to make more established links with other movements across the country; ii) they are co-opted by the centre and the official unions, which offer greater benefits in keeping with clientelism; or iii) they have been repressed. Brazil's workers' movement, which erupted onto the scene in the late 1970s, is a marked exception. It survived, despite having developed during a military regime, and went on to form the basis of the Workers' Party (PT), which has become a viable electoral force. The PT incorporates other social movements and it enjoys high levels of female involvement.

Traditional unions have generally not been very welcoming of women and at present the tough conditions have helped marginal-ize women's issues, which are on the whole not perceived as important as wages and job security. It is hardly surprising, then, that women should take little interest in union affairs and see them as alien to their own needs and interests. Gabriel and Macdonald (1994) argue that unions need strategies which look beyond the workplace if women's issues are to be addressed adequately. Another contributing factor to the image of women as disinterested in unions is that they are concentrated in activities which are characterized by high levels of job insecurity. There is a perception that women are less keen to engage in confrontation, partly resulting from their more vulnerable position in the labour market. Martens (1994) suggests that women's more holistic approach to demand making, including a combination of workplace and domestic issues, makes them more conservative in labour disputes and likely to show a preference to negotiate rather than engage in confrontation and strikes: this is reflected in Amado and Checa's (1990) study on the Argentine teachers' movement.[11]

The precariousness of their position makes women wary of mass collective action which may jeopardize their jobs. In Uruguay, one activist, Teresita, commented, 'There was no union and we never got involved in any union activity. I had a child to bring up, I was alone and when you're in that situation you only think about the child and how you're going to survive economically. Most of us were in the same position, bringing up children alone' (in Fisher, 1993: 50); her comments are echoed by other women in the study.[12] Furthermore, many women work from home or in domestic service, which separates workers, making it more difficult to develop a collective identity around which to mobilize. Finally, as Cook (1996) demonstrates, the participation of women in unions is not considered as important as that of men. In her study of the Mexican teachers' union, in households where both adults were teachers, she found that it was nearly always the man who attended union meetings.

Nevertheless unions do have a role in the defence and promotion of women wage earners: as the feminist activist Ana María Flores in Mexico comments, 'the issue isn't whether or not we want unions, but rather what kind of new unionism do we want. What alternative can we develop to patriarchal, paternalistic unionism? What are we going to do about demands for productivity? We've been talking about a democratization campaign – but we've been in that very struggle for decades now, and the independent unions are full of the same practices as the authoritarian ones' (in Gabriel and Macdonald, 1994: 555).

Mainstream (malestream) unions

The established unions have tended to hold patriarchal attitudes to women workers and have generally refused to see 'women's issues' as central concerns. In Peru, Scott (1994) notes that women have participated in union activity but generally under male leadership. Unions have been active in those industries where women dominate, such as textiles, but often the leaders are still men. The labour movement has helped reinforce traditional gender roles through the acceptance of a gender division of labour apparent in some unions (Cortina, 1990; Scott, 1994). Cortina (1990: 260), studying Mexico, remarks, 'it is revealing that the officially sanctioned participation of women in the union occurs primarily through social events organized by the leadership.' In Uruguay one activist, Moriana, comments,

> In 1973 the CNT [National Labour Convention] created a Women's Secretariat, headed by a textile worker. However, it didn't have a feminist focus and its main objective was to get women doing solidarity work during strikes. In 1969 there had been a long bank strike and one of the difficulties which the leadership of the bank union perceived was that the wives of bank employees were pushing their husbands to break the strike, in the traditional role of 'don't get involved, think about the kids' etc. This was, I would say, the first time the union movement saw the need to work with women – but note, seeing women in terms of workers' wives, not as workers themselves. (in Fisher, 1993: 48)

These attitudes have reinforced arbitrary boundaries between public and private arenas to the detriment of female representation in unions, since women are seen in their social rather than in their worker identity. The large unions and confederations have been dominated by men, although there have been some shifts in perspective, with an increase in women's sections, particularly since the early 1980s, reflecting the role of women in other forms of political mobilization.

A common problem throughout the region is that the more established unions have frequently more to do with the self-aggrandizement of labour leaders than with representing workers. Union leaders become as much a part of the political system as the parties and as divorced from the daily grind of their members: hence women's antipathy towards 'official' unions documented in Peña's study (1987). Furthermore, as Cook (1996) asserts, the presence of a woman leader does not necessarily improve the situation. This is echoed in a regional report on unions: 'the existence of women at national level or within the top leadership of unions does not necessarily imply a way out or a solution to women's issues' (Rigat-Pflaum, 1991: 25). The author later comments that the solitary position of women within the leadership is also a problem for furthering women's issues.

Given that women have not been highly visible in the labour movement, there is a shortage of studies regarding the early days of their participation. Nevertheless, there are indications that women were active in unions, albeit not in large numbers, both in general confederations and in women-only organizations, from the end of the nineteenth century.[13] Some of the demands were gender specific, such as action against sexual harassment (Navarro, 1985). Valdés and Gomáriz (1995) suggest that women's participation declined after the unions became institutionalized in the region around 1930. What these studies show is that women had great difficulty in being acknowledged as workers and that the male trade unionists tended to have an overly stereotyped idea of women and their needs and interests, many of which still persist (Navarro, 1985; Amado and Checa, 1990; Cortina, 1990; Bareiro et al., 1993).

Much activism was in pursuit of protective legislation, which is a double-edged sword for women in their struggle for labour rights. In Argentina there have been quite generous gains made around maternity and child-care, but frequently in a way which is prejudicial to women's longer-term interests. Currently employers have to provide nurseries if they employ more than fifty women: Norma Rial, who works on labour issues and advises the government, argues that this leads to a situation where nurseries are underutilized and that the onus is still on mothers as carers.[14] It also makes women workers seem more expensive to employ: laws aimed to protect end up discriminating against those they are designed to help.

Rial considers that male trade unionists are resistant to change and still haven't engaged with women's issues, and so set them to one side. Mirta Henault, who has a long history of union activity in Argentina, talked of the developments over the decades. She suggested that women were joining unions in the 1960s and 1970s, particularly the professional unions which were more progressive, but with a worker rather than gender perspective. In the 1970s women's sections began to appear, but without a feminist perspective. Enough women were engaged in union activity to warrant two organizations: the Mesa de Mujeres Sindicalistas (Union Women's Table) and the Movimiento Nacional de la Mujer (National Women's Movement). To date, however, their success has been limited. Henault also commented that the main union confederation, the Peronist Confederación General de Trabajadores (CGT), has a Women's Secretariat – headed by a man![15] In the case of Argentina, I would suggest that the founding of the PPF (Peronist Women's Party: see Chapter 4) undermined women's activity in the labour sector. Bianchi (1993) and Deutsch (1991) both indicate that the members of the PPF were young women who worked. Belonging to the PPF may have given women access to the political arena, but it was short-lived, while the Peronist labour movement still mobilizes and has (waning) influence.

As with institutional politics, the changing debates on gender which emerged in the democratization process of the 1980s have had an impact on the attitudes of some trade unions towards women. The fact that women have gained a greater profile in public life owes much to their participation in the popular protest movements in the 1970s and 1980s. There has been a reassessment of women's roles in society resulting from the greater 'public' visibility of women and the uncovering of their participation in all forms of collective action. Unions have responded to this change. There are training courses and women's sections, including in the CGT (Henault, 1994: 200). In the Argentine teachers' union there has been an increase in women holding office, and training courses have been developed by the Women's Department of the union; however, there is antipathy on the part of some men for the need for a women's department in a union dominated by women (Amado and Checa, 1990). Similar antipathy is evident in Uruguay, where male unionists consider women's sections and separate organizations divisive of the movement (Fisher, 1993).

Despite the continued difficulties it is important to acknowledge the advances: some unions have set up women's groups or branches to address particular problems that working women face; there have been specific programmes to educate women about their rights and the roles of unions; in Argentina there is talk of the quota law for political office being extended to trade unions;[16] and certain women-dominated professions have gained union recognition for the first time, particularly domestic service, where the particular needs of live-in employees were discussed (see below). In many cases the existence of a women's branch gave women their first representation on union national executives. Not only have unions been opening up, or forced to create, spaces for women's issues, but women trade unionists have also been organizing themselves in separate groups to make links between unions, and sometimes social movements, to discuss common gender issues (Amado and Checa, 1990: 15; Carrillo, 1990; Henault, 1994).

Union activity is changing as the work environment changes and there is a development of non-traditional industries. The large-scale factories of the 1950s and 1960s are no longer the major employers they were. Union activity appears to be less working class and more middle class, reflecting deindustrialization: in the mid-1980s 70 per cent of strikes in Argentina were in the state sector (Amado and Checa, 1990: 26), but this does not mean greater gender awareness. There is still the lack of an integrated, holistic approach to the role of unions in today's society. Workers may also be antipathetic towards unions which are closely identified with the state, which does not mean that they are against workplace organizing (Peña, 1987), but alternatives may be limited. It is evident that unions do little to attract women workers and are not receptive to alternatives to the male work pattern. It is not surprising, then, that the majority of women do not use their participation in the labour force as an introduction to collective action and the development of political subjectivity, particularly from a gender perspective.

Grassroots and independent organization

Independent, grassroots organizations have occurred in many sectors and many countries in the region. In some countries they have been part of the democratization process of the 1970s and 1980s and linked with other social movements. In many social movements women's participation has been a central feature, sometimes resulting in a reassessment of gender relations. There have also been examples of internal 'democratic currents' within some of the larger, more established unions, such as the Mexican teachers' union, the SNTE.[17] On the whole the ability of these unions to consolidate themselves once the initial reason for organization had passed has been limited, since it requires high levels of commitment from the members. For women, the problems have been exacerbated by the nature of the work they do and the isolation of many, given that they frequently work alone. Despite this, however, a number of women-only or women-dominated unions have emerged over the years, including several vibrant domestic-service unions. The aims have been to regularize the conditions of work, particularly as regards working hours and days off. Unionizing live-in domestic workers is particularly difficult, since the women are dependent on their employers not just for work, but for housing as well. Furthermore, it is often young women and recently arrived rural migrants who have the worst conditions and the fewest number of contacts for support. There are also a number of unions in the textile industry and the *maquiladoras*.

By examining the cases of domestic workers, garment makers and workers in export processing zones (EPZs), we can come to some conclusions about the advantages, as well as the limitations and constraints, of such organizations. Unless indicated to the contrary, this discussion includes a Brazilian domestic workers' organization (Anderfuhren, 1994), a Mexican domestic workers' organization (Joffre Lazarini and Martínez, 1994), a Uruguayan domestic workers' association (Prates, 1989), *maquiladora* activists (Peña, 1987), rural workers' organizations in Central American EPZs (Delgado González, 1994) and the 19th September Garment Makers' Union in Mexico (Carrillo, 1990, and Tirado, 1994). In assessing their different experiences we can conclude that, far from being apolitical or disinterested in workplace collective action, women make good union members. They are prepared to take radical action to defend and promote their interests when the issues are right. Nevertheless, they still participate in fewer numbers than men, and frequently their issues are simply ignored and thus they reject unions.

A common problem which union organizers encountered was that women often did not see themselves as workers, particularly domestic workers. The union activist Moriana comments, 'perhaps one of the areas we've worked on most is the guilt felt by many women workers. If women are guilty about working outside the home, it's also a serious obstacle to their participation in unions' (in Fisher, 1993: 63). As women have developed a greater worker identity, there is an acknowledgement of rights, reflecting a shift in political subjectivity. Resulting from this was the demand for pro-fessionalization of work, with the formalization of hours – again a particular issue for domestic workers. For factory workers, a further issue was equality between women and men in the work-place, including equal treatment and equal pay. In countries which are immersed in clientelistic relations, this assertion of an identity with concomitant rights must not be underestimated. A second common characteristic was the importance of training, which often developed skills and provided information. This training and information encompassed educating workers in the role of unions, including the larger confederations; the development of leadership skills; advocacy work; professional training (of considerable benefit if women are to earn more); and identifying women's rights as citizens and workers. Finally, these organizations also provided support networks, particularly important for immigrant women.

Many independent unions enjoy support from external organizations. The key to good relations between support organizations and union members is encouraging women to take as active a role as possible, both in developing the agenda for action and in assuming positions of responsibility. In many countries there has been a welfarist attitude towards workers, which makes members passive recipients of aid and reinforces clientelistic relations. Support organizations fall into two main categories: union activists from other organizations and members of the women's movement, sometimes with the support of international organizations.

Obviously being both a feminist and a union activist is not necessarily mutually exclusive, as Carrillo (1990) shows, although there is generally a difference in emphasis. In her study on the garment workers and their supporters in Mexico, she comments that the supporters among the women with union (CRI) backgrounds tended to be working class, while the women from the feminist organization (MAS) tended to be middle class. The difference in perspective is that the CRI women 'identify themselves as labor activists with a focus on sectors that employ a high proportion of women', while 'MAS advisers view themselves first and foremost as feminist activists whose activism is directed towards the concerns of wage-earning women' (Carrillo, 1990: 222). The increased interaction between feminists and unions has great benefits for both in developing strategies for a more gender-sensitive and inclusive socio-economic system, and is mutually beneficial in terms of raising awareness of new issues and strategies. The emergence of the NAFTA has opened new possibilities for interaction among women wage earners in Mexico, the USA and Canada (Gabriel and Macdonald, 1994).

A common problem where feminist organizations have become involved is the emergence of certain class antagonisms; this is particularly the case in domestic workers' organizations, since some feminists who support the groups also employ domestic servants. In the cases in the literature presented here, however, initial problems were, for the large part, resolved in a way which allowed the workers to engage with an alternative way of understanding their subordinate position. A Uruguayan activist, Mabel, comments, 'the majority of women who came back from exile came with new ideas and even if it was European feminism, it attracted us. They began to work with groups here. There was no friction. They'd had their experience from outside and we'd ours from inside. There were conflicts but we discussed them with a lot of respect. There was a good relationship and we could work together' (in Fisher, 1993: 54). Nevertheless, it appears important to most of the women to maintain their class analysis at the centre of their activism (Scott, 1994; cf. Craske, 1993, on popular movements).

Even where there is a well-developed programme for supporting women's workplace organizing, change can be slow. In a study of a women's centre providing support for women workers on Mexico's northern border, Kathleen Staudt (1987) concluded that women achieve a sense of personal empowerment as a result of their activities in the centre.[18] The role of support networks and organizations seems, if not vital, then a significant advantage for the long-term success of the movements, but it must be recognized that the support organizations themselves also have an agenda to pursue, which will promote a certain vision of the world.[19] A feminist consultant may see her involvement as part of a consciousness-raising exercise to promote feminism, rather than women's labour rights, although these are clearly linked.

The organizations examined here demonstrate that certain characteristics can be identified as auspicious for women's workplace organizing. These are small-scale groups, with a holistic approach to women's needs, including a clear training programme and a women-centred focus. The more intimate focus helps lead to empowerment for women and gives them the confidence to assert their rights, and, in cases, to become leaders themselves. Good relations with external organizations can offer valuable support and advice. There are, however, still problems. Firstly, the aforementioned tension between class and gender can rupture good relations. Secondly, some groups fail to break away from the welfarist approach: providing a service is not a problem in itself but can undermine the assertion of rights. Thirdly, some groups lose impetus when the immediate goals are achieved. Finally, as Staudt (1987) identifies in her study, it has proved difficult to move beyond personal empowerment to organizational empowerment. This suggests that change will not have an institutional political impact in the short term.

It appears that the grassroots organizations succeed in generating support from women, despite their difficult working conditions, because the issues are not divided implicitly along a public–private dichotomy; rather, they are viewed in a dialectical fashion whereby work problems cannot be separated from domestic needs (cf. Cubitt and Greenslade, 1997). By linking their activities in the public and private spheres, and not seeing one as subordinate to the other, but both as equally important parts of their lives and identities, women are taking political action around these identities. This can lead to empowerment for some as they demand and defend rights integral to citizenship.

Non-formal workplace collective action

Not all workplace resistance is overtly organized collective action. Indeed it is common for resistance to take forms which undermine employer practices rather than those which involve direct confrontation, where the potential costs are very high. The notion of everyday forms of resistance, popularized by James Scott (1985), is useful in analysing these informal methods of resistance. Perhaps the best-documented accounts of this kind of industrial action in Latin America again come from the *maquiladoras* in northern Mexico. An interesting element of the development of the border industries, and indeed similar types of industrial production across the globe, is the explicit nature of the gendering of the production procedure (Peña, 1987; Pearson, 1991; Gabriel and Macdonald, 1994). Women are employed almost exclusively as shop-floor workers, while men have been overrepresented in the supervisory and managerial roles.

There has been much written about the reasons for the high proportion of women workers in these assembly plants, and authors examining different countries point to the supposed greater dexterity of women at doing detailed close work, the relative cheapness of employing them rather than men and the lesser likelihood of their taking industrial action.[20] *Maquilas* are generally wary of unionization, and the need for work is so great that women would rather not organize than lose vital wages. One plant manager commented, in relation to the promotion of women to line supervisors, 'The ones who don't make it are the more political ones.... Because we have promoted the ones who accept measurement, they also discard those who don't fit into the same profile' (in Peña, 1987: 139).

The reasons given for employing more women are based on myth and stereotypes of female and male characteristics. It is important to note the construction of skill utilized to reinforce gender hierarchies in the workplace: although women are supposed to be dextrous to be shop-floor workers, they are not considered skilled and therefore can be paid less. This reinforces other gendered notions, because it appears that women's work is secondary to, or less important than, men's and by implication this reinforces the breadwinning status of the male (cf. Wilson, 1993). Furthermore, women's wages have declined more sharply than men's in the current economic downturn (Wilson, 1993: 68) – again reinforcing the idea that women's work is less important than men's.

Devon Peña's (1987) study of shop-floor struggles gives an insight into the attitudes both of the factory managers and of the workers. Despite the difficulties in maintaining independence and developing strong organizations, some unions have emerged in these factories and played important roles in campaigning for political changes and defending rights. The shop-floor workers, however, are divided, with some being assigned as group leaders where there are some benefits in kind but where wage rates are the same (Peña, 1987). To help group leaders set the pace, employers deliberately speed up the production process, which further encourages competition among the women. Refusing to co-operate with the speed-ups is a common way of resisting manipulative working practices. Frequently this resistance requires organization and interaction between the shop floor and the group leaders. Many leaders are returned to the general production line as a result of participating in resistance strategies. One worker commented, 'she helped us to organize ways of getting around the standards [increased output] ... by working slower, damaging components, and hiding pieces. Eventually, management caught on to what we were doing. They fired several workers and demoted her back to the soldering line' (in Peña, 1987: 142). But all such action had to be organized carefully: 'The group from the start was clandestine. Our action in the factory was invisible up till the time we hit with walkouts and sabotage. Sometimes it was necessary to meet after work since they watched over us closely.... We made little groups [*bolitas*], had dinners and parties. We talked about the problems and made plans for the next day at work' (in Peña, 1987: 143).[21]

These informal resistance activities tend to produce two

opposing views from analysts: there are those like Scott and Peña who see them as demonstrations of political consciousness which can redefine power relations. But others are much more pessimistic in their analyses, seeing little that is radical about such forms of resistance and identifying them as part of short-term responses to difficult situations, which does little to undermine or change power relations.[22] I suggest that we take a sober but not overly pessimistic view of these strategies. While it is unlikely that they will form the basis of radical collective action and social change, women who are able to assert their power through these strategies are more likely to defend that power.

An important factor is whether workers are conscious of their resistance and the reasons behind their actions. We must also be able to contextualize the activities; they have often taken place in an authoritarian or semi-authoritarian system where labour organizations have played a key role in upholding the state and where independent activism has been co-opted or repressed. When becoming involved in action, the workers are aware of this and are constrained further by their need to maintain family income: taking public action against a situation requires considerable courage, and the more disadvantaged the worker, the more serious the implications. Also activism tends to come in waves with ebbs and flows; consequently a decline in activity cannot be seen as a permanent retreat or a failure on the part of the activists. Another point worth noting is that the ability to assert some kind of control over one's work environment, however limited, can help personal empowerment, which in turn can be translated into other situations such as the domestic arena. It is difficult to assess the level of consciousness of resistance of those engaged in these actions, but the more aware the actors, the greater the political impact.

The political implications of work

In this chapter I have demonstrated that workplace collective action offers women only limited opportunities for developing a political identity and that traditional trade unions have not responded to the needs of women workers. The problem of Latin American trade unions is that found in many European countries: work issues are seen as separate from reproductive issues and unrelated to the primary concerns of most women. Grassroots unions, which are smaller scale affairs and focus more on the informal labour sector, appear to offer women greater scope for expressing themselves politically. There are problems, however, since gains made in general labour law are difficult to enforce in the informal sector (Fisher, 1993). For most women of the popular classes paid work is largely a response to economic need rather than the desire to pursue any personal agenda. There is evidence, however, that they welcome having an independent income and, where applicable, enjoy the daily contact with others.

Furthermore, for some women, participation in unions can lead to engagement with feminist discourse and a new understanding of the constraints in their lives. Under military governments, many trade unionists were exiled: as one, Moriana, says, 'I had my first contact with feminism in Mexico [in exile] and only then did I begin to recognize the discrimination women faced in their work and in the unions' (in Fisher, 1993: 54).

The nature of work influences the development of political identity associated with it. For middle-class women a career is more common and can contribute to their identity in a significant way, not least in that they have a 'public identity', but there is still the tendency to see this work as secondary, and many give up outside work on marriage or childbearing. Furthermore, there does not appear to be a greater tendency among professional women to unionize than among those engaged in other types of outside work. Teachers throughout the region form a peculiar profession in that women are well represented, and teachers' unions have often been at the forefront of industrial disputes (Amado and Checa, 1990; Bareiro et al., 1993; Foweraker, 1993). Given the centrality of education policy to governments at different moments of the twentieth century, this sector has had more industrial-relations muscle. There is no doubt that the women who are least likely to organize, and see their worker identity as positive and central, are those engaged in domestic service or home work which is seen as an adjunct to their domestic tasks. The shifting labour market has created new realities which are reflected in gender roles both in the workplace and in personal relationships.

Gender relations

The renegotiation of gender relations is not easy. Many women do not wish to admit the degree of their income-generation activities if it undermines their partner's contribution, particularly when men are still perceived to be the major income earners. These changes are frequently slow and sometimes are impeded by the work experience itself. Gabriel and Macdonald (1994: 537) argue there are strong links between women's wage-earning work and their domestic work: 'the reasons for employment of women often centre on their gender-ascribed characteristics.' Wilson (1993) suggests that many small-scale workshops become an extension of the domestic sphere, reproducing similar gender relations: the more informal and clandestine the workshops, the more the gender relations resembled domestic production (cf. Safa, 1995). This helped constrain worker identity for the women involved, but Wilson argues that there may be a greater impact on gender relations as young women are able to claim some rights in the home to reflect their earning status.

The small workshops are frequently part of the goal to have as flexible a workforce as possible, following the Japanese 'just-in-time' model; consequently work is insecure and low paid, and the degree of exploitation is greater (Roldán, 1993). In such conditions the relationship between work and empowerment is weak (McClenaghan, 1997). Women make up the majority of the workers in these workshops, and again the type and location of work reinforces the secondary status of women workers. Benería and Roldán (1987) argue that wage earning does not necessarily help redress the gender relations in the home. Similarly, in the Dominican Republic, McClenaghan (1997: 29; cf. Gabriel and Macdonald, 1994) finds that in many instances 'patriarchal values are actually being reinscribed.' She points to Elson and Pearson's assertion that, even where there are changes in domestic relations, it is a shift in private power, 'which is by definition not collective and unlikely to be reproducible outside individual contexts' (McClenaghan, 1997: 26). Furthermore, as others comment, unions often reproduce traditional gender relations themselves (Scott, 1994; Cortina, 1990). The deepening of the neoliberal economic model would indicate that the labour movement generally will continue to be weak, and will be sidelined by governments which are keen to encourage international investment – which, in turn, demands a quiescent labour force and political stability. This model also depends upon the private provision of labour force reproduction and therefore needs women to focus on the domestic sphere as their primary responsibility.

Class and gender issues are apparent in women's union activities, but, in Scott's (1994) comprehensive study on Peru, it appears that women initially mobilize with a class rather than a gender perspective. In women-only unions gender obviously takes a more central role, but in domestic workers' unions class is clearly a key element, since in many cases the employer is also a woman. But gender is unlikely to be at the forefront of labour struggles while gendered ideologies influence hierarchies which place formal-sector work as more important than home work or local workshop subcontracting. This endorses the view that women's work is secondary to men's and that the primary responsibility of women is reproduction, regardless of their other obligations (cf. García and de Oliveira, 1997; Wilson, 1993).

The mothering role reinforces the relegation of wage labour and the suppression of a worker identity, although, as McClenaghan (1997) points out, being able to provide materially for your children is seen as part of good mothering. The trade unionist María Julia comments, 'if the most important thing for [women] is to be a good mother and if the only jobs available are those with the worst pay and conditions, they're not going to feel very positive about their working life' (in Fisher, 1993: 57).

Again it is the state-sanctioned links between motherhood and social reproduction which help undermine the links between the identity 'worker' and collective action for women. Only a holistic approach which does not compartmentalize peoples' lives will help make politics more inclusive of women's experiences. That women seem to prefer a more holistic approach regarding engagement in political activity again demonstrates the limitations of the liberal conception of citizen. The emphasis on the public (male) individual leads to men's identities being fractured and fragmented, since an essential part of their lives (the private) is ignored.[23] The current neoliberal economic model, however, reinforces a public–private distinction which makes a more holistic approach difficult. While the ideological construct of a public–private distinction prevails in a way which leaves women responsible for the private, women's work will serve as much to constrain and oppress as to liberate. If their worker identity is seen by women as secondary, it will offer only limited potential for collective action.

Empowerment and political participation

There are, however, other political implications of work around shifting gender relations and personal empowerment. A combination of issues have resulted in working women being accepted and acceptable: the economic crisis has forced women to take an ever larger role in income generation; increased educational attainment has given some women greater choices; shifts in industrialization patterns have had an impact on the labour market, with more 'women's' jobs such as those in the assembly plants; and women now see work as a part of their worlds. As women are earning more and are possibly in the home less, gender relations are changing. Although engagement in exploitative capitalist practices may be a problem, this is not an entirely negative experience: it can create valuable new opportunities for women in the public arena (Kandiyoti, in Rai, 1996: 31).

Similarly, wage earning can increase women's participation in domestic decision making, particularly around expenditure (Chant, 1993; Safa, 1995). Safa argues that, given the traditional status of women in the home, it is easier for them to challenge men in this arena rather than in the 'public' sphere: 'women have gained more negotiating power in the household than at levels of workplace and the state' (Safa, 1995: 35). The problem remains, as identified by McClenaghan above, that these developments are generally individual, when it is collective improvements that are needed. Safa similarly acknowledges that there remain strong links between women's wage-earning role and their domestic work: 'most of these women now consider paid employment part of their domestic role, because they are working to contribute to the household economy rather than for their own self-esteem or personal autonomy' (Safa, 1995: 47). This identification with serving and providing for others will continue to militate against development of citizenship.

Conclusions

Evidence of the relationship between the workplace and institutional politics is patchy. At a national level the experience appears to have little impact. Few female politicians have come to national prominence as a result of their involvement in the labour movement. The country where the potential for this might be greater, Argentina, channelled women's activity through the PPF. It appears that the women who have come to national prominence in labour disputes have been the wives of strikers (Domitila Barrios in Bolivia and Sandra Dodero, the police officer's wife in at the forefront of the 1994–5 strikes in Uruguay (see Perelli, 1994), are but two examples). At the local level there is a paucity of studies which examine the link between the workplace political activism of women and their participation in political parties or electoral campaigns, or their voting intentions. But, given that collective activity often feeds into the development of political subjectivity (see Chapter 2), where the work environment, in whatever form, leads to collective organization there are political implications. The state-endorsed female and male gender constructions, however, will inform the ambit of work and therefore the types of workplace activity in which women and men tend to participate.

Although work is a central part of women's lives, we know surprisingly little about how it informs their political identity. From the examination of material presented here, I suggest that unions do little to encourage women's participation and are narrow in their views of workers' issues. Furthermore, they reinforce the idea that women are not 'real' workers. Where work is having a greater impact is within private power relations, which can have political implications, but change is slow and uneven. In the following chapter collective action in the neighbourhood is examined. Although women again appear to prioritize class over gender, the different terrain of struggle and mobilizing identity means that the impact is greater at both the personal and the institutional level.

6

Social Movements: Consumer and Human Rights Organizations

> I joined the CoMadres in 1978; I had never been involved in any political work nor did I know if the CoMadres were a political or humanitarian group. All I knew is that they understood my suffering.
>
> *María Teresa (in Schirmer, 1993: 45)*

Introduction

The exclusionary nature of political systems in Latin America reached its height under the military regimes in the 1970s, particularly in Argentina (1976–82) and Chile (1973–89). Even civilian regimes such as that in Mexico, however, practised authoritarian methods which made autonomous political expression difficult. Despite this, different kinds of collective activity have occurred regularly throughout the region. In this chapter I examine the emergence of social movements in the 1970s and 1980s where women played a key role. There are a number of interrelated arguments I make here. First, these movements demonstrate the clearest examples of the connections between motherhood and political participation. This helped to broaden the political debate and make it more inclusive of different experiences. The tight links between motherhood and social reproduction, however, are evident, and for many motherhood remains an apolitical identity. Furthermore, the non-negotiable stance of many motherist demands is anti-politics, since negotiation and compromise are at the centre of politics. The limitations of using motherhood as the basis for female political action is apparent.

Second, motherhood may be an identity which crosses class and ethnic boundaries; nevertheless, women in these movements, particularly consumer organizations, tend to prioritize class over gender. For the majority it was a defence of a gender division of labour and issues more in keeping with practical gender interests which encouraged their participation in social movements. Third, participation in social movements provides women with an important entry into politics not forthcoming through engagement in work and parties. Participation can lead to the development of political subjectivity and citizenship through establishing rights more inclusive of women's experiences. Fourth, empowerment, more often at the personal than the institutional level, can result from participation in social movements as people become aware of their political efficacy.

Motherhood's role as a catalyst for political involvement, as 'mobilizing referent', is demonstrated throughout the chapter. But antipathy towards politics remains and is reflected in the strategies and tactics women use. There are tensions in the relationship between social movements and the institutional political arena, which, in part, accounts for the weakening of social movements as electoral politics has re-emerged throughout the region. For most people, participation in politics is an ambivalent experience which requires compromise and negotiation, whereby relationships with other political organizations is one of exchange. Despite the important role they played in the democratization process, a combination of factors contribute to the continuing distance between social movements and political institutions. One is that the corrupt and clientelistic practices of many institutional political actors means that social movements frequently guard their autonomy and independence highly (Munck, 1990). The other issue for women is that gender constructions are developing slowly and political participation remains something which is related to crisis or exceptional situations. Nevertheless, participation in social movements has had considerable impact on women's empowerment and has led some to deepen their political participation. With the shift to electoral politics, however, we also see how conservative and resistant political institutions are in incorporating new demands.

The rise of social movements

Popular protest falls into two main categories: firstly, consumer organizations, which generally focus on standards of living in terms of both goods and services; and secondly, human rights organizations, which have been particularly important in Argentina, Chile and Central America. I discuss their development and focus below on the actors, the issues, the terrain of struggle and the leadership–base relationship. Many countries have experience of both human rights organizations and consumer groups: since the latter were often perceived as consisting of opposition activists, they were themselves often targets of repression. Despite the importance of these movements in the challenge to authoritarianism, they have been side-lined as civilian regimes have re-emerged in the 1990s. Governments attempt to demobilize anything which challenges the new consensus of the post-military regimes (and largely succeed in doing so). This includes demanding justice for victims of human rights abuses or questioning the skewed economic distribution arising from the economic project. The neoliberal model reaffirms the distinction between public and private which social movements helped erode. This clearly has gender implications since women are more likely to participate in movements than in parties, despite the recent changes highlighted in Chapter 4.

Although social movements centre on specific agendas, it is the longer-term political implications which have proven challenging. The political education of the actors and the impact on political systems generally are of greatest importance in this analysis. Movements can develop from being localized low-scale groups into sophisticated and politically astute organizations. At their most successful they have introduced new actors and practices into the political arena, have challenged the modus operandi of authoritarian political systems, and have contributed to the democratization of many regimes. Social movements represented civil society, which was a 'training ground of democratic rule' (Volk, 1997: 9).[1]

These groups must not be romanticized, however: they are small in number, wax and wane, and find it difficult to sustain themselves under multi-party electoral systems as parties reassert themselves as the principal political actors. As Hellman (1997) reminds us, not all social movements can be seen as progressive and democratizing. It is important to remember that they differ widely in practices and goals, and even the most successful sometimes have a limited impact on the most important decision-making arenas. Furthermore, many reflect the political culture in which they have emerged, and incorporate clientelistic tendencies. Their importance lies in their ability to undermine persistently even the most authoritarian regimes, and to provide an alternative political education and experience for those who are generally marginalized from the formal political arena.

The development of consumer organizations

Although the region's economies had been growing, particularly in the 1960s, the highly skewed income distribution meant that many people were not benefiting from economic growth; some people's lifestyles were actually deteriorating. The combination of the economic crisis, structural adjustment and past failures of governments to address inequality, despite the years of growth, resulted in a response from 'ordinary people'. The neighbourhood became a key battleground, since the responses to crisis were often communal. More traditional responses through parties and unions were rejected, either because these arenas were seen as unhelpful or because they had been repressed by military regimes.

Initial responses to the economic conditions were often to engage in collective survival strategies. These included the establishment of communal kitchens and the development of informal child-care groups, self-help housing projects and shopping groups. At first these were simply extensions of the domestic work already being done, but they helped forge a collective identity. As austerity measures increased, so too did the demands and protests from these groups. There were strikes and demonstrations and organized petitioning of local authorities for services.[2] In expanding the activities, groups formed alliances and linkages with one another to increase their efficacy. This development of strategic capabilities reflects Foweraker's (1989, 1997) analysis of the development of citizenship. Further linkages were made with facilitating organizations which helped strengthen the organizational capacities of these movements; these included the Catholic Church, NGOs and local civic associations.

The collectivization of domestic tasks gave women a key role in these movements, and they saw that their organizational capacity in the home could be used in a broader context. In many cases the position and authority of men were weakening as a result of unemployment, and they were sometimes side-lined in these communal movements (Fisher, 1993). This resulted in shifts in gender relations in homes and in the organizations. The movements were important in the anti-authoritarian struggle and also contributed to the development of feminism (see Chapter 8).

The number of these movements was immense, but the majority did not go beyond their original goal of alleviating the worst excesses of the economic crisis. Furthermore, the repressive context in which many of them emerged did not make development easy. The majority of the movements being discussed here are from lower-income neighbourhoods, where there was a need for services and where the impact of the crisis was the most severe. There were, however, middle-class housewives' organizations which protested at the rapid increase in the cost of living in Argentina, particularly as the economic crisis deepened (Fisher, 1993; Feijoó and Nari, 1994). Linkages were also made through NGOs and other organizations, discussed below, which further blur class distinctions within the movements.

Human rights organizations: the origins

Extreme levels of human rights abuse occurred in Argentina during the so-called Dirty War (1976–82), in Chile in the first few years of the Pinochet regime, and in many Central American countries over the past thirty years, although no country is immune. The rhetoric of the authoritarian regimes of the Southern Cone centred upon medical metaphors of a sick society which required radical surgery; this consisted of killing ('exterminating') perceived subversives. The rhetoric was highly gendered as well; motherhood was promoted as a patriotic duty, reflecting the discourses of fascist parties (Deutsch, 1997; cf. Pateman, 1992). Since women were seen as 'naturally' apolitical, they were spared the worst excesses of human rights abuses at the outset.[3]

Those targeted for 'disappearance' were activists in political parties, trade unions and student organizations. While women featured in all these, men made up the majority.[4] Feminist organizations were also targeted and many women were exiled. This led to their involvement with emerging feminist debates in other countries, which in turn influenced local developments when the women returned after the re-establishment of civilian rule. Certain universities were targeted, with 'radical' academics being forced to leave the country. Exiles went to many different places – some to other Latin American countries, others to Europe (many Chilean socialists and communists went to the Eastern bloc, and Italy was a destination for many Argentinians) and the USA.

The most common tactic used by the military in Argentina and Chile, which had learnt by Brazil's 'mistake', was to arrest people, but without taking them to police stations for formal questioning; if there were no official records of an arrest there could be no writ of *habeus corpus*. In the first days of the regimes in both countries, thousands of people were killed indiscriminately to instil fear in the population at large – a tactic which worked. In Central America (Schirmer, 1993) and Peru (Poole and Rénique, 1992), villages often suffered massacres, but this was carried out in a very visible way, as a warning to others; disappearances also occurred.[5] In other countries the scale of the abuse was not so great, but it was incessant, and over the years incidents numbered hundreds.

In Argentina and Chile women kept coming across one another when they were searching for husbands, sons and daughters. The task of finding people was almost impossible, since there were no official records and the women had to depend on sightings by other people who may have been held with them. The authorities made life yet more difficult by sending the women to places they knew the victims would not be. The usual grisly tour for the women would be the police stations, the army barracks, the hospitals and the morgues. As María del Rosario in Argentina describes, 'at the police stations and the barracks we stood in queues for hours and they turned us away, they played games with us, they laughed at us' (in Fisher, 1993: 105). Some women began to recognize one another in their traipsing around and formed groups to present their lists of disappeared.

The organizations emerged to give support and to make the search more efficient. In Chile the church played a key role as one of the few institutions left relatively untouched by the repression. In Central America the groups were hampered by the rural–urban divide, since many of the abuses took place in the countryside. Indian women had even less experience of dealing with the authorities than their urban counterparts in Chile and Argentina. This was exacerbated by racism and language barriers: many of the victims were indigenous peoples, while those organizing the abuses were white (reflected in the events in Chiapas from 1994).

Although women featured heavily in these organizations, for reasons explored below, men also participated. In Argentina, one organization, the Asamblea Permanente de Derechos Humanos (Permanent Assembly for Human Rights: APDH), was keen to be seen as non-sectarian, and encouraged men and women alike to be members. At the outset the public face of the APDH was male, and the majority of directors are still male, but over time there have been changes. In the initial organization the focus was on disappearances, but after a while the remit of human rights grew to include indigenous peoples' rights, police violence and youth issues, and a women's commission was established in 1987 to tackle the specific problems women faced. Within this commission the main policy areas are the work environment, domestic violence, and the promotion of the UN Convention on the Elimination of all forms of Discrimination Against Women (CEDAW). Although the APDH does work with the Las Madres de la Plaza de Mayo (the Mothers of the Plaza de Mayo) on joint campaigns, it is critical of the 'sectarian' nature of women-only organizations and considers its own organization to be much broader.[6] The Mothers choose to emphasize the natural rights that motherhood gives them. They argued that their demands are unique and above politics, very much in keeping with Kaplan's female consciousness.[7] As was the case with the consumer organizations, human rights groups moved on from being local support groups to become sophisticated bodies, many with international profiles.

Structures and organization

There are a number of reasons why women were major participants in the social movements. These reflect the mobilizing identity, the issues, the terrain of struggle, and the leadership–base relations.

Identity

Women in both the consumer movements and the human rights organizations were responding to their practical gender interests as dictated by the prevalent gender discourse (see Chapter 2). They were defending the gender division of labour and generally had little previous experience in collective organizations. They did not start with an idea of a political protest. They were keen to fulfil their roles as mothers, but their participation subverted that identity, and they became, in Alvarez's terms, 'militant mothers'. In human rights organizations, theirs was a desperate attempt to find out some information about loved ones: the onslaught against the family triggered the 'female consciousness'. For women, the emphasis was unequivocally on mothering. In Chile a woman from Agrupación said, 'We are *mothers*, not women' (emphasis in the original: Schirmer, in Jelin, 1996: 194, fn 5).[8] The Mothers in Argentina, another women-only group, was strongly defensive of this.

Women were able to be invisible simply by being women. In a country where a group of more than three was banned as a public meeting, women could meet in groups because this was perceived to be harmless gossiping (Bouvard, 1994; cf. Jelin, 1997). Clara explains, 'we'd meet in a cafe and so no one would realise what was going on, we took paper and pretended to be copying dress patterns.... Or we'd pretend we were celebrating a birthday' (in Fisher, 1993: 108). This invisibility was put to good use in leafleting campaigns and the placing of stickers around cities asking for information about missing people.

Eventually, the women decided to take their demands to the most public of places. A weekly march took place in the most important square in central Buenos Aires, the Plaza de Mayo, which was flanked by some of the most important buildings in the city: the presidential palace, the metropolitan cathedral, the cabildo (town hall) and the city hall. They met every Thursday afternoon and marched silently, wearing white headscarves embroidered with the names of missing relatives: they became Las Madres de la Plaza de Mayo (the Mothers of the Plaza de Mayo).[9] The symbolism of the silence and the white headscarves was an illustration of the powerful use of 'female apoliticalness' – tactics also used in Central America (Schirmer, 1993). Soon, when it became apparent that pregnant women had been abducted and their children born in captivity and adopted by 'decent' citizens, these women were joined by grandmothers of the disappeared.

While most consumerist organizations included women and men, there were some which were consciously women-only movements, 'in order to prove they were as capable as men', and thus they questioned gender relations directly (Chuchryk, 1994: 69). Even in groups which were not gender specific, women made up large numbers. In Chile, as in the Argentinian case above, it was considered that women would find it easier and safer to protest than men, since the patriarchal ideas of the military would not see women as politically threatening (Feijoó and Gogna, 1990). Women-only sections also emerged within mixed groups to allow women to discuss gender-specific issues, but also 'because when we put forward ideas in the meetings, no-one took any notice' (Flora, an activist in Argentina). Similarly, in Paraguay, Magui comments, '[we] set up women-only meetings to encourage them to take part in the organization. When there are men around women don't speak' (both in Fisher, 1993: 179 and 83).

Women's identity was shifting from 'mother' to 'woman', and a more gender-aware approach was being established. This included women having the right to participate in organizations and to have a voice. Mobilizing around motherhood allowed them to participate collectively without challenging gender stereotypes. It is clear that women responded to the claims being made in the name of motherhood, and that the authorities also acknowledged, to some degree, the legitimacy of such claims. Motherhood in these cases becomes a strategically useful identity to generate a movement.

Issues

The issues involved were generally not perceived as political, but both consumer organizations and human rights groups directly confronted state policy in key areas of the economy and over security issues. As Massolo (n.d.) identifies in the Mexican case, the movements developed and the focus of the struggle shifted from the original issues to demands for transparency and accountability of the authorities. This eventually resulted in the demand for democratization. The distinction between social and political concerns was blurred. Female consciousness and the 'ethic of care' approach are perhaps best illustrated by the human rights movements. The women who campaigned against the military were responding in a very direct way, with the desire to protect human life, and they generally protested the innocence of the disappeared and arrested people (Bouvard, 1994; Fisher, 1993): this contradicted the military's writing of history and their understanding of what was subversive. Although the basic demand was to have the disappeared returned, since this was frequently impossible, the struggle for democracy and accountability became central. The human rights protests highlighted the brutal nature of the regimes: coercion was such a chief part of their modus operandi that to curtail repression meant a change of regime.

The consumer movements were fundamentally linked to family welfare and often developed out of survival and co-operative networks: as such, the women were organizing around their practical gender interests. Some organizations protested against declining standards of living resulting from austerity measures, while others demanded the extension of existing services.[10] Since most governments were pursuing similar economic policies, these movements were challenging the heart of government policy. The right to a 'dignified life' (*vida digna*) was incorporated into citizenship discourse. The role of women as household managers put them on the front line: Teresita in Mexico observes, 'the man has his life which is work, and that is his responsibility. He comes home with the money. For the woman, the house is hers, and things such as no light and no water are part of the home, so it is her fight' (in Craske, 1993: 114). It is at this moment that the links between caring for others and citizenship are apparent, since these demands can be translated into rights. Such activity, however, conforms to rather than challenges gender divisions of labour, and does not necessarily introduce women to political engagement in others' arenas.

Terrain

The organization and early development of social movements were evident in a variety of terrains, but all were private in the sense that they were unseen by the authorities. The local organizing frequently took place in non-political spaces which women already inhabited and thus reflected a domestic character. The economic crisis had led to the development of communal kitchens, which seemed apolitical; however, they became the focus of political organization in many countries, particularly Chile, Peru and Uruguay. In Uruguay, 'the night-time *apagones,* when entire districts of Montevideo turned off their lights, and the *caceroleos,* the banging of pots and saucepans that could be heard echoing across the neighbourhoods around the capital, were intended as constant reminders to the military authorities that the spirit of resistance had not been broken' (Fisher, 1993: 52).

The local nature of these organizations made it easier for women to participate, given that their freedom of movement is limited by domestic responsibilities and social norms. But it wasn't long before women – most notably the Mothers in Argentina – took their protests into the public arena, from 'the *casa* to the plaza'. The reality of human rights abuses rips through the private domestic arena: the state has penetrated in a brutal fashion the 'sanctity' of the home, denying it its private function. On the one hand the NSS were reinforcing public and private distinctions, with the emphasis on family values. On the other, however, they made the distinction meaningless by circumscribing public space and actions and invading private spaces: arrest could come at any moment and one never knew who was an informant. The consumer movements also challenged the boundaries between public and private space through the collective activities taking place in domestic space. Homes and communal kitchens became places of political organization, while public places (such as parish halls) housed communal kitchens.

Leadership–base relations

Some consumer organizations were initiated by people with experience in organization, while most of the human rights organizations emerged in direct response to people's experience of losing someone, so there was no automatic leadership. Those with charisma and skills tended to emerge as the spokespeople, although some organizations appear to try and maintain collegial decision-making structures. Relations with the institutional sphere were not always warm: in Argentina the Mothers were keen to keep a distance from all parties in the transition period (Feijoó and Gogna, 1990).[11] In Chile, however, the distinct party tradition allowed for closer, though not completely amicable, relations between parties and women's organizations, including those supporting human rights organizations (Frohmann and Valdés, 1993).

As with other organizations, however, certain women have emerged as leaders in the popular consciousness, especially outside their own countries: in Argentina it is Hebe Bonafini and Nora Cortiña; in Central America it is Rigoberta Menchú. The success of the movements, however, reflects the efforts of many who remain nameless and invisible to the outside world. The importance of working together and of everybody being valued equally is evident in the comments of América (from El Salvador's Co-Madres):

> One thing which motivated us a lot was that they [from the city] respected very much the opinion of the *madres campesinas* [peasant mothers] ... they respected us: there has always been a mutual respect among us, and I believe that mutual respect has allowed us to exist until today. There is no devaluing our opinion because one

or other of us hasn't studied. The one thing that unites us is the problem of [finding] our relatives. (in Schirmer, 1993: 35)

In consumer organizations, women and men frequently participated together; there is some evidence to suggest, however, that men are more likely to emerge as leaders (Stephen, 1989; cf. the APDH discussed above). Nevertheless, women remained important actors, and they seemed encouraged by smaller and tightly networked groups which allowed those with little previous political experience to feel comfortable and gradually take on responsibilities (Craske, 1993; Barrig, 1994). The small organizations where women dominated tended to have a less hierarchical structure and to collectivize responsibilities, as demonstrated by the women-only group in Chile (Chuchryk, 1994). In some cases a divide has emerged between the base and leadership, and traditional practices of *caudillismo* (strongman politics) have emerged, with some leaders using social movements as a launch pad for a political career (Craske, 1993; Jaquette, 1994b). The issue of maintaining independence from the traditional party-political sphere is more important in those countries, such as Mexico, Brazil and Argentina, where parties have been seen as part of a corrupt system, rather than those (Chile and Uruguay) where the parties themselves were not seen as so problematic.

The strength of movements in the 1970s and 1980s reflects, the ways in which issues diversified and multiplied and linkages were made with other groups. Also, as the campaigns developed, there was a professionalization of protest. This included linkages with established organizations, including churches and NGOs, which have provided valuable support, but which also introduced their own perspectives and agendas which influenced the development of social movements. The role of social movements has become more complex with the return of civilian governments in the region. The terrain is more difficult since political stability is paramount and parties are not keen to pursue the issues. Many people want the truth about human rights abuses, but not if it destabilizes the civilian government to the point of collapse. The military is still a major actor in many Latin American countries. Similarly, few are protesting against the continued austerity measures, and are focusing instead on daily survival.

Facilitating organizations: professionalization of protest

The two types of social movement reflect certain things in common. Most marked is the erosion of traditional boundaries and dichotomies, but also the way in which the social movements were supported by a broad array of organizations – support which was invaluable. Despite the importance of human rights groups and consumer organizations in breaking the silence around the abuses, and in demonstrating that women, even if 'apolitical', could not be ignored, the role of international organizations was important in getting the women's voices heard. These organizations included international 'solidarity' groups, well-established human rights organizations such as Amnesty International and Americas Watch, development NGOs and churches. Given the military's insistence on Christian patriotism, the backing of the Catholic Church was important. In Chile the Vicariate of Santiago set up a centre to monitor human rights abuses and to put pressure on the regime for information. Similarly, in Central America the Catholic Church was an outspoken critic of the abuses. Inevitably, perhaps, it was easier for human rights rather than consumer organizations to gain international attention, but the movements' success meant that the women themselves were to become targets of the security forces (Schirmer, 1993; Fisher, 1993).

Help came in different forms: organizational skills, advice on strategy, links with other groups, knowledge of legal systems, finding markets for locally produced goods. The involvement of some outside organizations, with the introduction of paid support workers, could be seen as the 'professionalization' of social movements. Local NGOs and 'civic associations', such as mothers' groups, trade unions, feminist organizations and popular education projects, have also played an important support role. The ease with which the organizations can operate depends on their history and the local conditions. Here the discussion focuses on the Catholic Church and NGOs.[12] An important issue is the relationship among these organizations and the groups themselves. How much autonomy do the organizations have and how do they seek to support the women in their activities? To what extent do these organizations have their own agendas and gender constructions? In many cases the role of facilitating organizations has given social movements a greater public profile – particularly on an international scale, which was important during the military dictatorships.

International NGOs have generally focused more on development issues, and have their own gender discourses, as will be addressed below. The relationship between a support organization and a social movement should ideally be one of exchange, where both can benefit. But this requires a clear understanding of each other's agenda and arena of action. In Latin America there have been tensions generally around class, since many of those working in facilitating organizations are middle-class professionals. Tensions also emerge as actors in social movements develop personally, but there have been successes as well. Despite the problems, the organizations have generally helped social movements consolidate themselves, but it is important that social movements are not taken over by the support groups.

The Catholic Church

The history of the Catholic Church in Latin America has been mixed, but over the past thirty years its support has been a significant help in the development of social movements, most particularly in the struggle to defend human rights. There has also been significant activity in low-income neighbourhoods by sectors of the church, particularly those who embraced the 'option for the poor' endorsed by the Second Vatican Council in the early 1960s (see Alvarez, 1990: 60–2). The church increasingly struggled against poverty in practical and campaigning ways (Fisher, 1993; Schirmer, 1993; Schild, 1994), which did not always have a directly religious content (Machado, 1993). There was also the development of liberation theology, influenced by the writings of the Brazilian pedagogue Paolo Freire. This 'progressive' church was not distributed evenly across the region; Brazil and Central America were the most receptive, while Argentina's church was the most supportive of the military government. It must be remembered that the church is not a homogeneous institution, so reactionary clergy may be found in all countries.

The potential of members of the clergy as allies was great, especially in military regimes. Since these governments espoused commitment to a Christian patriotism, the church had significant room for manoeuvre, which also protected parish groups from repression; the regimes did not want to be accused of acting against the church. This was particularly important in Chile,[13] although the church's status has not always saved outspoken clergy from repression, as events in Central America attest.[14] But in Argentina, Clara recounts, 'I grew up fearing God, respecting priests and the Church. What did they do? They went into the concentration camps and blessed the tortured youngsters and then they told us they knew nothing' (in Fisher, 1993: 112).

The clergy, both women and men (it must be noted that there are many more nuns than there are male clergy), often promoted the teachings of the Second Vatican Council through popular education projects, utilizing the ideas of Freire (Alvarez, 1990). Here people were encouraged to relate events in their daily lives to their education, generally basic reading and writing skills. For some this led to a questioning of the charitable basis on which poverty was previously tackled, and the issue of justice became key (Machado, 1993). This experience often led them to challenge accepted realities regarding the rich and poor in their societies and the belief in a natural hierarchy (which also underpins corporatism and many aspects of traditional Catholicism). The educational process also involved Bible-reading exercises, with an emphasis on analysing daily experiences. These reading groups often introduced women to collective organization and networking. In most church-based groups women outnumbered men, which was frequently reflected in subsequent social movements. Not all Bible-reading groups developed into collective action groups, but a large number did.[15]

The importance of church support was in legitimizing activity; it was difficult for partners, parents and the authorities to criticize women for participating in something endorsed by the church. The domestic nature of the campaigns did not present the church with any conflict in its teachings of gender roles; in many ways they affirmed the Christian ideal of womanhood, with a focus on improving the welfare of the family or defending life. For many women there was the added advantage that partners would not only not object, but the church would possibly intervene on other issues such as alcoholism and domestic violence. The commitment to the 'option for the poor', through the struggle for social justice in this life rather than waiting for the hereafter, was not shared by all clerics, however, either in Latin America or in other parts of the globe. A series of Latin American bishops' conferences first promoted, then reined in, the changes, and Pope John Paul II has discouraged what he sees as inappropriate political activity (despite his own support for the Polish Solidarity trade union in the early 1980s).

Despite the obvious advantages that the clergy gave to protest campaigns there were obvious disadvantages as well. Firstly, some clergy came into conflict with their superiors and were removed if it was considered that they had become politicized. Secondly, the church was limited in what practical aid it could give women in the long run. In the early stages the campaigns were compatible with church teaching, but as demands developed the potential for conflict grew. Issues such as reproductive rights and divorce would inevitably test the relationship between parish activists and clergy, and many women felt abandoned by the church at the very moment when the situation became tougher.[16] For some it seemed as if the church, through its liberation theology, had encouraged the women to think and act for themselves, but when they questioned marriage and why they should stay in abusive relationships, the church could offer no solution – other than that they remain in the relationship, or, at most, separate from their husband but remain married. As a consequence, some women in this situation became cynical about the whole process of collective action and personal autonomy and withdrew completely from participation (Craske, 1993). Others braved potential ostracism and pursued alternative political action away from the church.

For many women, parish-based organizations might be an important first step towards collective action, but some can be left with ambivalent experiences. For the church, there are clear boundaries about legitimate activity, and gender roles cannot be challenged at the deepest levels (Mohr Peterson, 1990). The ultimate female icon remains the impossible virgin mother, although for human rights groups the tensions between this ideal and involvement in the movements were not so great. Although the Catholic Church has changed its discourse on women to some extent (see, for example, the Pope's letter to the world's women before the 1995 UN conference in Beijing), the central focus on motherhood remains.

Non-governmental organizations

The positive impact of NGOs is fivefold: i) they are able to give local campaigns an international profile through solidarity work; ii) they can be of practical use in offering expertise in project development and resources; iii) many have well-developed 'gender-sensitive' programmes which help ensure that women are central to the projects; iv) they frequently bring other women into the community who can act as role models; and v) by supporting women's community initiatives they are demonstrating the public importance of the private roles of women.

The role of NGOs throughout the world has increased enormously over the past few decades. Conceptually the picture is blurred somewhat, with almost any organization being eligible for NGO status and there being great differences between international agencies and local organizations. NGOs have been particularly active in the field of Third World development, as governments and aid donors have been unable to deal with all the needs facing them and NGOs sometimes fill the breach. Many NGOs are small-scale organizations focusing on a single issue, while others are massive with enormous budgets and large staffs. It is difficult for NGOs to have a political character, particularly if they wish to work in the international arena. It is important, therefore, that they present themselves as promoting social welfare, rather than political, projects.

Many NGOs have supported self-help initiatives which emerged during the economic crisis, providing financial and logistical services. Developments in the 'home' countries of these NGOs and the impact of the United Nations Decade for Women have made gender analysis and gender sensitivity increasingly important; thus the role of women in projects sponsored by NGOs has been promoted. Frohmann and Valdés (1993) indicate the importance of the increased presence of NGOs and the links with the 'women's movement' (loosely defined) in Chile. Since the early 1970s, when the field of women in development emerged and later challenged the work of the gender and development scholars, the role of women in the development process has been much discussed and increasingly promoted by the UN and others.[17] Much of the language focuses on empowerment, which introduces its own problems (see Chapter 2 for further discussion on empowerment). Through their focus on women, NGOs have provided a valuable space for tackling gender issues (Schild, 1994), but they are not power-free organizations, and the NGO/aid structure is fraught with problems around who controls the programmes and who are the clients (Arellano López and Petras, 1994).

Despite the positive role NGOs can play, there are tensions. Social movements tend to have a campaign element, which might be overtly political in an oppositional sense, and a practical project, which is where the self-help element is important. It is in these latter social welfare projects where NGOs are active, in supporting

such things as the construction of health centres, popular education projects, low-cost housing, and income-generation activities.
This self-help philosophy is popular not only with NGOs but also
with supranational organizations such as the World Bank and the
IMF: indeed, the new civilian governments in the region are also
happy to utilize the organizational strategies developed by social
movements, since they help to take the load off government
finances (see Craske, 1998; cf. Barrig, 1994). Despite the 'gender-
sensitive' approach, in many cases the projects have fed into a
more traditional reading of femininity. As Barrig (1994) points out,
encouraging women through aid agencies to plug the gaps in food
provision only serves to reinforce the gender division of labour.

Schild (1994) also comments that there is a class element, since
the staff of both local and international NGOs tends to be middle
class and the 'clients' poor. With the return of civilian governments, many aid agencies which had dealt directly with local
organizations shifted their funding to national governments to be
distributed along national development lines. Indeed many local
NGOs, some helped by international agencies, became the
providers of government services. They were favoured for their
self-help philosophy and because they were private organizations,
but this also meant that their autonomy and role in putting pressure on governments became compromised (Arellano López and
Petras, 1994). Furthermore, their involvement has shifted responsibility for service provision away from the state to the private
sector and reinforces the reliance on women's ability to adjust to
new challenges to maintain family welfare. In these circumstances
the women-dominated social movements become providers of services rather than being involved in the decision-making process,
effectively disempowering them, as well as reinforcing their nurturing role. Finally, depending on the NGO concerned, there can
be issues of accountability (Arellano López and Petras, 1994).

Facilitating organizations can be invaluable, but they too are
complex social organizations with their own agendas, internal
power hierarchies and gender discourses. They have been important for supporting groups and at their best have contributed to the
empowerment process, but they do not guarantee successful outcomes for social movements. The Catholic Church is constrained in
helping social movements, and particularly women, by its own
agenda and ideology, but it has been an extremely important ally
in many countries. The exchange between social movement
activists and NGOs has sharpened the analysis of best practice in

development and aid work, including 'gender-aware' approaches. There has been a move away from the vision of poor people as clients and victims in need of help towards one which sees them, and particularly women, as resourceful and committed activists who are engaged in a struggle for change on many fronts. The most successful relationships are those where the social movements maintain a measure of autonomy and the organizations facilitate rather than dictate.

Political implications of social movements

Participation in social movements has provided women in particular with a political education which has not been so forthcoming in the institutional arena or the workplace (as seen in chapters 4 and 5). I stress here two main political consequences of social movements: i) the impact on our understanding of what constitutes politics, not least because of the high levels of female involvement; and ii) the development of citizenship, which is more inclusive of women's experiences and a challenge to gender relations.

The scale of social movements in Latin America had an impact on the democratization process. In all the countries social movements, of all types, positioned themselves in opposition to the authoritarian governments and challenged their coercive, depoliticization tactics. There are of course many interpretations and theories to explain the transitions to democracy, not all of which place much emphasis on social movements, or indeed on the role of women within them: as Waylen (1996a) comments, much of the literature on democratization has little to say about gender relations. Nevertheless, the presence of social movements was important in undermining authoritarianism, and the change in the attitudes within the institutional political arena towards the 'woman question' indicates that women's increased political participation has filtered beyond the social movements arena (see Chapter 4). The importance of social movements in a general sense is that they kept civil society alive when it was under siege, or, as in the Mexican case, helped develop one outside of the corrupt electoral sphere.

Reconstituting politics?

Social movements began as 'apolitical' groups, and for some women this remains an important principal. Consequently, their activities challenged the meaning of politics, particularly around key issues of the erosion of dualisms: public/private, social/political, and, formal/informal politics. As I argued in Chapter 2, most women's lives have not conformed to rigid distinctions around public and private, but the distinction has been used as an ideal type. Social movements highlighted the ways in which this is an arbitrary divide, and both how 'private' or domestic issues can become very politicized and public and how political (public) organization can be very private. Similarly, the issues on which women focused were not the usual concerns of parties and governments, but they have moved onto the political agenda as a result of social movement activity.

The construction of an apolitical feminine identity played an important part in the strategies and tactics of both consumer organizations and human rights groups. Firstly, in the main, both types of organization avoided traditional political practices of confrontation and negotiation. They also attempted to stay clear of hierarchically organized structures and stressed a language of civil and human rights as opposed to partisan discourses. Most women in the various case studies emphasize how their involvement did not begin as a political act in their own understanding of 'political'. Women were responding to their 'female consciousness' and their practical gender interests. They were not challenging the gender division of labour but defending it, but for many their perception of their interests changed as the movements developed. Furthermore, as Molyneux (1998) identifies, strategic struggles can help satisfy practical interests. While motherhood remains a central feature, women have questioned many aspects of their subordination, both in the domestic and in the institutional setting. 'Militant motherhood' has subverted the traditional passive, suffering role of motherhood into a more assertive and proactive identity which has conferred *political* rights. The presence of women in these movements and the emphasis on 'women's issues' has had an impact on the institutional political arena as witnessed in the shifting discourses and new women's ministries (see Chapter 4).

Women and citizenship

Social movements also encouraged the development of citizenship and political subjectivity – and more particularly with a gender perspective. Schild (1994: 64) suggests that, by challenging the pre-existing boundaries of appropriate behaviour, there is the development of a 'gender-specific culture of citizenship'. Fisher (1993) indicates the importance of breaking the isolation as collective identities develop, resulting in a challenge to authoritarianism. It is the development of collective identity outside of official channels and the linkages constructed between different groups which demonstrate different, more critical, interpretations of everyday life for the participants. Nora Cortiña of the Mothers talked of her personal development and stressed how her concerns moved beyond the immediate needs linked to maternity, solidarity with others being a key part of the process: but women can confront new realities only if they feel it inside (*tienen que sentirlo adentro*).[18] The Chilean women's movement deliberately linked the demands for democratization at the national level with women's subordinate position in the home, using the slogan '*democracia en el país y en la casa*' (democracy in the country and in the home). This associational element of social movements, rather than their material gains, poses the greater challenge to the political systems. As Foweraker (1989) underlines, it is this moving beyond isolation of individual experience that contributes to political subjectivity and a language of rights, which in turn challenges the culture of clientelism.

Renegotiating gender relations

Women's gender consciousness was focused predominantly on their nurturing roles, but this changed and broadened as different advantages and disadvantages of gender construction prevalent in society became apparent (see, for example, Corcoran Nantes, 1993; Craske, 1993; Fisher, 1993; Machado, 1993; Schirmer, 1993; Jaquette, 1994c; Rodríguez, 1994). As experiences in social movements lead to empowerment for some women, they have questioned other issues, including domestic violence, family planning and freedom to work. As one Paraguayan activist, Eulogia, stated, 'it's a hard battle against the men. But now we're struggling to get out of prison! We're trying to change the men. Being in the organization has changed us. We don't go to church any more. There's too much machismo, they go around with their eyes closed. After fifteen children, I said that's it! The factory's closed!' (in Fisher, 1993: 100).

A broader interpretation of gender and politics is developing beyond that available in the institutional political arena. Women are combining what might be perceived as traditional gender discourses around motherhood with more 'second-wave' feminist analysis concerning women's subordination in the workplace and political arena. They learnt to use and abuse such gender constructions but also found that, at times, these limited their ability to become involved in political activity. But many feel empowered and more able to assert their rights. In some organizations the women-only sessions, which have encouraged women to develop their political skills, allowed them the space necessary to gain confidence to speak in public – a skill which they seem to think that men automatically have (Craske, 1993; Barrig, 1994).[19] For some women, learning to speak also meant learning Spanish in order to deal with political authorities (Schirmer, 1993). In addition these spaces gave them the opportunity to discuss issues which concern women, both as activists and within the home. The issue of domestic violence was the catalyst for a women-only section in one Mexican organization (Cubitt and Greenslade, 1997). But women-only spaces can create ghettos; the strategy has to be re-evaluated regularly to maintain maximum impact.

Much of this points to the increased empowerment of women. They have become more assertive as a result of their participation. They have acquired a confidence which encourages them to think of their skills as positive characteristics to be valued. As the comment of Eulogia above demonstrates, they are no longer prepared to provide the same 'services' as usual. In speaking of her experiences in a Mexican social movement, Carmen observes,

> Carmen [of four years ago] didn't go out, spent all her time at home, a Carmen who didn't know anything outside of Carmen.... I've grown in this respect, I'm no longer afraid to speak to the [state] governor ... at times, just before I go in, I don't even know what I'm going to say, but more than enough words come out. Four years ago, when did Carmen get involved with all this? (in Craske, 1993: 130)

The empowerment in part develops as women acknowledge their rights, both as women and as citizens. In this respect, political institutions (such as constitutions) can provide the structure for the empowerment: 'I, for instance, didn't know that there existed rights or a constitution.... And upon hearing [about laws], I became very animated because it means that we aren't doing anything against the law, that we are within our rights [to make demands]' (María, a Guatemalan activist, in Schirmer, 1993: 55).

But, as María demonstrates, it takes people to make these empowering structures mean anything, and often this involves great personal cost.

Constraints

Assumptions should not be made, however, about the links between social movement activism and political subjectivity. The negative impact can stem from the reinforcement of certain roles for women; Perelli's article (1994) on Uruguay provides a good analysis of 'unconscious resistance' whereby women protest but it has little impact on their political development and makes no substantial challenge to gender subordination.[20] Barrig (1994) also suggests that many neighbourhood organizations in Peru serve to reinforce the gender division of labour and can further burden women by making them responsible for crisis management through their free labour. Similarly, the domestic focus might reduce opposition to their participation in the short term, but women may encounter greater opposition if they wish to move beyond this (Craske, 1993; Machado, 1993; Mohr Peterson, 1990). There have been occasions when women find their way forward blocked either by domestic constraints or by the facilitating organizations which supported them at the outset (Mohr Peterson, 1990); this has been particularly problematic for those who have close links to the Catholic Church and may wish to campaign around reproductive rights or divorce.

Although social movements have provided women with a more accessible political arena, there are a number of problems. Despite church involvement to legitimize women's participation and the reliance on 'feminine' interests, there can be pressures on the women to limit their participation: some have pointed to an increase in violence once a woman becomes involved in collective action (Jaquette, 1994c), although it is difficult to know the extent of the problem. Secondly, although women generally have more flexible timetables, they do not have more free time (despite the popular conception held by many men!). On a global scale women work two-thirds of all working hours (Tiano, 1984), which limits their options for participating in other activities. As the burdens of participation increased so did the time necessary to become involved. For many women political involvement in the community represented a triple burden: reproductive tasks, income generation and then collective action. Unsurprisingly, some women have found this demand on their time too much. Some families complained that women were prioritizing their new-found political interest over their families; motherhood may have been the spur for their political participation, but for some participation resulted in their being criticized for forgetting their role as mothers. Their participation is only acceptable while it responds to crisis and doesn't detract from their primary task. To that extent, participation in social movements often reinforces the links between womanhood, motherhood and social reproduction.

As the movements progressed, the amount of time and effort needed to maintain momentum increased dramatically. In addition to the tensions created by balancing the other tasks and responsibilities in their lives, women increasingly had to deal with worries over tactics and strategies and the prioritization of demands. These issues became more important as authoritarian regimes gave way to elected governments which returned parties to their central role. Relations between parties and social movements have been problematic in most countries. Many movements feel that parties undervalued them and were interested in the issues only as a way of co-opting the dynamic groups. Parties formed the basis of government in these new polities, but the issues remained challenging problems. For many movements there were stark choices to be faced: it was much more difficult to challenge a democratic government than an authoritarian one (Waylen, 1993; Taylor, 1996, Craske, 1998).

Although most people wanted the new governments to survive and the democratization process to progress, they also wanted governments to address their demands. Many civilian governments continued with the neoliberal economic projects initiated by the military, and in many cases deepened them, especially in Peru under Fujimori and in Argentina under Menem. The Chilean government largely adhered to the same economic policies as General Pinochet and has accepted his appointed senators, and Mexico, still under the PRI, has embarked on paradigmatic neoliberalism – though not without problems.

Women in particular were wary of the promises of political parties. Given the strength of social movements, it might be expected that high-profile leaders would be courted by parties. There are few examples, however, of women engaging in representative politics at the national level as a result of their participation: Graciela Fernández Meijide in Argentina and Benedita da Silva in

Brazil are remarkable exceptions. As Hellman (1997) points out, the expectations that actors will maintain the momentum indefinitely is unreasonable. Mobilizations are time-consuming and the returns are often limited: they played an important part in challenging authoritarianism, but the organizations are not perfect and are prone to the same weaknesses as all collective organizations, in particular succumbing to factionalism, clientelism and *caudillismo*. As discussed in Chapter 3, the new liberal democracies are highly exclusionary elite settlements, with citizenship being focused on electoral participation rather than the programmes and policies which might address the demands of the activists outlined here. This apparent lack of response can also fuel women's decisions to withdraw from mobilization.

Conclusions

The rise of social movements was important in broadening the political debate and incorporating new actors onto the political stage. Women, in particular, were central to this process in part because of the issues, but also because of the geographic location and the unusual circumstances of state terror and economic collapse. Women, on the whole, did not involve themselves in order to make a political statement, but to fulfil their traditionally prescribed roles, and in doing this they absorbed a language of rights. The important point in recounting the relationship between women and politics in Latin America is how the movements developed beyond the local and immediate into political organizations which challenged authoritarianism at its most extreme. Consequently they were part of the democratization of the region in the 1980s. They contributed to the development of civil society by encouraging political subjectivity and a sense of empowerment among the activists.

Given the decline in social movements with the return to civilian politics, Staudt's (1987) comments that organizational empowerment is difficult to achieve are borne out, although personal empowerment might be more resilient to changing political conditions. The involvement of social movements has helped 'engender' politics (Alvarez, 1990). A major repercussion of this was the politicization of motherhood and the acceptance of women as political actors with distinct needs and interests, reflected by the shifts within the institutional political arena and changing attitudes towards political parties (Corcoran Nantes, 1993; Craske, 1993; Waylen, 1996b). Some women continue to make a distinction between good and bad politics: they participate in organizations when the issues are 'good' and moral, but less so in parties, which are 'bad' (Craske, 1993). This reinforces a monolithic reading of motherhood and, I suggest, also constrains women in the long term by limiting their options. Despite the importance of militant motherhood as a mobilizing identity, women stress their class links rather than their gender identities.

Despite the moves forward, there are limitations. The movements often developed in response to crisis. In the case of consumer organizations, the economy has not improved, and social movements have become a permanent feature of crisis management but without giving women any extra say in the decision-making arena. As a more permanent character of some of these organizations emerges, mobilization fatigue becomes a problem. In some cases social movements have merely reinforced the perception of women's participation being legitimate as a response to crisis. Furthermore, many do not question traditional gender roles, but elevate the rhetorical commitment to women's 'superior' morality while keeping power within parties and bureaucracies. Finally, as civilian governments have reasserted themselves, social movements have been demobilized, and the positive things they brought with them have sometimes been lost in the process (for example, women still have little representation in congresses). Indeed many governments have absorbed the crisis-management techniques in their own public policies (Craske, 1998).

If we look critically at the movements themselves, we must acknowledge that they emerged in political cultures where corruption and clientelism have been key characteristics, and it would be unreasonable to expect them to avoid any of these negative characteristics. They may contribute to democratization, but we must not assume internal democratic dynamics or that women do indeed make 'morally superior' political actors because of their female consciousness – a point to which I will return in the concluding chapter.

The success of the social movements indicates the potential of grassroots political organizations, but their weaknesses highlight the need for the continued engagement in negotiations to form alliances. These alliances have to give greater access to the major power arenas: that is, social movements need to make more effective links with political parties. Their failure to do so is particularly problematic for women. For the longer-term political fortunes of women, the development of the female political subject needs to move beyond militant motherhood. Such an approach has clearly enriched political debate and practice, but the political identity of women cannot be limited to this field of action.

7

Revolutionary Empowerment?

Nicaraguan feminism was born in the revolution, it grew in the revolution, and has grown at an accelerated pace since the end of the Contra war.

Sofía Montenegro (in NACLA: Report on the Americas, 31/1, 1997: 45)

Introduction

Latin America has experienced considerable political violence over the decades, including a number of revolutionary movements and four revolutions this century: in Mexico (1910–20), Bolivia (1952), Cuba (1959) and Nicaragua (1979). There have been many attempts to understand revolutions, and one classic analysis, by Theda Skoçpol, suggests that 'social revolutions are rapid, basic trans-formations of a society's state and class structure; they are accom-panied and in part carried through by class-based revolts from below' (in Bush and Mumme, 1994: 345). But, as Bush and Mumme point out, this ignores the ways in which gender and gender rela-tions both shape and are changed by the revolutionary process. Indeed, most writers on revolution ignore the issue of gender and family relations in their analyses, despite the fact that both Marx and Engels wrote on the condition of women and ways in which revolution would alleviate their oppression. This omission, however, is not limited to analysts, but is also made by revolution-aries and politicians, as I indicate below.

The revolutionary experience is similar to the transition to democracy discussed in the previous chapter on two counts. Firstly, periods of transition, such as revolutionary struggle and the establishment of a new state, represent moments of fluidity in political structures where gains can be made. Once the systems begin to consolidate the opportunities for change decrease: indeed, in some situations women's gains are often eroded. Secondly, motherhood is a 'mobilizing referent' (in the same way that Alvarez (1990) identified in relation to social movements); consequently strong links are made between women's needs and mothers' needs.

The new political institutions which are forged in the post-revolutionary settlement can become structures for empowerment, and in the cases of Nicaragua and Cuba there is evidence of state feminism, discussed in greater detail in the following chapter. But it is clear that such structures need pressure to be imposed from outside to maintain a women-centred focus.

The first principal argument I wish to highlight is that gender relations were central to the revolutionary processes; related to this, I wish to stress how women were involved in the struggle itself, although they are often invisible in subsequent accounts. Second, I argue the failure to address gender relations is a common feature of revolutionary movements and regimes: the insistence on maintaining the centrality of motherhood and other domestic roles by many who claim to espouse women's rights has generally led to women's gains being limited and easily sacrificed. Although both Cuba and Nicaragua pursued many policies aimed directly at improving women's status, neither succeeded in attaining gender equality. Indeed, as Molyneux (1985) identifies in the Nicaraguan context, the promotion of women's interests had to be in keeping with the perceived priorities of the revolution – that is, national development – rather than be priorities in themselves. Attempts to erode public–private distinctions have not succeeded, in part because it is financially too costly for states.

Third, gains can be made through state action, and revolutionary regimes have tried to promote women's rights. However, an independent women's movement is necessary to provide alternative agendas and strategies, which in turn maintain pressure on the regime and represent different aspects of women's lives: the struggle for citizenship must be multifaceted. Once the state becomes the only terrain on which to advance women's rights, there are problems of competing interests and the co-optation of key actors which can undermine the project. Even the most 'women-friendly' regimes seem to harbour an antipathy towards feminism, particularly among the male leadership; consequently an independent, grassroots movement is needed to promote this particular perspective.

Finally, the experiences highlighted here demonstrate the limitations of a state-sponsored development of political subjectivity (see Chapter 2). When women benefited from state policies, it was often as objects of the process rather then as actors who had developed demands and strategies. Cuba and Nicaragua have favoured top-down policy making and have tried to co-opt independent women's movements where appropriate. Autonomous organizing has often been perceived as counter-revolutionary (at worst) or introducing tangential issues (at best) onto the serious agenda of national construction (also apparent in Mexico and Bolivia earlier this century).

In this discussion of revolutions and counter-revolutions in Latin America, it must be noted that they took place over a twenty-year period during which time the debates around gender relations and the political role of women changed rapidly; consequently it is not always possible to compare the experiences directly. What is clear, however, is that women have played important roles in all revolutionary and counter-revolutionary movements, albeit not always with a gender perspective. After the Cuban and Nicaraguan revolutions, analysed here, women's rights were established in public policy, which was not the case in the Mexican and Bolivian revolutions before them.[1] Despite this, women's responsibilities were constructed around their domestic roles: regardless of the radical social transformation taking place, gender relations generally remained relatively unscathed.

I also assess the policies undertaken by the new government and the gains and continuing problems facing women. The chapter ends with a discussion of women's participation in the counter-revolutionary movement in Chile between 1970 and 1973, in order to examine the similarities and differences in general discourses on women.

The armed struggles

That women were active as combatants in all the revolutions and also in many other revolutionary movements is generally acknowledged, although somewhat downplayed, and the focus is often on individual women portrayed as exceptional.[2] In Cuba some of the revolutionaries in the Sierra Maestra were women, including Celia Sánchez (later a member of Council of Ministers and on the Central Committee of the Cuban Communist Party: CCP), Vilma

Espín (who became first head of the Federación de Mujeres Cubanas: Federation of Cuban Women: FMC), Haydée Santamaría (subsequently a member of the Central Committee of the CCP and Council of State) and Melba Hernández (who became Cuba's ambassador to Vietnam). Santamaría and Hernández had taken part in the first revolutionary attack on the Moncada Barracks in 1953 and Espín had been head of the entire province of Oriente for the underground forces (Randall, 1981).

In Nicaragua the struggle had first emerged between 1926 and 1934, when Augusto César Sandino led the revolutionary forces.[3] Women were active in both front-line combat and support activities (Fernández Poncela, 1997; Randall, 1994), and participated in subsequent opposition activities until the overthrow of the regime in 1979 (Fernández Poncela, 1997). During the final struggle leading to the successful overthrow of the dictator Somoza, women made up some 20 per cent of armed combatants (Chinchilla, 1994), and women were commanders of units. One, Mónica Baltodano, became one of the highest ranking members of the revolutionary army and was one of the commanders in charge of the final push into the capital, Managua. When the National Guard surrendered she went to negotiate with one guard, who refused to speak to her because she was a woman (in Randall, 1994: 23). Another woman, Dora María Téllez, occupied the important city of León, which established a liberated zone where the new coalition government could be installed (ibid.: 37).[4]

Women were also combatants in the armed insurrections in Peru, El Salvador, Guatemala, Argentina, Uruguay, Colombia and contemporary Mexico.[5] But men have made up larger numbers in these revolutionary movements, particularly in the field. In Nicaragua the perception is that women were heavily active, yet only 7 per cent of women participated in the uprising against Somoza in 1977–8, against 93 per cent of men (Fernández Poncela, 1997). Women's participation in insurrection was concentrated in so-called support roles: keeping safe houses, acting as messengers and decoys, transporting weaponry and communications equipment in the guise of going to market. Although perceived as secondary, they are, of course, vital to any armed struggle and highly dangerous activities if one is caught: torture rather than death in battle is the more likely outcome for such activists.

In the prolonged open warfare that made up the bulk of the Mexican revolution, women were also camp followers who carried on with the 'domestic' life of cooking, doing laundry and providing sexual relationships to service the male combatants (Soto, 1990). In Nicaragua women protested against human rights abuses and organized and protested on the streets against Somoza through AMPRONAC (the Nicaraguan Association of Women Confronting National Problems) (Chinchilla, 1994; Smith, 1993). Despite their limited but notable role in combat before 1979, women were demobilized during the Contra War, although they participated extensively in the neighbourhood militias (Chinchilla, 1994; Randall, 1994): this is discussed further below.

In these extreme circumstances, women often took on socially inappropriate roles for women of their times, and were able to forge themselves greater autonomy and a voice for themselves – something mirrored in social movements. But, as discussed below, in the period of consolidation after the armed struggle, more traditional gender constructions re-emerged, frequently sanctioned and promoted by the revolutionary governments themselves. In the Ejército Zapatista de Liberación Nacional (EZLN) in Mexico women are combatants, spokespeople and activists of the movement. To engage so fully in such activities challenges dominant gender constructions not only in Mexican society at large, but also within the local indigenous cultures: the majority of participants are Indian. The centrality of the 'women question' from the outset indicates the significant shift over the course of the century regarding the legitimacy of women's demands. But, as the example of Cuba in particular demonstrates, rhetorical commitment to women's rights is not always reflected in reality.

The revolutionary states

Cuba and Nicaragua present contrasting perspectives of the role of women in revolutionary society. Both have promoted certain policies with the idea of liberating women and making them full citizens in society. Obviously the twenty-year gap between the two revolutions does mean that there are differences in issues and policies, but in other ways the socialist underpinnings of both countries result in some common features. Both states established women's sections early on and saw the mobilization of women as a fundamental part of establishing a new society. Particular attention was paid to incorporating women into the labour market, along with attempts to make some 'private' tasks public. Like Mexico and Bolivia before them, both states prioritized class over gender and were antipathetic towards feminism. Both countries have had to deal with unfavourable economic conditions and international pressure: Cuba suffered the US embargo and Nicaragua was engaged in a violent counter-revolutionary struggle, also backed by the USA, from 1984. Latterly, along with the rest of the region, both have had to embrace structural adjustment. In Nicaragua this occurred once the Frente Sandinista de Liberación Nacional (FSLN), which had formed the revolutionary government in 1979, lost the 1990 elections to a coalition favoured by the USA. Cuba's economic reforms accelerated after the collapse of the Soviet bloc in Europe, when traditional markets and supplies of aid dried up. In both cases the economic conditions have put strains on the revolutionary societies and have had a gendered impact: households fill the void left by a reduction in social services, and domestic reorganization occurs to lessen the impact of structural adjustment.

Cuba

The case of Cuba demonstrates the importance of the commitment of the political leadership in promoting women-friendly policies. The armed struggle in Cuba was a guerrilla affair which took place over three years in the Sierra Maestra (1956–9) and received important support from localized urban social protest. Women were part of the guerrilla team, but not in large numbers, and frequently their participation was seen as supporting their fighting partners rather than representing their own political beliefs (Miller, 1991). The charismatic leader Ernesto 'Ché' Guevara considered women indispensable as part of the revolutionary struggle and acknowledged the important part they would play. Nevertheless, as he wrote in *Guerrilla Warfare*,

> the woman can also perform her habitual tasks of peacetime; it is very pleasing to a soldier subjected to the extremely hard conditions of this life to be able to look forward to a seasoned meal which tastes like something. One of the great misfortunes of the [Cuban] war was eating cold, sticky, tasteless mess. Furthermore, it is easier to keep her in those tasks; one of the problems in guerrilla bands is that they [masc.] are constantly trying to get out of these tasks. (in Miller, 1991: 146–7)

Regardless of this demonstrated lack of the leaders' attention to gender roles, women began to organize. Despite Guevara's lack of gender sensitivity, in 1961 Castro did establish a women's depart-ment, the Federación de Mujeres Cubanas (FMC), within the Ministry of Youth, Women and Culture, headed by Vilma Espín. (The next such ministry in Latin America did not appear until 1981 in Guatemala.) This radical aspect of Castro's new Cuba was not particularly popular: Espín herself was antipathetic to the idea, suggesting that discrimination did not exist. The wife of Fidel's brother Raúl, and a combatant of the revolution, she questioned the need for a women's ministry: 'Why do we have to have a women's organization? I had never been discriminated against. I had my career as a chemical engineer. I never suffered' (Molyneux, 1996: 6, fn 19).

Nevertheless, the FMC was founded and tried to encourage women to take an active role in constructing the revolutionary society. The commitment and leadership of Castro in developing women-friendly policies has been very important, if restricted. Before the 1959 revolution, women had made significant gains in Cuba: the 1940 constitution included laws on divorce, maternity and other benefits for working women, civil equality with men and the vote (Deutsch, 1991; Lutjens, 1994). Despite lower female university enrolment, women's literacy was slightly superior to that of men (Deutsch, 1991). Nevertheless, there was still a marked distinction between public and private spheres, also by mediated ethnicity, class and the rural/urban divide (Lutjens, 1994). Thus there was still much the new revolutionary society could do to improve women's position in society. But any initiative which was to emerge came from the top (Molyneux, 1996).

Targeting women

Castro's commitment to improving the lot of women concentrated on introducing them into the workplace and on the collectivization of domestic tasks as a way of addressing gender inequalities. The Cuban economy could not absorb the increase in the labour force immediately but incorporated many women into the revolutionary effort by mobilizing them in voluntary work brigades. This gave them new skills which could be used when the labour market expanded; in the meantime it provided free labour for the revolu-tionary effort. Women were gradually incorporated into the paid labour force, but the voluntary brigades returned with renewed vigour with 'rectification' (Lutjens, 1994).[6] Another problem was the cost of welfare services needed to allow women to participate fully in the labour force: when it came to economic priorities for government spending, child-care frequently came second (Nazzari, 1983). This voluntary effort for the revolution also occurred in the political arena, where women were encouraged to participate in community schemes and in the Comités de Defensa de la Revolución (Committees for the Defence of the Revolution: CDR) (Molyneux, 1996). Thus women's new role after the revolution included significant involvement outside the home, much of it unpaid.

The obvious gains of the revolution were the improvements in education, health care, an increase in live births and improved life expectancy, which, while they benefited all, had particular repercussions for women. Since women were expected to cope with sick relatives and children without schools, the improvement in public services had particular advantages for them in responding to their practical gender needs. Women did enter the labour market in greater numbers and frequently in professions which had previously not welcomed them. Women's wages, however, still remained lower than men's, which was to leave them in a more vulnerable position when rectification set in.

A major problem, however, lay in the failure to address gender inequalities in the private sphere. Women were still more likely to be responsible for reproduction in the household, so the paid and voluntary labour were adding double and triple burdens to their days. This was recognized by the leadership and led to the promulgation of a new Family Code in 1975, to coincide with International Women's Day in International Women's Year (Azicri, 1979). Modelled on East German legislation, it was designed to increase male participation in household duties (Molyneux, 1996; Deutsch, 1991). There are obvious problems with such a law, not least how to police it, but there are two points which should be emphasized: one is that the code reinforced the nuclear family, with its roots in pre-revolutionary society; and the other is that it made parents responsible for the support of minors, contrary to the spirit of the public provision of private services which had underpinned earlier revolutionary legislation (Azicri, 1979; Nazzari, 1983). Nevertheless, it gave institutional legitimacy to the demands to redress gender inequalities within the home: unfortunately its only partial success has since been eroded by the demands of structural adjustment and rectification.

The Federation of Cuban Women

The centrality of women to Castro's vision of a new Cuba was also manifested in the FMC. This was the only official channel through which women could mobilize. In common with the political structures throughout Cuba, it was a top-down organization that was conceived by the leadership. The appointed leader, Vilma Espín, was part of the revolutionary elite and has remained a key player ever since. The FMC was an important tool in the mobilization of women into the voluntary work brigades and the training of women with new skills for a new society. But, while the FMC did much to further the position of women in Cuban society, it brooked no alternative channels through which women could express and represent themselves: issues of gender had to be within the confines of the socialist project itself (Molyneux, 1996: 19). Indeed, any notion of feminism was, for the Cuban hierarchy, an anathema, since it was inextricably bound to 'imperialist' US and Western bourgeois values: Espín herself insisted that the FMC was feminine rather than a feminist organization (Molyneux, 1996: 12).

The 1975 UN Decade for Women was a catalyst for a new perspective of issues of gender. The role of NGOs became increasingly fashionable, and they were accorded a new status in the discussions and structure which emerged. At this point the FMC 'converted' itself into an NGO to capitalize on this energy at the international level and potential UN funding, but still remained the only official channel for women's mobilization (Molyneux, 1996). The grassroots challenge to the FMC came in the late 1980s as a new generation of women, some educated abroad, began to question its efficacy, its ability to represent women and its authoritarian style. Furthermore, rectification was having a particular impact on women, and again they were to be mobilized into the voluntary brigades in order to defend the gains of the revolution, but this again placed extra burdens on them. As we saw in Chapter 3, structural adjustment programmes depend on households adapting to the new constraints, and women generally make the bigger adjustments as they engage in more income-generation activities and cope with the reduction in public welfare services (cf. Craske, 1998). The rectification period in Cuba had similar repercussions: the priorities were economic development and defence of the revolution. This period witnessed the reassertion of the public–private distinction, which had been eroded during the first two decades of the revolution with the public provision of domestic services and the greater incorporation of women into the labour market, although this was never as great as had been anticipated.

Implications of rectification

The response of women to rectification has led to a shift back towards some of the social relations seen before the revolution, with women more likely to spend longer hours on food production, housework and child-care (Molyneux, 1996; Lutjens, 1994). The challenge to the FMC came also from those who accused it of not championing or defending women in these critical years. Some thought that it no longer responded to or reflected the needs of the majority of Cuban women: 'The FMC not only lacks analysis, it also lacks a sense of its own purpose: this is why it is perceived as irrelevant by the mass of Cuban women whose lives have changed so dramatically' (quote in Molyneux, 1996: 26).

But the FMC has been changing, and, in some instances, engaging in a more overtly feminist discourse. Referring to changes which had taken place in the 1980s, Lutjens suggests,

> among the signs of a stronger and more critical FMC are its advisory relationship to central policy makers, participation in studies on the condition of Cuban women, and involvement in the implementation of such innovations as the municipal commissions created to coordinate women's employment in the early 1980s. (Lutjens, 1994: 374)

However, she also acknowledges that there have been calls for a renewal of grassroots participation and less top-down control over the direction of the FMC in order to regenerate it, particularly when it needs to be able to mobilize support for the regime in these difficult years. The economic situation has begun to improve from the crisis in the early 1990s, but the future is by no means secure.[7] Some successes could be the development of a women's studies programme at the University of Havana, the establishment of Women and Family Houses (Casa de la Mujer y Familia: these act as refuges), the re-emergence of the federation's journals, and the extension of the discussion of gender across to other party organizations (Molyneux, 1996; Lutjens, 1994).

Political representation

Despite the advances that women have made in the economic and social sphere and official encouragement to participate in all aspects of public life, their political representation has not been so positive. Women have been better represented in Cuba than in most of the region, peaking at a third of representatives in the National Assembly and currently ranking eighth in the world (see Chapter 4), but in the local political structures women's representation has been weaker. The highest level, the municipal level, was at 17.1 per cent in 1986 (Véliz and Aguilar, 1992: 97). Since rectification women's participation in formal political decision-making bodies has declined, possibly explained by the increased burdens of domestic reproduction: these burdens have been given as a cause for their decreased participation in wage labour (Molyneux, 1996).[8]

Despite the greater involvement of women in Cuba than is the regional norm, those who have made it to decision-making positions express challenges similar to those active in non-socialist countries (Stubbs, 1994). Tackling the issue of political representation has not been easy: in 1990 the FMC had a radical agenda for its fifth congress around questions of political promotion and the family, but 'discussion was stymied at the congress when the FMC leadership shifted from an exciting gender agenda to one of defense and production for reasons of national political expediency' (Stubbs, 1994: 197). Despite Cuba's good record regarding numbers of female political officers, its neighbours, particularly the newly democratized countries (see Chapter 2), have been catching up as they embrace more women-friendly discourses. Cuba has been slower to engage with new theorizing on women and power, although there has been some opening up, reflecting the influence of the UN Decade for Women. Cuba is no longer the role model for women's political participation it might once have seemed.

On balance it must be remembered that Cuba remains the only country in the region with free access to abortion and a progressive attitude towards reproductive rights, women's labour rights and the sharing of domestic duties. Despite the difficulties in challenging 'traditional' gender constructions, the 'feminist state'[9] has resulted in a much greater number of women professionals, and access to certain social goods is much better than in most other countries in the region. Furthermore, the state remains central to women's lives, with 98.3 per cent of women working for the state (marginally higher than the percentage of men at 91.1 per cent) (Véliz and Aguilar, 1992: 43).[10] But the reality is that Cuban society is still highly gendered and that women still have to tolerate more difficult daily conditions than their male compatriots. The worsening economic situation in Cuba has made life much more difficult for the majority, and women are often supporting families alone as men attempt to find work abroad.

Furthermore, whatever the gains made by Cuban women, these have been achieved within the context of a non-democratic state. Little opposition to Castro is tolerated and his position as Cuba's leader has not been ratified by a popular vote. There are increasing numbers of independent feminists who are campaigning to further women's position in society, but independent organizations do not have freedom of movement so advances can be slow. Over the period of the revolution gains were notable, and were often achieved in difficult conditions. The challenge now is to allow for a more independent and critical women's movement which will challenge the state and maintain a gender-sensitive debate. While this is by no means assured, there are already a number of organizations and initiatives which indicate that many women are ready to engage.

Nicaragua

There are many parallels between the situations in Cuba and Nicaragua, and the latter's revolutionary government which came to power in 1979 attempted to learn from the mistakes of Cuba. Specifically, it aimed to avoid being heavily identified with one of the superpowers, although this was very difficult given the attitude of the United States, which sought to undermine the Sandinista government from the outset. Like Cuba, before the revolution Nicaragua had been ruled by a brutal dictatorship backed by the United States. National liberation had a distinctly anti-US flavour, but the incoming government recognized the need to maintain good relations with its powerful neighbour, not least for trade purposes. But, as in the Cuban case before it, the USA saw the new government of this small impoverished nation as a threat to regional security and worried that it would encourage rebels in other Central American countries to follow suit. The initial years of the Sandinista government were tough, not least because of the socio-economic challenges of physical reconstruction it faced, but relations with the USA deteriorated with the election of Ronald Reagan as president in 1984, which resulted in the escalation of the Contra War, backed morally and financially by the USA.[11]

In terms of assessing the revolution we can separate it into three main phases: the initial stage (1979–84) of reconstruction of a country following years of brutal neglect by the previous regime;[12] the second phase (1984–90), which saw the deterioration of living standards as the war deepened; and finally the period since 1990, after the Sandinistas lost the elections and became the party of opposition. Here we will concentrate on the first two stages, since these assess what a revolutionary government can do to support and further women's status in society.

Women organizing for change

As established above, women were active in opposing the Somoza dictatorship. The FSLN was founded in 1961 to pursue the armed struggle against the Somoza regime, although it suffered defeats in the early years. At this time, the first attempts at organizing women began with the Socialist Party's Organización de Mujeres Democráticas de Nicaragua (Nicaraguan Organization of Democratic Women: OMDN), but gradually its founders moved to the FSLN (Randall, 1994). In 1966, 'on direct orders of the national directorate', Gladys Báez made another attempt to organize women from the popular classes in the Alianza Patriótica de Mujeres Nicaragüenses (Patriotic Alliance of Nicaraguan Women: APMN), and the first national meeting was called in 1969 (Randall, 1994: 17). Again this attempt lacked success, but in the same year the FSLN established its Historic Programme, which committed it to,

> full support of women's emancipation [promising] to 'pay special attention to the mother and child' [with] day-care and maternity leave provision. 'The Sandinista people's revolution will abolish the odious discrimination that women have been subjected to compared to men; it will establish economic, political, and cultural equality between woman and man.' (Smith, 1993: 199)

The first successful women's organization was not initially connected to the FSLN. AMPRONAC emerged in 1977 as a cross-class alliance to defend human rights (Fernández Poncela, 1997), but in

1978 the members voted to become a Sandinista organization (Smith, 1993). After the FSLN victory, women who had been at the front returned and were not going to accept the old gender relations they knew. In the desire to construct a new society, the FSLN leadership formed another women's organization: the Luisa Amanda Espinosa Nicaraguan Women's Association: AMNLAE.[13] The activists were enthusiastic and the organization grew rapidly, with the aim of integrating women into the revolutionary process as a way of improving their social condition (Randall, 1994). A problem which is identifiable with all the FSLN women's movements, the APMN, AMPRONAC and AMNLAE, is that they were 'still part of an overall plan of struggle and ultimately responded to the FSLN's top-level, all-male leadership' (Randall, 1994: 17). This was to have repercussions for the development of a feminist organization and/or agenda.

In the first stage of the revolution the energy directed towards reconstruction was remarkable, and many international brigades of volunteers went to support the process. Women participated in popular education projects and health-care initiatives, and in other projects in 'defence of the revolution', and living standards rapidly increased. Given that women began from a worse position relative to men, these general gains benefited them particularly. The Nicaraguan regime was also different in that it did not denounce feminism as counter-revolutionary, and some women officials publicly expressed enthusiasm (Molyneux, 1985).

AMNLAE grew during the 1980s, particularly among the popular classes, although many preferred to organize in other, non-gender specific bodies, and increasingly participation in all these organizations represented a triple burden for women (Chinchilla, 1994). Although there was an acceptance of feminism, the issues which the AMNLAE leadership put on the agenda avoided 'an explicit critique of sexism', with some issues being deemed too feminist (ibid.: 179). Women were still seen as an important constituency, but increasingly the focus was on motherhood and domestic roles and participation in national development. The ex-president Daniel Ortega argued that a woman who 'aspire[s] to be liberated by not bearing children negates her own continuity and the continuity of the human species' (in Chinchilla, 1994: 185).[14]

Nevertheless, there were a series of legal changes concerning women's status. Fernández Poncela (1997: 50, fn 12; see also Randall, 1994) lists a number of laws passed, many of which focus on the rights of mothers and partners, particularly those in free unions, with emphasis on the domestic arena. There are, however, other important laws in the area of work and production. The outlawing of the degrading use of women's bodies in advertising demonstrates the range of the issues under discussion. The problem with many of these legal changes, however laudable, and one encountered in many countries, is that they were difficult to enforce. The government established the Women's Legal Bureau to assert women's rights in 1983, which became a catalyst for bringing new issues into debate: one observer considered it to be the 'first feminist institution' (in Chinchilla, 1994: 183). There can be no doubt of the importance of these initiatives: women's lives improved both materially and symbolically as a result of having more defensible rights. But there was a limit to the questioning of gender relations, and debates shifted as more traditional gender discourses emerged and the influence of the Catholic Church became more apparent.

The impact of the Contra War

The re-emergence of more traditional gender discourses was particularly evident in the calling-up of soldiers for the Contra War. Women could claim space in the public domain in support of the war effort, but this did not include combat roles, despite their pre-1979 participation (Chinchilla, 1994). Women did participate in the militias, but in the development of the draft law only men were to be called up. The FSLN maintained that women were still responsible for family welfare since the government had been unable to establish all the child-care facilities necessary and the resources were being directed elsewhere: furthermore, the war complicated things. For the first time, AMNLAE voted against the FSLN, but the latter had its way (Randall, 1994). As in the case of Cuba, women's issues and demands were frequently seen as secondary to defence and development, which was obviously reinforced by the privations of war. Nevertheless, the debates continued and increasingly 'taboo' subjects were discussed publicly: voluntary maternity, reproductive rights, sexual harassment, power relations in the family, tolerance of machismo, sexist education and feminism itself (Chinchilla, 1994: 183). Inevitably there were trade-offs between the deepening of feminist demands (the shift towards strategic interests) and the competing interests of conservative forces of the Catholic Church.[15] In 1987 the FSLN's Proclamation at AMNLAE's Third National Assembly reviewed the Sandinistas' historical commitment to women and the gains that had been made since 1979. It also declared its commitment to combat sexism and to promote women's leadership, but at the same time it accepted the family as the fundamental unit of society. It made no reference to contraception, sex education and abortion, and, perhaps most significantly, 'guaranteed not only biological and social but cultural reproduction, a view associated with the Catholic Church and conservative social theorists' (Chinchilla, 1994: 185).

Women were active in the area of political representation, but, again, increased female participation was an issue. In 1983 women made up 21 per cent of the party membership and 56 per cent of the official posts: Fernández Poncela (1997: 40) explains this disparity as the result of men's greater holding of positions in government and the military. Women were similarly well represented at the executive and judicial branches at this moment.[16] By 1989, however, women held only 3 per cent of executive positions but half in public administration and the service sector. Women's representation in the national assemblies of 1984 and 1990 stayed virtually static (13 against 16 per cent) (ibid.: 41–2). Fernández Poncela concludes, 'the discourse and statements of principle promoting female "integration" in the framework of the revolution, the legal reforms, and the creation of institutions, were not sufficient to boost women's participation of formal politics' (ibid.: 42).

In 1985 Maxine Molyneux had suggested, 'the program of women's emancipation remains one conceived in terms of how functional it is for achieving the wider goals of the state' (Molyneux, 1985: 251). Fernández Poncela reached a similar judgement in 1997: she maintains that insufficient attention was given to questioning agendas, timetables, organizational structures and work styles. She also points out that women themselves were often responsible for reproducing these structures.[17] Although women entered the public workplace in much greater numbers and were represented in organizations such as parties and unions in larger numbers than pre-1979 days, the changes in gender relations themselves were limited. The reproductive roles of women were still seen as a priority by most – women and men – and the state had need of this particular gender construction.

The 1990 elections

The 1990 election marked a watershed for Nicaraguan politics: firstly, it heralded the end of the Contra War; secondly, it meant a different focus, economically and socially, which deepened structural adjustment with its gendered impact; thirdly, it allowed for a reassessment of Sandinismo and its relationship to feminism. As regards this third point, many women had been concerned with the FSLN's 'misogynist campaign slogans' during the 1990 election campaign, and the defeat at the ballot box allowed women to question their party loyalty in ways difficult beforehand (Randall, 1994: 35). There have been a number of interesting initiatives coming from women outside the Sandinista hierarchy, and more women are willing to identify publicly with feminism and recognize the diversity of women's interests.

Times are tough, however, with daily survival for the majority very difficult: the US aid expected after the Sandinista defeat was not on the scale anticipated. These conditions make organizing for any cause a time-consuming distraction away from the struggle for daily life. But the Nicaraguan feminist movement is alive and developing in ways which reflect the needs of 'real' women and are not solely dictated from a male-dominated leadership. Electoral defeat has allowed greater opportunities for independent feminist activity within Sandinismo. Women are active in rapprochement between Contras and Sandinistas in the east of the country, and there are initiatives emerging around cultural expressions of womanhood, feminism and sexuality. While the revolution provided both opportunity and constraint for Nicaraguan women, its end has demonstrated that there might be new problems, but also that there is considerable energy at the grassroots, which makes feminism an important element in the country's life.

In terms of improving the status of women's lives, both the Cuban and Nicaraguan governments did much from a practical perspective by making their traditional domestic tasks easier to perform. The improvements in social welfare had a greater impact on women's lives: these improvements are very important and should not be underestimated. While women did not always question gender relationships fully, state provision of 'private' goods did allow women greater personal freedom, and some legal changes did undermine certain gender stereotypes about women's and men's duties and responsibilities. Although the provision of state welfare has not necessarily challenged gender roles, there are 'strategic' implications, since the focus on practical issues has led some to question the gender division of labour: a truly transformative approach will be both practical and strategic.

In both countries women's rights were newly enshrined in the constitution and easier to defend with the aid of official organizations. Although attempts were made to challenge heterosexist attitudes, the success of this is difficult to measure and machismo remains a serious problem. Currently, women's lives are deeply affected by economic crisis rather than by deliberate attempts to undermine their status. This is reinforced by the continuing gender construction which sees motherhood as synonymous with responsibility for social reproduction. Revolutions have failed to break this link.

Counter-revolution

It is clear that women have been central to the development of revolutionary movements and societies in Latin America. They have made gains in terms of political representation and socio-economic welfare, but they have also been active in counter-revolutionary movements in the region. Here the discussion focuses on Chile during the Allende administration (1970–3). As in the counter-revolutionary struggle in Mexico during the 1920s, the defence of motherhood and the family played an important part in the logic of participation. The women mobilizing against the revolutions did so in defence of their interests, informed by class and religion. They rejected socialism, which they saw as undermining women's natural role. In Chile the linking of patriotism with Christianity became more apparent after the fall of President Allende (Mattelart, 1980). The imagery around motherhood played an important part in the discourses. This examination of counter-revolution demonstrates that politicized motherhood can give rise to reactionary as well as revolutionary activity: it shows that politicized motherhood works in multiple directions.

In Chile there was an emphasis on the links between Christianity and nationality. The country had experienced one of the most stable and liberal political systems in the region, with clearly defined political parties and distinct platforms and supporters. There had been regular elections where party competition was healthy from the 1950s. As in many countries, there had been significant feminist organizations and women participated in the major parties. Although apparently stable, the Chilean system was in fact becoming dangerously polarized around three main groups: the Christian Democrats, with Eduardo Frei; the Conservatives and Liberals, led by Jorge Alessandri; and the Socialists and

Communists around Salvador Allende. In the 1960s the Frei administration revitalized the network of Mothers' Centres, where middle-class women taught working-class women the skills of sewing and other domestic tasks. These centres encouraged political support for the middle-class women's preferred party, the Christian Democrats (Supplee, 1994).

Allende's presidency

In 1970 Allende came to power, with 36.2 per cent of the votes, a smaller percentage than in 1964 when he lost, and, significantly, with much less support from women than from men (30.5 per cent of women's vote): Frei had won 63 per cent of women's vote in 1964 (Mattelart, 1980). Allende was the first elected Marxist president in the region, but almost from the outset his administration ran into difficulties, resulting, in part, from his weak electoral mandate. His radical reform project was also affected by external hostile forces, culminating in covert action by the USA. But perhaps his most difficult opposition came from women, who saw his government as a threat to their status.

Despite Allende's Marxist ideology, his views on women were of a more traditional hue and centred on motherhood (see Chapter 2, note 6). He did little in his own favour by harbouring suspicion of the Mothers' Centres, which he associated with the Christian Democrats. The women who protested against his policies began organizing from the outset of his administration. An early demonstration was the march of the empty pots: starting in December 1971, this became a regular feature of Chilean life throughout the Allende administration. The women organizing the marches were generally professionals and often had relatives in positions which would make demonstrating against the government difficult. The organization El Poder Femenino (Women's Power: EPF) was formed as a branch of the far-right Fatherland and Liberty group: it came to dominate the anti-Allende demonstrations and was the most renowned association.

Class and gender: a challenge

Although they were defending class interests, the gender element of the movements was clearly evident in the focus on consumption and the tactics of using domestic symbolism to make the point: the use of pots and pans gave the participants the name *las caceroleras*. Some women threw chicken feed into the barracks to goad soldiers into taking action against the government. The women also employed scare tactics in media campaigns to terrify Chileans into opposing the government. The most established right-wing paper, *El Mercurio*, wrote editorials encouraging the women and emphasizing their duty as patriotic mothers:

> The Chilean woman, through her sufferings, her humiliation, and her heroism, has safeguarded the libertarian hopes of Chile ... [she] understands that the reconstruction of Chile will be an undertaking worthy of a disciplined and patriotic people. It is for this that *Women's Power* calls upon all Chilean women to demonstrate once more their unflagging spirit of sacrifice. (Mattelart 1980: 290)

Although the EPF might be at the more extreme end of women's protest, the Mothers' Centres, identified with the centrist Christian Democrats, also spoke out against the Allende government (Supplee, 1994). As the government became increasingly beleaguered by strikes, protests and an unofficial blockade, it was unable to further any of its plans. With the country in almost complete collapse, the military took over in one of the bloodiest coups in the region. The new government, led by General Pinochet, quickly demobilized the EPF but did acknowledge the important support of women. He established a women's agency headed by his wife, and more women were appointed to political positions during his administration than were elected afterwards: indeed women's political representation in Chile has not been high despite its strong history of feminism (see Chapter 4).

This example of counter-revolutionary activity shows that women have a clear idea of which political structures best correspond to their interests. Given the pervasive way in which women are encouraged to focus on the domestic sphere and the primacy of motherhood, it is not surprising that they mobilize to defend the status this gives (cf. Kandiyoti, 1988). Women were allowed a legitimate space for public action, but it was clearly delineated. Allende failed to take advantage of the potential contribution women could have made to his administration. His own attachment to the links between women, motherhood and social reproduction meant that he failed on two accounts. Firstly, he limited women's political autonomy and the development of their political subjectivity. Had he engaged in more imaginative ways with gender constructions he might have generated support for his regime from a broad range of women. Secondly, given that his target was women as mothers, he failed to use effectively the already established Mothers' Centres. He saw these as too closely tied with the Christian Democrats and his antipathy towards them alienated them. It is clear that the EPF mobilizations were unprecedented and, as such, were of great symbolic value. They also reinforced the idea that women legitimately mobilize in a crisis but retreat to the domestic sphere when 'normality' returns. Many of the active women believed that they were moral custodians protecting the country from godless communism, but the consequences in this case put a rather sinister spin on the idea that women have a 'unique valorization of life' which informs their collective action. The EPF encouraged a military coup, and, although they could not have predicted the extreme levels of violence, it was clear that there would be bloody consequences. The women here acted out of self-interest to protect their class and gender interests, but were not motivated by moral superiority. Despite the sorry outcome, the similarities in gender constructions between counter-revolutionaries and Allende supporters is evident. These are also seen in the revolutionary discourses of other Latin American countries discussed above.

Conclusions

What the discussion of revolutionary activity demonstrates is that women are important to the success of revolutions, both in terms of the armed struggle and in the consolidation of the new regime. They are active and have clear reasons for identifying with the struggle which cannot be explained solely in terms of following where their partners lead. Women may not always mobilize to promote or defend their gender interests, but if they are ignored as actors they can be important allies for the opposition. Women, like men, will tend to support political movements if they can see benefits for themselves; whether they see benefits will depend on how they view their own interests. Revolutionary regimes have generally failed to address gender relations per se. Both Cuba and Nicaragua attempted to address key areas such as the domestic division of labour and the employment of women's images for commercial exploitation, but these issues were not prioritized and were easily sacrificed in difficult times.

It is clear that the gains made can be significant, but they need to be defended, and thus an independent women's movement is necessary to maintain the momentum for change. If there is not an external source of pressure, women often become objects of state policies and their political autonomy is threatened. Given that revolutionary states tend to be more interventionist and privilege state actions, it is perhaps not surprising that there is an antipathy towards independent activists, especially in Cuba and Nicaragua, where feminism has often being depicted as a bourgeois distraction from 'real' issues.

The attention of revolutionary governments to the domestic sphere generates support, and many demands will emerge from women wishing to address domestic issues. Women who are mothers clearly have an agenda which reflects this identity, but such an agenda also depends on other things, including access to the workplace, the need of women to work, their desire to engage in other activities and their personal histories. Furthermore, the centrality of motherhood can be a double-edged sword. In both Cuba and Nicaragua the governments used this to legitimize limiting women's participation in national life, including armed combat, both implicitly and explicitly.

Accepting the importance of motherhood to women's identity, political or otherwise, should not cause problems for analysts. The problems arise when motherhood displaces everything else. Frequently, the desire to improve family living conditions (rather than issues of national sovereignty) might be the impetus for women's involvement in revolutionary struggle (or other forms of political action), but inevitably for many things move on. Women have demanded changes on other issues linked to sexism, labour laws and equality, and consequently participate in an array of organizations. Governments' fears at addressing all the issues which emerge from women's participation reflect the radical implications much of this would have. The economically beleaguered governments of both Cuba and Nicaragua were forced to acknowledge how important women's traditional reproductive roles had been and how the reprivatization of domestic tasks would benefit them greatly. In the earlier cases of Bolivia and Mexico, women were only on the periphery of the revolutions in terms of articulating gender interests (notwithstanding the important feminist debates going on in Mexico at the time), but neither government would have welcomed a penetrating debate on gender relations to 'detract' from the real revolutionary business.

It is apparent from the examination of revolutions that men do not relinquish power easily. Individual men may support and indeed encourage women to take a greater part in the decision-making arenas, but few would stand aside for women. It would appear that revolutionary states are as resistant as other states to the participation of women. Most members of the revolutionary governments appear to think that women's best interests were served by the general aims of the revolution: it took some time before it became apparent that many gender issues remained unchanged. Indeed, from a gender perspective, these societies look remarkably similar to others in the region. Even in revolutionary societies, where women's interests have been considered, women's lives are more burdensome than men's. The persistence of *marianismo* is notable and, while militant motherhood might be evident, autonomous feminist organizing is less welcome, since it challenges power relations to a greater degree. Despite this, independent feminist organizations have emerged which campaign to put pressure on states for change and to defend the gains already made.

8

Feminisms in Latin America

Latin American women tear open the national curtains in order to proclaim – in a thousand ways and a thousand languages – the validity of their dissent and their emancipation ... no matter where it was born – whether from the harsh processes in which violence is deeply rooted or from other, tangled up in more subtle machinations.

Julieta Kirkwood (in Vargas, 1992: 195)

Introduction

The development of feminism has had an impact on politics in Latin America as in other parts of the world. Its evolution has been difficult on account of the stereotyping of feminism by political parties and other activists and the failure of feminists themselves to develop an inclusive agenda. The perception of feminism in the region is largely negative, and feminists are seen as elite, professional women with few interests in common with 'ordinary' women. As such, there have been serious tensions around class and ethnicity. Nevertheless, as feminism has developed there have been attempts to reconcile the different issues and engage in a more inclusive discourse which addresses the role of motherhood and domestic concerns, and not just equality with men.

The Latin American experience illustrates how political institutions can be useful as structures of empowerment for women, but that they are not enough on their own. The political environment in which the feminist organizations operate is very important in terms of achieving their aims: the openness of the state to external organizations; the dialogue between political parties and civil society groups; and the degree to which political practices militate against independent political organization. The growth of feminism reflects the ways in which these, and other local experiences and debates, interact with developments taking place at an international level. Given the difficult terrain on which feminism has evolved, its influence, particularly at specific moments such as the transition to democracy, is impressive. Furthermore, it is clear that feminism is not merely an imported discourse forced onto women activists in the region, but one which has been enriched by practice and theory in Latin America, and a movement which has its roots in struggles at the turn of the century. Nevertheless, there is still a pervasive antagonism to feminism in the region, and this negativity comes as much from women as from men.

The development of feminism over the twentieth century has not been smooth anywhere; questioning gender relations in society requires the undermining of most, if not all, power relations. Thinkers and writers concerned with the condition of women's lives, and particularly their lack of legitimate power, long considered the limitations placed on women, but it wasn't until the nineteenth century that feminist movements could be discerned. Marx saw that relations between women and men reflect the cultural development of society (McLellan, 1977): as society develops, so gender relations will become more equitable. As with feminist movements in other regions, the early feminist organizations in Latin America generally were concerned with three main issues: the vote, protective labour laws and education.

Despite its occasionally exclusive and exclusionary character, latterly feminism has engaged with other analyses of oppression, particularly class and race, to bring a more nuanced account of women's lives into view. Women's gender identity is no longer seen as the pre-eminent oppression they suffer, but this shifts depending on context and needs. These developments have led to the distinction between feminist and feminine movements, discussed below. This distinction is simultaneously useful and awkward, as is the case with most dichotomies, and demonstrates the degree to which feminism itself has become a contested term.

The challenge of popular feminism has both enriched and brought problems to feminism as a movement in the region. Indeed, there is a question of whether feminism remains a useful concept when discussing the lives of Latin American women. I argue it is, but that the term needs to be used advisedly and that assumptions about 'proper' feminism are unhelpful and merely serve to silence women who did/do not conform to this set of ideas. The vibrancy of and tensions within feminism in Latin America were demonstrated in the 1980s with a series of biannual Regional Feminist Meetings bringing together diverse groups of women.

The present situation is one of consolidation and reconsideration about the future of feminism in the region and the role it has to play within the institutional political arena. The diversity currently evident in Latin American feminism, I suggest, indicates the strength of the movement, which no longer has to concentrate on unity and single-issue campaigns. Although few women identify with it openly, they claim many of the gains made through struggles as rights. In this chapter a number of issues are explored: how feminist discourses emerged in the region; how the actors concerned engaged with the state and other institutional political arenas and actors; the debates emerging from the five regional feminist meetings; the role of state feminism; and, finally, an assessment of where feminism is at the end of the twentieth century.

Feminist or feminine?

For some time now there has been a debate about the differences between 'feminist activity' and other forms of women's political participation, which, while reflecting their gendered interests, might not be called feminist. This has led to distinctions such as feminine/feminist, practical and strategic gender interests, feminist movement and women's movement. This clearly reflects the antipathy towards feminism in the region, but it also implies that there are women's interests which are not feminist, which leads to the question 'what is feminism?'.

The problem here is that there is no answer, or, at least, no answer which is complete. There are many feminist analyses which try to explain women's subordination and, consequently, to devise strategies for women's 'emancipation': these are broadly liberal feminism, socialist feminism, radical feminism and maternal feminism.[1] It is impossible here to give an adequate discussion of the differences, but what is clear is that feminism is not so much a theory as a critique of existing theories. Nevertheless, these analyses do, of course, all have serious theoretical implications which enhance our understanding of politics. The different approaches offer alternative strategies about how women should act in order to change society in a way which benefits them. Attitudes towards the state differ greatly, with some seeing it as the most important tool to advance women's interests, and others shunning it as a masculine construct which will always act against women's interests. To an extent the strategies and tactics used will depend on the social, political and economic make-up of the country: the feminist movement is influenced by the forms and structures of other political organizations. In Chile parties have played an important role, as would be expected; in Brazil it is grassroots organizations which have been key; and in Peru independent organizing is more common.[2]

Feminist and feminine in Latin America

All types of feminism are evident in Latin America, although the popular perception of feminism owes more to the extreme radical feminism of the early 1970s than to anything generally espoused by the region's feminists. Socialist feminism has been influential, since many of the early feminists in particular combined their feminism with leftist party activity, particularly in socialist and anarchist parties. Liberal feminists, however, have also had an impact, and their emphasis on equal opportunities, with special help to allow women to 'catch up' with men, has also been influential. Maternal feminism as a concept, paralleling 'female consciousness', emphasizes women's contribution to national life through their '[devotion] to the protection of vulnerable human life' (Elshtain, in Dietz, 1989: 11). This clearly resonates with the relationship between motherhood and political organization in social movements, although activists tend not to refer to 'maternal feminism' as such. Popular feminism, which emerged from social movements, concentrates on class and gender, rather than motherhood per se.

While the divisions between these different perspectives can lead to heated debates, witnessed during the regional meetings (see below), there can be common goals. Most people who would claim to be feminist are interested in changing the position of women, and 'feminism in general [is] to attempt to transform women from an object of knowledge into a subject capable of appropriating knowledge, to effect a passage from the state of subjection to subjecthood' (Delmar, 1986: 25). This parallels the development of citizenship in the region. This definition, of course, could include many who would spurn the label feminist. Similarly, there are women's groups which appear to have the same demands, some of which would use the term feminist and others which would not. It is indeed difficult to give a fixed definition to the term, particularly given that it has become increasingly contested over the years. Here I refer to feminists as people and organizations who question women's structural subordination within society and seek not just to ameliorate the conditions but to develop an alternative set of structures which would undermine such subordination. So why has there been the development of distinctions highlighted above?

Women who began to question in a consistent manner their subordination tended to be 'exceptional', no matter what their class. By this I mean that they engaged in activities generally thought to be inappropriate for women, whether pursuing higher education, education in 'masculine' fields, travel, political participation, or work outside the home, and they often acted as role models for others. This is not to say that women who did not question gender roles were unaware of gendered power relations, simply that they chose not to struggle for change for whatever reason: perhaps the costs were too high or they were involved in other struggles, or they accepted their positions as natural – women's destiny is to suffer.

As feminism has developed over the century, so the questioning of gender relations has permeated many other debates. A major problem which has prejudiced feminism as a movement in the region is the perception that it is anti-men. Women in social movements are often struggling alongside their male counterparts to effect social and political change and do not wish to be in conflict with men (Craske, 1993; Scott, 1994). There have also been problems in that in some cases professional women have exploited women themselves, as domestic servants, in order to further their own positions while demanding equal rights with men.

A clear problem, as Molyneux (1985) observed, is that there is no consensus on the content of 'women's issues'; consequently the struggle of feminists to change conditions to effect subjecthood has developed in many ways, leading to tensions between the different perspectives. As Chapter 2 demonstrated, the separation of gender interests into practical and strategic can help us understand the reasons behind political participation and the strategies and tactics employed. It is assumed that struggling for strategic (feminist) interests requires a consciousness of gender position and is thus a challenge to gender relations, while the struggle for practical (feminine) interests may not challenge dominant gender roles. It is clear, however, that the two are frequently related and that for many issues there are both practical and strategic implications. Any struggle requires the prioritization of the demands, which reflects needs, available resources and costs. For those women more involved in practical struggles it reflects their priorities as much as a lack of consciousness of gender subordination.

For the purposes of this discussion, movements which do not challenge gender roles are not considered feminist, although many 'maternal demands' can still be included in a feminist agenda. Even feminine movements, however, may still struggle for a greater recognition of women's 'traditional' roles, which challenges the values we give to women's and men's assigned roles, so there are political implications. Even among feminist organizations 'a critical distinction which can now be made is between women's movements which premiss their strategic vision on the minimization of the difference between the sexes, and those which argue for the enhancement of women's place in society through an appreciation of the differences between the sexes' (Molyneux, 1998: 237). It is clear from this chapter that there are many variations of feminism and women's activism in Latin America, all of which affect the development of politics and citizenship in the region.

The roots of feminism in Latin America

I argue that the development of feminism responds to trends and debates globally, but there are also facets which reflect the particular developments and history of Latin America. Although there have always been individual thinkers, writers and activists who have striven to understand, theorize and change women's status in society, feminists and feminist movements in the region emerged in the latter half of the nineteenth century. They were concerned with women's civil status, labour laws and education. In the late nineteenth century many men in the region were not enfranchised, so while there were demands to have women's citizenship recognized on the same footing as that of men, feminists saw educational equality as key to the improvement of women's lives. The focus on education has remained throughout the century, with many involved in the 'gender and development' field still advocating it as a principal way of combating women's subordination. In keeping with this focus, it seems natural that it should be teachers who were the first groups of middle-class women to develop a

gendered critique of society, linking education with access to political and economic power (before this the individuals questioning
gender relations had tended to be upper-class women) (Miller,
1991).

The issue of civil status was important since women were
subject to their husbands' jurisdiction and had few individual
rights. In some countries women under the age of thirty could not
leave the parental home except to marry. The restrictions on
women were often shared by their European contemporaries, and
the struggles and debates often went on in parallel.[3] Women had
interests in the area of labour legislation: despite the idea that paid
labour was men's concern, women, of course, worked long and
hard in factories, as domestic servants and in the home. Without
their contribution, both paid and unpaid, families would not have
survived, but there was no security of labour, few contracts, and
little concern about separate needs that women might have, such
as maternity leave (many of these problems still exist: see
Chapter 5).

Many women who belonged to women's groups were also
members of political parties, generally socialist or anarchist. The
International Feminist Congress in Buenos Aires in 1910 was
attended by women from all walks of life in the region who, while
they had differences, saw that they had common goals which
could cross class divides. A common theme was the equality of
women and men while accepting women's different mission:
Miller (1991: 73) comments,

> the belief in women's 'different mission' lies at the heart of feminist
> movements in Latin America and differentiates it from the predomi-
> nant form of feminism that developed in England and the United
> States, where equality with men was the goal, and gender differ-
> ences were denied or at least played down. In the Latin American
> context, the feminine is cherished, the womanly – the ability to bear
> and raise children, to nurture a family – is celebrated.

Consequently, the campaigns were often to protest against laws
which affected their ability to fulfil these roles, something which
echoes throughout the century. Although this is not universally the
case, it does demonstrate the centrality of motherhood even to
many feminist constructions of womanhood: this may seem ironic
given that the popular perception of feminism is as anti-family and
man-hating. The platform approved at the congress had eight
main policies around divorce, education and labour laws. The

challenge then was to get these points onto the policy agenda of the legislators. At the time Argentina was undergoing political shifts and new alliances were developing: male suffrage was extended in 1912, but no mention was made of female suffrage – change was going to be slow.

Six years later, in Mexico, a feminist congress was called (by a man, Governor Alavardo of Yucatán, who also set the agenda) to discuss Mexican women's status as the revolution raged. As in Argentina, teachers were well represented, and many demands centred on access to education. One delegate shocked the assembled women by suggesting that women were men's sexual as well as intellectual equals (Miller, 1991). As in the rest of the region, there were great divisions between the different groups of women assembled, with opposition to women's greater participation in public life coming from Catholic women's organizations. Nevertheless, unlike in Argentina, suffrage was a central concern of the delegates.

In the Second Congress (November 1916), divorce, marriage and education were also key issues. In the 1930s there were a series of national congresses of women workers and peasants where the old debate between prioritizing class or gender produced tensions, but the delegates did agree on the need for an eight-hour day, paid maternity leave, support for single mothers, sanctions against perpetrators of domestic violence and greater work opportunities for women (Ramos Escandón, 1994). As we saw in Chapter 4, the franchise was not to include women fully until 1953, but the 1917 constitution, while denying women the vote, did improve the rights of married women in key areas, particularly regarding their legal relationship with their children and access to family resources.

Other countries in the region had similar gatherings to those in Argentina and Mexico, reflecting similar concerns and demands. In some countries, particularly Peru, race also played an important part in the divisions which were evident in emergent feminist discourses. It is apparent that there was considerable international interaction in the debates, and Latin American women were active in Pan-American associations (Miller, 1991). What is clear from these early encounters is that women were aware of their subordination and were keen to address the structures of their powerlessness. At the same time, however, there was not a consensus on goals and approaches: there was a tension between those who saw women's legal and social equality with men as essential and others, particularly those more closely associated with the Catholic Church, who were more concerned to elevate women's traditional roles and to distance themselves from the corrupt masculine world of politics. Regardless of the different views, all Latin American women were enfranchised by 1961, and increasingly women were accorded legal equality with men in many areas.

In the middle decades of the century, women became increasingly visible in public life: more worked outside the home, they were members of political parties and stood for office, they participated in revolutions and armed struggles, but their legal status was rarely the same as that of men. They continued to be paid less, were outnumbered in parliaments and congresses, had fewer rights to child custody and material resources in the event of divorce, and generally had more cultural restrictions placed on their lives. For many, their lives deteriorated with the advent of National Security States in the 1970s (see Chapter 3), many of which ended public provision of contraceptives, changed divorce laws, and targeted feminist organizations as subversive. In this earlier period, one high spot for women's political participation was the Women's Peronist Party, which identified with a particular reading of womanhood.

Evita: the legacy for feminism

Even those women who achieved positions and succeeded in public life did not always promote feminism or women's rights. In Chapter 4 I discussed the development of the Partido Peronista Femenino (PPF) in Argentina, which was established to draw women into the networks of Peronist supporters. Forty-five years after her premature death from ovarian cancer, the legacy of Eva Perón is mixed, and her name still evokes great passions both for and against her. The main thrust of Peronist legislation focused on maternity or on women as 'organizers of domestic consumption' (Bianchi, 1993). Little in the way of promoting other aspects of women's lives through legislation occurred, and neither Eva nor those who still identify with her could be classed as feminist: indeed most of them would reject the term.

In the 1990s the wife of the Peronist governor of the province of Buenos Aires, Hilda González de Duhalde, reflected many of Eva Perón's tactics: she had established a Liga Femenina within the Peronist party in the province to encourage women's political participation, but she believes that women should not reject their natural role as 'protector of the nuclear family, the central axis of the family'.[4] An obvious admirer of Eva Perón (there were photographs on the wall of her office), she commented that Eva had made an enormous contribution to Argentine political life, but 'never from a feminist position: Evita was never a feminist. Evita always spoke of working alongside men, with men.' When asked about the influence of feminism in Argentina, she responded,

> luckily feminism still hasn't had much influence. I believe that feminism as such has been a current of thought which has not learnt much, what's more, it hasn't succeeded in catching on in society generally, because, I believe, common sense tells us that things aren't black and white ... To defend women's rights or equal opportunities doesn't mean separating ourselves from men, or leaving to one side all those things which God or nature has set out for us. ... I believe that feminists have made a mistake in being so extreme, women prefer to be feminine, prefer to struggle for equal opportunities but naturally they want to carry on being the central axis of the family, the protector of life, the carer of their children. I believe, naturally, that women have a vocation for these tasks and that feminism only represents a tiny minority of women ... in our country or other countries of the Americas.

Obviously this is only the view of one woman, but González de Duhalde has influence within the Peronist party and her views are not unusual. She demonstrates a rejection of feminism which caricatures it, and is patently unfamiliar with the debates which have been taking place within feminism over the past twenty years, both in Latin America and at an international level. But she also highlights feminism's failure to combat the caricatures and to respond to a wider agenda more effectively. A similar caricature was evident some years earlier in Pinochet's Chile when the National Women's Bureau (headed by Pinochet's wife) published a pamphlet extolling the virtues of motherhood as women's natural destiny and anything else as a rejection of her feminine identity. Here feminism is defined as the opposite of machismo: 'the desire to impose female dominance over men' (in Miller, 1991: 211). Nevertheless, González de Duhalde's use of the language of equal opportunities indicates the impact of feminism, in that such claims have become uncontested and largely accepted: these terms have moved beyond a feminist agenda into the mainstream.[5]

Second-wave feminism

Since the late 1960s a feminism has developed and become more diverse. Virginia Vargas (1992: 199) suggests there are three main 'streams': the feminist stream; the stream of women in political parties; and the stream of women from the popular classes. In the following section I discuss the feminist and popular women's stream and the impact of the UN International Year and Decade for Women (1975–85), which proved to be catalysts for many activities.

Feminist groups

Feminist groups concentrated on an analysis of women's subordination and developed during the 1960s and 1970s. There are feminist groups throughout the region, which is reflected in the growth of the Regional Feminist Meetings discussed below. Some feminists were influenced by writings coming out of Europe and the United States, but many women were drawn to feminism as a result of the failings of other kinds of political activism, particularly those of leftist political parties, to address women's specific needs.

When discussing revolutions we saw that many on the left considered feminism to be a bourgeois distraction and thought that women's subordination would automatically end with the development of socialism. Women's issues as such were at best peripheral to the central debates and at worst counter-revolutionary. Many women saw, however, that the culture of machismo had permeated leftist politics as much as any other social structure and that the agendas of political parties frequently failed to include issues relating to private and domestic arenas. As Sternbach et al. (1992) comment, many on the left distinguished between 'good' and 'bad' feminism, where bad feminism was bourgeois and not seen as relevant to working-class women's needs and good feminism put the needs of the revolution first. It soon became apparent, however, that sexuality, reproduction and domestic violence were as important and relevant to working-class women as they were to their middle-class, professional sisters. Women drawn to feminist organizations initially tended to be those who were politically aware and active, and who were 'stereotypical' inasmuch as they were generally upper-middle-class, highly educated professionals who, in many ways, led privileged lives. Several women's groups were centred around universities, and international influence was strong. Many feminists were exiled during the military regimes, which brought them into contact with alternative debates and lifestyles. The demands and issues at the centre of these movements – voluntary maternity, divorce law reform, equal pay and generally greater personal autonomy – are not necessarily peculiar to Latin America.

There are many differences across the region: Chile is perceived as being a country with an active women's movement and one which, since the return to electoral politics in 1990, has good relations with the state. This is true to an extent: there are many independent feminist organizations and many researchers have become incorporated into the state apparatus at times.[6] There are a number of women's studies programmes at universities and the women's ministry is active and involved in many projects. There are still many outstanding concerns, but the omnipresence of parties in the political structures makes identifying autonomous spaces difficult. Feminists tend to belong to a party, and consequently they have their dual militancy to consider: it can be seen as negative to be too closely associated with feminism.

There are only nine women deputies in Chile, and few are identified as feminists.[7] The Socialist Party (PS) deputy Fanny Pollarolo stressed the importance of parties in Chilean life and commented that there has been significant interaction between women activists and the parties, with parties on the left more open to women. Nevertheless she pointed out that the internal quota for the Socialists (and the Party for Democracy) is only 20 per cent, and that the gender-aware programmes and workshops organized by the vice-president for women's affairs of the PS, Vivienne Brachelet, has been limited to educating women, and men are not included in this.[8] Nevertheless, there has been dialogue between political actors and feminists, and feminists have had an impact on legal changes implemented since 1989: these affect everyone.

In contrast, Argentina is not seen as having a strong women's movement, and even professional women who might be stereotypical feminists in other countries are resistant to being identified as feminists.[9] There are many examples of grassroots organizations, but they do not generally have the profile of Chilean organizations. However, the Argentinian government does have a women's council (Consejo Nacional de la Mujer: CNM), similar to that in Chile, but it does not have ministerial status. The suggestion that

Argentinians are too individualistic and are adverse to organizing collectively (see note 1) was undermined by the evidence that they could organize impressive campaigns and demonstrations around specific issues, although people would retire to other activities afterwards. This was illustrated in the campaign for the quota law (see Chapter 4), when women exerted considerable pressure on the mainly male deputies to pass the law.

The women's co-ordinating organization Multisectorial de Mujeres is key in bringing women together for specific campaigns; it was behind the series of national women's meetings over the past decade, which have grown considerably. The political scientist Nélida Archenti comments that the meetings are often invisible to most Argentines, since they are not reported in the media, and that she considers that the meetings have become dominated by party activists with their own line on an issue: one debate she feels has been debilitated by party involvement is the legalization of abortion.[10] Sternbach et al. (1992) suggest that in Latin America generally, at the outset, the focus of feminism was 'outward-oriented' rather than inward, as was the consciousness raising popular in the early feminist movements in the USA and Europe. This, they argue, reflects the particular economic conditions and political repression which Latin America experienced.[11] Despite the country differences, the debates and impact are visible through changes in legislation and the way in which other people, women and men, have incorporated feminist discourse into their language.[12]

The heavily repressive regimes of the militaries limited all political organizing but could not repress it completely. Many activists became heavily involved in opposition activities, some in parties (or what was left of them), others in social movements. The feminist struggle became very much intertwined with anti-authoritarian struggle. Chilean feminists in particular stressed that authoritarianism was the highest form of patriarchy.[13] Different countries had different contexts in which collective organizations developed. Women's organizations grew in Brazil's less repressive military regime, particularly during the liberalization process (decompression), which began in 1974. The feminist movements which emerged tended to be influenced by left-wing political parties and were economistic in focus (Alvarez, 1990). Likewise in Chile, where repression had kept any kind of collective action dormant for years, a socialist feminist collective began to publish its own magazine, *Furia*, in 1981 (Chuchryck, 1994).

Similar groups emerged throughout the region. One of the key debates which arose was the linking of patriarchy in the home with the patriarchal state, which had expressed itself in its most basic form through the military governments. Thus the feminist struggle became inextricably linked to the struggle for democracy, and the two fed off each other. Feminists who had not engaged in party politics began to see the institutional political arena as one which could bear fruit for the advancement of women. Similarly, women who became involved in anti-authoritarian politics without a gender agenda often developed a more gendered perspective as a result of their participation, particularly where male activists ignored the role of women. Pinochet did not have the monopoly on anti-feminist rhetoric: María Antonieta Saa, a Democracy Party (PD) deputy in Chile and feminist activist, commented that the successful 'No Campaign' which eventually ousted Pinochet was 'horribly machista' (in *Doble Jornada*, 3 October 1988).

The degree to which there was interaction between parties and feminist organizations has depended on a number of factors, not least on the general perception of the efficacy of political parties. In Argentina and Mexico, where they are frequently seen as corrupt by definition, feminists have tended to keep a distance from parties, but in others a more positive relationship has developed. This is reflected in Jutta Marx's comments that Argentine feminist groups have focused more on private/intimate issues than on questions of political representation.[14]

In Peru the situation was particularly difficult for any political organization at the height of Sendero Luminoso's violent campaigns in the 1980s. Nevertheless, links were made between feminists and parties, particularly left-wing parties, and socialist feminism became the strongest tendency (Barrig, 1994). Many women have assumed a 'double militancy' of party and feminist organizing. Some have chosen to prioritize one over the other, leading to tensions between *políticas* (party activists) and *feministas* (feminists), which will be explored further below, in the discussion on the Regional Feminist Meetings of the 1980s. For the present it is worth noting the comments of the Peruvian feminist Virginia Vargas:

> The meddling of the parties and political institutions often obscures and acts as a barrier to the important advances of the women's movement.... It is discouraging to take part in the marches celebrating [Women's Day, March 8], because although it is true that there is an undeniable presence of women from the popular sectors,

they do not make their demands as women, but instead present the
positions of the parties converting these marches to a polarization
between 'feminists' and party 'classists'. (in Barrig, 1994: 161)

The issue of autonomy from political parties remains a point of
tension and concern for many Peruvian feminists.

Social movements

The social movements discussed in Chapter 6 indicate another way
of introducing and developing feminist ideas. Social movements
have proved to be a fertile ground for linking class and gender
issues: 'women of the "popular" classes ... in their roles as
mothers, are gaining their citizenship and becoming aware of their
gender subordination' (Vargas, 1992: 199). At times a popular or
grassroots feminism has emerged (Fisher, 1993; Chuchryk, 1994).
This is a result of an increasing awareness of gender subordination
on the part of activists, as their experiences illustrate their
disadvantages more clearly. Many social movements are women-
only or have women-only spaces where participants can reflect on
their particular concerns. Sometimes these activities are supported
by feminist organizations, which has helped 'desatanize' feminism.
In El Salvador, Cecilia comments, 'I don't have a problem with the
word "feminist"; I understand that a feminist movement fights to
regain possession of rights of women as a gender, right? ...
Although, I will say that there are women who fight against the
man, and feminism for us is not that' (in Schirmer, 1993: 47). This
quote demonstrates both how the discourse of rights has become
widely used, and how there remains a nervousness towards feminism if it is seen as being anti-men.

On occasions special links are developed, and feminists seek out
grassroots organizations to offer support or special services to
poorer women. After the 1985 earthquake in Mexico City which
left thousands dead and many more homeless, feminist activists
became involved in helping women from the affected neighbourhoods to learn skills needed for reconstruction and to negotiate
with the authorities for compensation and resources (Massolo and
Schteingart, 1987). Other examples include feminists supporting
women in workers' organizations (see Chapter 5); a programme
for empowerment in northern Mexico (Staudt, 1987); and, in
Argentina, the establishment by Mabel Bianco, a member of the
first Sub-secretariat for Women, of a health education programme

focusing on AIDS awareness, which goes out to the poorest regions of the country and liaises with local activists. There are of course hundreds of other examples of this kind of interaction between self-defined feminists and other grassroots women's activists in different fields.

There are those who criticize this kind of activism as being merely welfare, a version of lady bountiful, but the feminists involved argue that it does make a difference to some women's lives, and that if a longer-term strategy of structural change were the only goal many of the women currently benefiting would be lost. Also, the women activists at the grassroots use self-help strategies and seek help from outside if they need it: should they be ignored because of the welfare implications?[15] Vargas (1992: 201) suggests that the interest of feminists in organizing with women from the popular classes in part stemmed from guilt and the 'need to prove that we were not merely influenced by foreign feminism. We were eager to demonstrate our sensitivity to the reality of poverty and inequality.' Whatever the cause, it helped contribute to the increased diversity of feminism, which, of course, introduced its own tensions.

These developments have helped diversify feminism in the region by moving beyond 'traditional' feminist concerns of professional women, and they have shown how sexism and gender subordination have an impact on all. The impact of social movements illustrates the interconnectedness of strategic and practical gender interests. Benedita da Silva comments, 'today the women's movement is much broader and there is greater understanding and solidarity across classes. Now there are women's groups all over Brazil focusing on all kinds of issues – women's health, reproductive rights, domestic violence, affirmative action. These issues not only cross class lines, but international boundaries' (Benjamin and Mendonça, 1997: 116).

Gender oppression, however, may not always be of central concern to women: at times their race or class may be the focus of their mobilizations. Women from social movements have demonstrated their commitment to feminism by their participation in the regional meetings. Paradoxically, engagement in movements centred on a defence of the gender division of labour frequently led women into roles that challenged this. Some became leaders and spokespeople, others engaged in activities which took them away from their 'normal' lives. While it is only a small minority who, like Nora Cortiña of the Mothers in Argentina,[16] go on to

identify with feminism, the increased awareness of the disadvantaged position of women is clear. Along with the new opportunities
is the increased status given to women's traditional roles, although
this appears to have had little impact on encouraging men to take on
a greater domestic role.[17] This is in contrast to the increased devaluation of jobs where women are participating in greater numbers.

Although there have been fruitful exchanges between feminists
and social movements, most social movements include men, so a
fine line has to be taken between challenging gender roles and
alienating men. There is evidence of the problems for individual
women resulting from antagonism from partners (Jaquette, 1994c).
Similarly, the chapters on work, social movements and revolution
demonstrated that many women had a greater class awareness, or
at least prioritized their class over gender needs: indeed the debate
over whether class or gender was the ultimate cause of women's
subordination emerged in the regional meetings (Vargas, 1992).
Hence there continues the antipathy towards 'traditional' feminism, which many women see as being against men.

The impact of the UN

The UN International Year and Decade for Women proved to be
catalysts for organizations to examine their gender awareness and
gave feminists a tool with which to put pressure on governments,
university faculties and other institutions to pay greater attention
to women and their specific demands. Many countries in Latin
America and beyond became signatories to the UN Convention on
the Elimination of all forms of Discrimination Against Women
(CEDAW), which focused on a number of areas where women
were particularly disadvantaged: one area which is rarely discussed is the section on women's political representation.
Although the CEDAW does not call for quotas to be established,
the wording does emphasize that women should have equal rights
in the political arena:

Article 7.
States Parties shall take all appropriate measures to eliminate discrimination against women in the political and public life of the
country and, in particular, shall ensure to women, on equal terms
with men, the right:
(a)   To vote in all elections and public referenda and to be eligible for election to all publicly elected bodies;
(b)   To participate in the formulation of government policy and

the implementation thereof and to hold public office and perform all public functions at all levels of government;

(c) To participate in non-governmental organizations and associations concerned with the public and political life of the country.

Article 8.

States Parties shall take all appropriate measures to ensure to women, on equal terms with men and without any discrimination, the opportunity to represent their Governments at the international level and to participate in the work of international organizations.

Despite this, few countries have tackled the continued underrepresentation of women in the formal political arena.

In the preparatory meetings leading up to each of the four international meetings (Mexico 1975, Copenhagen 1980, Nairobi 1985 and Beijing 1995) agendas were discussed and acted as a catalyst for more legislation, more reports, debates and a greater understanding about women in national life. Things were not always smooth, and opposition was also galvanized into action – something that was particularly evident in the lead up to Beijing: Argentina demonstrated that such meetings could be hijacked by reactionaries when the term 'gender' was seen as undermining the very fabric of society, and the term was banned from the Ministry of Education.[18] But throughout the region meetings were taking place which became the stimulus for discussions.

Despite the difficulties, at least there was movement and a recognition of women: making women visible in all their roles has been one of the important results of feminism this century. Depressingly, it proved to be very difficult for Latin American women involved in the preparatory meetings to come to an agreement to take forward to Beijing, mirroring some of the problems at the 1994 Cairo conference on population. There are those who think that such enormous international meetings are counterproductive, since they are costly and too big and multicultural to make any serious, consensual decisions, and that much more could be done with the resources at the local level. The impact of the UN decade was notable for focusing people's attentions on the issues and for mobilizing governments to think about the issues, and the UN continues to be a catalyst for debate. But it is also a large and cumbersome organization which is slow to move forwards – another example of institutional inertia. The UN has helped reinforce the 'gender-aware' approach, which means that women are more visible in projects emanating from NGOs, the World Bank and the IMF.

These different elements – feminist groups, the UN and social movements – have interacted with each other in terms of discourses and strategies for action. While not all involved would consider themselves feminists or engaged in a feminist project, many actions and outcomes do respond to my usage of feminist as challenging structures which subordinate women and searching for alternatives. As such, they have contributed to women's empowerment. The exchanges that these different elements brought have contributed to contemporary feminism and are particularly evident in the regional meetings, to which I now turn.

Contemporary feminism and the Regional Feminist Meetings

In the 1990s feminism is firmly established in Latin America and is evident throughout the social, political and economic structures which frame women's lives. In the 1980s the struggle for democracy brought together women working in different areas, since accountable government was a common goal. This contributed to new exchanges and the emergence of more inclusive dialogue: nowhere is this more evident than in the series of Regional Feminist Meetings that took place in the 1980s.

The series of regional meetings (of Latin American and Caribbean women), which to an extent resonate with the UN meetings, is a testimony to the way in which feminism has broadened its appeal, how multifaceted it is, and how, as it has grown, tensions within it have emerged. While many are saddened and disheartened by the sometimes serious disagreements between feminists themselves or between feminists and other women activists, I would emphasize that this can be positive. Although it can represent a setback on a given project, it also shows that the movement is so wide and incorporates so many ways of being a feminist or a female political actor that such schisms do emerge: we would never expect men to agree on anything purely from a gender perspective. On the contrary, we expect men to be divided by many other considerations which override the fact that they are men. Maybe too much cohesion between women's agendas has been expected. This unified view, the 'sisterhood is global' approach, has been questioned over the past years, not least by women from the Third World. The debates coming out of Latin America throughout the 1980s are examples of this.

The roots of the regional feminist meetings are in the early days of the feminist movement. Vargas (1992: 203) comments that in those early days the region's feminists always met outside Latin America, 'in places that were friendly but still not entirely ours'. A group of feminists decided to organize a meeting within Latin America. The first regional meeting was in 1981 in Bogotá (Colombia) and was followed up every two or three years: Lima (Peru) in 1983, Bertioga (Brazil) in 1985, Taxco (Mexico) in 1987, San Bernardo (Argentina) in 1990, and Costa del Sol (El Salvador) in 1993.[19] At the outset these meetings were attended by fairly small numbers holding a fairly narrow interpretation of feminism, but by the end of the decade large numbers representing diverse issues were attending. There is no space to go into the detail of the meetings, but there are a number of points which merit discussion: i) the increase in numbers attending and *who* was attending; ii) the development of the issues; iii) the emergence of fault lines and tensions; and iv) the broader political implications.

The actors

The number of participants increased rapidly from 1981 to 1993. In Bogotá only 230 were present and most were Colombian. Furthermore, they were either women who considered themselves first and foremost feminists[20] or those who prioritized their party militancy. In Lima the numbers increased to 650, and on this occasion women from social movements participated, indicating the strength of such movements in Peru. The numbers rose to 1000 in Brazil and again included a large proportion of women from social movements. The location of Mexico in 1987 facilitated the attendance of women from the Caribbean and Central America, and the numbers rose to 1500. At this meeting new groups of women were present, including members of government ministries (demonstrating the increased importance of the meetings) and NGOs and Catholic feminists. The numbers doubled for San Bernardo bringing together an even more diverse group, including lesbians, ecologists, pacifists, indigenous and black women, and parliamentarians: 'veterans' were in smaller numbers, although it is not clear why.[21] The numbers decreased to 1300 for Costa del Sol, however, reflecting the difficult security situation in El Salvador, including death threats to the organizers.

The shift from a relatively small meeting of people from similar backgrounds to extremely large gatherings with a great diversity of actors clearly had an impact. Each session became more unwieldy and more formal, and the potential for disagreement increased as different groups had different priorities: this is discussed below. But it is impressive that the various organizing committees were able to maintain the meetings with such regularity.

The issues

The first meeting focused on the issue of autonomy in relation to political parties and 'double militancy': the issue of autonomy alienated some party members, who 'chose to stay outside this recently discovered sisterhood' (Vargas, 1992: 204). Another issue, however, did emerge at the meeting: domestic violence. The second meeting broadened the debate somewhat with the theme of patriarchy, which caused some antagonism for those on the left (there were no delegates from Cuba and Nicaragua). The issue of racism also appeared as central to feminist discussion; this was taken further in Brazil in 1995, when both race and sexuality were central debating points and for the first time lesbians organized a closed session. These debates led to the issue of multiple identities, which questioned the privileging of certain feminist identities.

The next step in Taxco was to question feminism itself: was there something definable as feminism which was separate from 'feminine' issues? – a difficult question, but one which demonstrates the broadening of feminism and its appeal over the years. In San Bernardo, with the presence of legislators from some countries, there was an emphasis on legal change. New networks resulted from the meeting to develop campaigns on issues including abortion and gender images in the media (IDB, 1995). In El Salvador human rights was a key theme (reflecting the country's history), along with the usefulness of quota laws and concerns about racism and discrimination within the women's movement.

The diversity of issues over time reflects new actors engaging with feminist debate and practice and the growing appeal and strength of feminism within political institutions. It also shows how feminism as a practice is always developing and that this requires self-examination. This of course highlights tensions and disagreements.

Tensions

There were a number of key divisions within the meetings, principally around political parties, race and social movements. Feminists carefully guard their autonomy against incursions by parties and many consider that parties compromise their position, while party militants promote a 'dual militancy'. This was deepened in Lima, when there were clashes particularly between socialist activists and veterans. Commenting on the slogan 'There's no feminism without socialism', Ana María Portugal, a founding member of the Flora Tristán Centre in Lima, argued:

> The slogan was intended to reignite the old polemic of the seventies, when to be a feminist in this continent was to fall out of grace with the party.
> But not for nothing have ten years passed, and for us, seasoned veterans strengthened by former political 'excommunication' and acts of contrition, it is time to break the cords that tie us down. The women at the conference responded that they would no longer give in to blackmail, guilty conscience, or labels of being 'petit bourgeoisie.' 'We ought not to fall into the game of conciliation,' a Colombian woman confronted the shouted proclamation, referring to a feminism that, in order to obtain the *nihil obstat* of the central committees [of the political left], must declare itself 'revolutionary,' 'anti-imperialist,' 'political,' 'of the masses,' 'identified with its own class interests,' 'not outside of society,' etc., etc. (in Miller, 1991: 219)

Many parties remain sceptical about feminism, and, given the record of parties in the region, feminists remain wary of them.

A second tension exists between feminists and the women's movement – that is, women who are active predominantly in neighbourhood organizations. These tensions were manipulated in Brazil when what appeared to be a staged event soured events: a group of black shantytown dwellers were denied free access and in the media feminists were accused of being racist. In Argentina, the veterans complained that the inclusion of the women's movement meant that the debate never progressed beyond the basics: effectively they considered that they had lost 'their' space to issues they saw as secondary to the feminist struggle. But the chants of 'we're all feminists' from women from social movements demanded that the veterans acknowledge the growth and diversification of the struggle.

The tensions are very real but have emerged out of strength as much as from internecine fighting. It demonstrates that the gender dynamic is evident in all areas of life and cannot be separated out into high theoretical debate, which can serve to exclude those who suffer most from sexism in social, economic and political structures.

Broader political implications

Over the course of the years legislators attended the meetings, so the debates had the potential to contribute directly to policy making. But more important is the development of debates and the linkages made across class, countries and ethnicities, no matter how difficult at times. This is reflected in the new networks established to campaign around specific issues. The meetings also fostered a broader debate regarding the gendering of society, which shows the multiple ways in which women are struggling to increase their autonomy and develop their political subjectivity, despite the constraints placed upon them. It also shows that this very broad approach of solidarity has limitations. As women make more gains in the personal and public power arenas, it is increasingly difficult to maintain cohesion across other cleavages. The 1980s was a moment of mass movements: the UN conferences, mass demonstrations against authoritarianism and the shrinking of the globe with world trade does not detract from the need to maintain activism at the local level. The 1990s is perhaps a period of consolidation, where local-level activism around key campaigns is more appropriate.

The continued diversity of feminist and women's movements in the region make further meetings organizationally difficult. The challenge is how to keep theoretical debates and practice vibrant as things change. The decade of meetings shows healthy, diverse and dynamic feminisms in the region, with continued challenges coming from race, ethnicity and class perspectives. Tensions remain between feminists and party militants, but there is greater interaction between the two. Many countries also have their own national feminist gatherings, which allow for smaller discussions. The massive meetings are not popular with everyone, and a more local perspective seems to be more in keeping with the political consolidation in evidence generally.

Although feminism has developed, it is still of interest to only small numbers of women overall, and less to the political class, women or men. So, while acknowledging its dynamism, it is important not to overemphasize its impact on institutional politics at large. An important point of the meetings is that feminism does have relevance and interest for women of the popular classes: they engage with feminist debates through choice. For many of these women, however, maintaining a class perspective is also a priority. The growth of feminism has resulted in an impact at state level.

State feminism

Given the inroads that women have made into state institutions, it is important to consider state feminism. The state has been useful for furthering women's issues, but the impact is not uniform across countries, given the different structures of women's ministries. Stetson and Mazur (1995b: 1–2) define state feminism as the 'activities of government structures that are formally charged with furthering women's status and rights'. In their edited volume the contributors consider the extent to which these agencies help undermine 'patterns of gender-based inequities'. Although none of the chapters examines Latin American countries, we can use some of the conclusions when considering the region. All Latin American countries have women's ministries of one type or another, but their different legal status will affect their potential impact. In their conclusions, Mazur and Stetson (1995) identify four typologies which explain the influence of women's ministries on policy and the degree of access to ministries of social organizations:

- type A: high influence/high access
- type B: high influence/low access
- type C: low influence/high access
- type D: low influence/low access.

Latin American examples

There is insufficient information to be able to categorize the influence of women's ministries in each Latin American country, but I suggest that Chile is an example of type C, while Argentina, where the Consejo Nacional de la Mujer has no binding role, is an example of type D – although greater attempts are being made there to liaise with feminist organizations. As far as our two revolutionary examples, Cuba and Nicaragua, are concerned, I suggest they are examples of type B, since they are not open to independent feminist organizations, and seem hostile to them. Nevertheless, both regimes have been conscious of the need to put women's needs into policy development, even if they have to fit in with national development agendas (see Chapter 7).

The women's ministries in Latin America, with the exception of that in Cuba, have emerged during the phase of democratization, when the institutional terrain was in a state of flux and there was more room for manoeuvre. Women had become highly visible in many different opposition activities and were able to make claims of the new states, but as the states have bedded down they have become more resistant to pressure. Georgina Waylen (1996c), in comparing Argentina, Chile and Peru, suggests that the political variables which have an impact on the ability of women's groups to influence the policy agenda include the relationship between parties and the state. Both Argentina and Peru have weak party systems, unlike Chile, where the parties are strong and clearly identifiable. These differences present opportunities and constraints for women's groups (ibid.).

The strong party system in Chile has contributed to the country's being type C, since there are good links between parties and social organizations, but SERNAM officials have found it difficult to influence other areas of government (see Chapter 4). In the cases of Argentina and Mexico the original women's ministries were disbanded and re-established. In Argentina the incumbent party has not established many links with women's groups, which gives such groups limited access to the ministries. In Mexico the tight links between government and the PRI means that it has been difficult for non-party members to access the state. The party prefers to establish its own organizations, frequently co-opting individuals from successful movements.

Even in Chile, where the relationship between SERNAM and independent women's groups is good, both the minister, Josefina Bilbao, and the sub-director, Paulina Veloso, had no direct experience of women's issues before their appointment, though none of the SERNAM staff I spoke with was critical of the women's commitment to their posts. But it does indicate that there is an antipathy towards having a women's ministry which is too strongly identified with feminism.[22] When SERNAM was founded it was opposed by the right, and even with the support of the Christian Democrats and the Socialists its agenda was limited by the Christian Democrats' emphasis on the family. The ministry is also hampered by 'its limited budget, unclear brief and a lack of formal machinery to oversee the operations of other government departments' (Waylen, 1996a: 129).

The context of state feminism

Given the political culture in Latin America, which still endorses a public/private division of society, it is not surprising that women's ministries still have limited influence. Waylen (1996c) illustrates the way political structures challenge the development of women-friendly policies and spaces. By employing Mazur and Stetson's (1995) four variables for explaining the effectiveness of state feminism, some of the constraints facing state feminism in Latin America are identified. The variables are: the politics of the establishment; organizational forms; conceptions of the state; and the politics of the women's movement. In the Northern liberal democracies Mazur and Stetson (1995) identified leftist governments as being more propitious for the development of type A state feminist organizations. A centralized office with a cross-sectoral approach with good co-ordination was the most effective organizational form. The agencies were also more effective where the state was perceived as a major actor and were less effective in highly decentralized systems, even if the state was considered important. Finally, the agencies were at their strongest in countries which had a vibrant independent women's movement, where women participated also in trade unions, parties and other social organizations and where there were different types of feminist organizations (radical, reformist, liberal, etc.).

With these criteria we can see that a major challenge for state feminism in Latin America is the state itself: in most countries it is structurally weak and not a major resource for furthering interests. In countries such as Mexico, which is still corporatist, despite some major political reforms over the past decade, authoritarianism remains a problem and new interest groups find it difficult to gain access to decision-making arenas. Such governments will prefer to co-opt rather than engage with new actors. Furthermore, there is great antipathy on the part of civil society groups towards the engagement with parties and the state, and few leftist parties (considered beneficial for state feminism) are in power.

In Brazil, which also has a corporatist tradition, the example of state feminism (the National Council for Women's Rights: CNDM) could be seen as another example of attempts to demobilize citizens and/or form a women's ghetto (Alvarez, 1990). In Argentina the suspicions of feminists regarding the motives of political parties and the state generally have undermined relations between the feminist movement and the institutional arena. Furthermore, the original women's ministry (the sub-secretariat for women) had been established as the Alfonsín government (1984–9) was in decline. Menem disbanded it and replaced it with the CNM, but took away its ministerial status. He also established a Gabinete de Consejeras Presidenciales, a shadow cabinet of women who advise the president. In both cases they have no binding role, and there are few who would vouch for President Menem's commitment to feminism, despite his support for the quota law. Even if feminist movements are strong, which is not generally the case, the state presents problems for promoting women's interests and challenging gender discrimination.

In a region which is fully engaged in economic reform and which is still consolidating the political stability of civilian regimes, the room for manoeuvre is small. The immediate aftermath of authoritarianism and the impressive activities of social movements did allow for a number of important legal changes in many countries, which demonstrated the state's potential in promoting the advancement of women as full citizens. In many countries the women's ministry was part of the same wave of legislation. But since then the political debate has become more narrow and structural adjustment is paramount: given that many of the demands coming from women's ministries require resources, the rhetorical commitment may be strong, but little is achieved materially. Considering the variables outlined by Stetson and Mazur, Latin America does not score highly: weak states, a socio-political culture which is not very open to feminism, antipathetic parties on left and right, and a feminist movement which is important but fragmented in many countries – and certainly not institutionalized in the way it is in effective countries such as Norway, Denmark and the Netherlands.

Yet feminists have not only infiltrated women's ministries but are active in other areas. Beatriz Paredes introduced feminists into the Mexican agricultural ministry when she was sub-secretary, before becoming governor for Tlaxcala in 1987 (Bourque, 1989). State feminism does exist in Latin America and has been important in key moments, but generally its influence is low and the opportunities it provides are not always accessible to women's movements active in the country. More work has yet to be done outside the state to maintain pressure on government agencies. The state can supply valuable resources and can be a structure for empowerment by providing a legal framework to defend women's rights. On its own, however, it is insufficient, and external pressure is needed to make the state work for women.

Conclusions: challenges to feminism in the 1990s

Although there has been much antipathy towards feminism in Latin America (as in most other countries) there have been many achievements, even if the agenda for further action is still growing. The transition to electoral government provided a key moment for women's movements to press for legal changes and access to the political arena. This political moment offered opportunities for feminism to reach new spaces and new women, who brought with them different experiences. There were still problems, however: 'some myths were revised, reformulated, confronted, although it was not possible to overcome a utopian vision based solely on a universal feminism' (Vargas, 1992: 208).

The number of changes in most countries reflects the importance of women in the opposition movements and the way in which certain demands had become mainstream as women, and many men, from all kinds of collective action organizations saw them as part of the democratization struggle itself. It is not unusual for women to emerge in much larger numbers in the political arena at exceptional times, then to decrease (Chaney, 1973), so we must view women's new political visibility in the longer term. It might decline but be on an overall upward trend, or the decline might reflect the 'business as usual' syndrome.

Countries which were not experiencing a transition, or undergoing only a limited one (Colombia, Venezuela and Mexico), also sustained women-dominated social movements whose members also contributed to international exchanges, through the feminist meetings, the development of new journals and magazines, and academic discussions. These, combined with the impact of the UN Decade for Women, proved to be a catalyst for change in these countries as well. The achievements throughout the region reflect the different strengths of state feminism, autonomous feminist movements, women's organizations, academic endeavour, the openness of political parties and international influences. Nevertheless, the ability of vested interests to defend their space

presents challenges for the future. It appears that the social movements focusing on practical gender interests have been marginalized to a greater degree than Feminist organizations, reflecting,
perhaps, the class composition of such groups.

The growth of feminism can also be judged in the way that the
language of equal opportunities has permeated most levels of
politics. Most parties are keen to stress the importance of women,
even if the understanding of women's social, political and economic role might be different: even the Catholic Church has indicated its awareness of the contribution of women to public life and
its own role in women's subordination.[23] But there are many problems. Women still have limited control over their own bodies, not
just in terms of extremely limited access to safe abortions and the
practice of enforced sterilizations, but in terms of adequate contraception generally and the continued legality of rape within marriage. Women's continued and generalized disadvantaged position
persists despite changes in governments, economics and the
impact of feminism. This of course is not limited to Latin America:
these criticisms could be levelled at almost any country in the
world. After the advances women have made over the past two
decades or more, there has, inevitably, been a backlash: as one
commentator ironically put it, 'After the millennium for men, we
have a decade for women.' The author Gabriela Cerrutti commented that post-feminism is premature in Argentina since that
country was still 'prefeminist'.[24]

The broad changes of the 1980s were easier at the time because
they were supported by the majority: the legalization of divorce,
and contraception and changes to child custody were not too contentious. Other issues remain highly divisive and the opposition
has regrouped. In Argentina the passing of the quota law was
radical and required a massive campaign by women from various
organizations and has resulted in the country having one of the
highest levels of female representation in the world. But alliances
made to push this through soon declined and the women deputies
have had limited impact in terms of promoting women's issues.

The 1990s has been a period of consolidation. Women's movements are not so visible at the national level but are still there,
becoming smaller and more focused on specific issues which are of
interest to the activists concerned. The terrain is tougher, with
ongoing economic crisis and the failure in some countries to consolidate party systems making political stability fragile. Feminism
is a multifaceted concept which includes many perspectives and

demands. Some women's movements may still eschew the term feminist and will still emphasize the complementary characters of women and men, which may limit the debate.

The feminist agenda, however, does not stay static, and over the past twenty years it has become much more inclusive. At the same time we must not label every kind of women's group feminist or consider it a force for the advancement of women: Perelli (1994) demonstrates that it is easy to mobilize without changing political views. The continued promotion of women requires the efforts of actors, both women and men, from all areas of national life. Feminists have a particular role to play as those who are interested in highlighting the gender implications of policy, and feminists, as Dietz (1989) explains, have a particular interest in democratic political practice. There has been a backlash, but the continued challenging of women's subordination in all areas of life is key to a healthy civic life. To do this feminists must liaise and negotiate with other political organizations, women's organizations and each other: as this chapter demonstrates, they have achieved much, but the tasks ahead remain considerable.

9

Conclusions
Politics: an Ambivalent Experience

In 1940 only five of Latin America's nineteen countries had extended the franchise to include women: in 1998 all women in the region have the vote; two countries feature in the world's top ten for the level of female representation in national parliaments; and three countries have experienced female presidents. As a result of women's political mobilization there have been numerous legal changes, women's ministries have been established and political parties court women voters and activists. The political context in which women have made these gains has been constantly transforming, frequently in the form of radical changes of regime, and women have also been important actors in these political developments. Latin American states have absorbed and reproduced some of the language of feminism, especially around equal opportunities, and they have acknowledged the need to defend and promote women's position in society by signing the UN Convention on the Elimination of all forms of Discrimination Against Women (CEDAW).

The Latin American cases amply demonstrate that times when regimes are in transition, such as during the democratization process and revolutionary struggle, offer moments of greater latitude for the winning of demands. The claiming of citizenship generally, and by women in particular, was facilitated by the renegotiation of many political structures and terrains. Through the examination of various arenas explored in this book, it is clear that the contribution of women to national life is broad, diverse and central: they are not bit players in the region's development. Despite the antipathy that women have traditionally shown towards the institutional political arena, important and lasting gains have been made which have facilitated their empowerment by opening up political structures and providing key resources.

There have been difficulties, however. Despite being a catalyst for collective action, the working environment continues to provide limited meaningful political participation for women; social movements and revolutionary societies are in decline, and, notwithstanding the many developments in feminism, women are not engaging in great numbers in feminist organizations. But however we look at the political landscape, the impact of women is evident. Furthermore, women are much more aware of their rights, in large part because the struggle for them has been arduous.

Over the past few years Latin America has entered a phase of political closure where the political spaces and agendas are tightly controlled; as a result the electoral arena has been prioritized as *the* political space and neoliberal economic reform as *the* policy issue.[1] This poses particular problems for women, whose representation in party politics is still lower than that of men and who have been particularly disadvantaged by the structural adjustment policies of neoliberal economics. This book has demonstrated how women as political actors have helped shape the structures which have developed, but it also illustrates how those structures offer both opportunities and constraints to actors in pursuing an agenda. In assessing women's political participation, it must be noted that there have been gains made at the general level which affect all women (and frequently men as well) and those which individual women experience as a result of participation: feelings of empowerment, a development of political subjectivity and a shift in gender relations at the personal level.

In these conclusions I wish to highlight two points: the shifts in gender relations and the implications of politicized motherhood; and the changing nature of politics and political practice. Change brings with it both costs and benefits: few advances that women have made over the decades have been without costs. Individual women may have ambivalent experiences as they engage more with paid labour, participate in social movements, or join revolutionary movements. Some have benefited greatly from change, and, as a group, women have made clear advances. But many women still face serious disadvantages as gender subordination interacts with other oppressions, including ethnicity, class and age. It is important to uncover the complexities and ambiguities which make up political practice.

Changing gender relations

In Chapter 2 I argued that there are exaggerated gender stereo-types which inform people's understanding of their role in Latin American society: for men machismo and for women *marianismo*. These are underpinned by a very clear notion of a separation of public and private arenas, onto which are mapped the categories male and female. Although none of these faithfully reflect lived realities, they influence how women and men participated in polit-ical life. The strict limitations placed on women as a result of these exaggerated types have been steadily eroded over time, but one element which has remained more constant has been the centrality to women of motherhood, as I discuss below.

Although gender relations still reflect the model of female home-maker and male breadwinner, the balance of power between these roles has not remained static. Women's increased empowerment through income generation, community organizing and the impact of feminism has changed the perception of what constitutes being a woman in terms of rights and responsibilities, even within tradi-tional boundaries. Domestic units are increasingly seen as partner-ships rather than family head plus (female) spouse and children.[2] The greater financial contributions of women to the family have increased their role in decision making, especially regarding household expenditure. Feminists and academics have highlighted the vital way in which women contribute to family income genera-tion through financial and other contributions. But paid work has proved to be a double-edged sword that brings increased burdens for many women. Frequently domestic gender relations are repro-duced in the small, informal workshops which account for a large number of women workers. This inhibits changes in gender rela-tions generally. Gender hierarchies are seen throughout the work-place, with men taking more supervisory roles. The advantages of work depend on the nature of the job, the levels of remuneration and the ability to reorganize and delegate other responsibilities.

Extreme socio-economic conditions pushed women into collect-ive action and gave new meaning to their traditional roles. In some social movements men were absent altogether, making a particular impact on gender relations. In consumer organizations women showed themselves to be the equals of men in terms of organizing and strategizing. Sometimes their participation had a direct and immediate impact on gender relations in the home when they confronted men in order to be able to participate. The rise of women-only spaces within social movements, influenced by feminist practices, has offered opportunities for discussing domestic violence and male alcoholism, resulting in greater sanctions against what has, in the past, been seen as 'normal' male behaviour. It would be wrong to suggest, however, that these problems have been eradicated. Indeed, we saw how women's political participation sometimes exacerbated the situation, yet, by making it a public rather than a private problem, attitudes are shifting.

The transformation of gendered power relations is also apparent in legal changes. In terms of gender relations, a significant legal reform was including women in *patria potestad*, whereby the claims of women and men to be guardians of children are considered equal. This undermines the patriarchal model which sees men as responsible for the other members of the family. Other important legal-institutional changes which reflect the increasing autonomy of women and recognize their political character include the legalization of contraception, greater access to divorce, women's programmes in state policies, women's ministries and the introduction of quotas within electoral systems.

The claim of women to take a full role in society is much more accepted, but there is still the expectation that they will only do so *after* taking care of the home. Information from the UK would suggest that shifting this perception is an extremely difficult task: women still do more housework than men, regardless of other commitments (Gershuny and Berthoud, 1997). While patterns in one country are not replicated directly in another, this does indicate the deeply entrenched nature of gender roles. In Latin America the experiences of Cuba and Nicaragua, where an attempt was made to collectivize domestic chores, show how difficult it is to find long-term alternatives to some kind of family unit for daily reproduction. A challenge for most countries, world wide, is how citizens can balance their various productive and reproductive roles without great social and economic costs to all, particularly in the current economic climate of state withdrawal. Women take on the greater burden of these chores. Maintaining the family unit as the basic cell of society responsible for reproductive tasks has reinforced the mythical status of motherhood.

The shifts in gender relations indicate a development of empowerment – a process whereby subjects increase their power to control their lives. This process is clearly constrained by social, economic and political structures, as well as by dominant gender constructions. But women are claiming rights and gaining a voice: they are no longer passive observers of the political process. The increase in female-headed households has allowed many women greater personal autonomy and more earning power has helped rebalance gender relations in the home. The many campaigns in which women have been involved have given them, in some cases, greater autonomy and power to decide their own futures.

Political motherhood

Throughout the book the importance of mothering has been demonstrated, both in women's gender construction in the region and in how it has informed political choices. In Latin American societies motherhood is a potent cultural symbol, reinforced by one of the most powerful political institutions, the Catholic Church. The initial impetus to protest and engage in confrontation with the authorities frequently conforms to an understanding of womanhood deeply grounded in caring. It has been used to explain why women engage in revolutions, support the political right, engage in wage labour, reject wage labour, participate in social movements and challenge feminism. It is clear, then, that the defence of motherhood and its associated interests does not lead to any one political conclusion in terms of a coherent set of interests or strategies. So while motherhood may dominate the construction womanhood, it is not a homogeneous and unitary construction but is understood differently by individual women as it reflects their experiences.

Constructions of identity are not purely arbitrary, however, but contingent, reflecting the institutions and structures around them. Employing motherhood as a political mobilizer has been strategically useful since it resonates with women's lives generally, and will therefore be attractive to women. Furthermore, since it already has a publicly recognized legitimacy, governments and politicians are predisposed to pay more attention to demands couched in these terms.

Motherhood, as an identity, interacts with other identities related to class, age, ethnicity, working environment and education. Similarities and common characteristics were evident in radically different movements which have claimed to defend motherhood and practical gender interests. The defence of the physical integrity of children is clearly demonstrated here as the motivation for many women's political involvement, especially at the outset. Once this identity became politicized, however, it had a number of implications, both radical and reactionary. Changes across the region (the rhetoric used by politicians, the activities of many women, and the analyses of academics) indicate the continued centrality of motherhood to women's lives. This book demonstrates that the values associated with motherhood, rather than simply the preservation of life, have informed many women's broader political involvement: hence the emphasis on nurturing and caring roles within institutional politics and revolutionary regimes. It also explains why women's increased involvement in politics tends to introduce more social issues into the political arena.

There are limitations, however. In emphasizing the uniqueness of women's 'female consciousness' – reflected in the need to preserve life – constructed gender differences are reified and limits are placed on women's choice to participate for other reasons. In these terms, motherhood predicts a specific agenda. Thus Kaplan's (1982) concept ultimately limits women's freedom to choose the nature of their political involvement in a way which reflects more than traditional perspectives. There are problems with the essentializing both of this singular view of motherhood and of womanhood itself. Even for those women who prioritize their mothering role, which is the majority, this is rarely their only identity, and other issues may motivate their political participation. Alvarez's (1990) discussion on militant motherhood acknowledges that motherhood is the 'mobilizing referent', but the content and meaning of motherhood do not remain static.

The emphasis on a particular view of motherhood does not only essentialize women's lives, it leaves open the question of whether a woman has to *experience* motherhood in order to participate in this way, or whether it is simply being female which gives her this unique valorization of human life. In Chapter 2 I argued that motherhood is not a biological function. Rather, its characteristics are culturally defined and mutate across class, generation, race and country. The core attributes around caring and nurturing become a set of learnt characteristics which most women absorb, regardless of whether they are actually mothers. These characteristics become associated less with motherhood per se and more with womanhood, so women are seen as responsible for social reproduction.

Although motherhood has remained a key feature of women's political involvement, it is increasingly accepted that women can combine motherhood with other activities, as workers and activists, and these identities will be reflected in their political engagement. The feminist debates which have developed over the past three decades have permeated political language and offered alternative ways of looking at women as political actors which do not rely solely on mothering. Despite antagonism from several quarters, the language of feminism has penetrated many debates. Equal opportunities, the right to work and to have access to adequate contraception, and fair divorce laws are not seen as particularly radical to most people today. Similarly, political motherhood has informed feminist debate, making it more inclusive and dynamic. The widespread struggles of women in different arenas have had an impact on political identity in broad terms, and many 'women's issues' are now perceived as citizens' demands, particularly in the 'new democracies'. Nevertheless, a gender division of labour still operates within the political arena and some issues still remain women's domestic obligations outside the concerns of citizens.

Discouraging empowerment?

Despite the way in which motherhood has been a central mobilizing factor for women, it is evident that there are many problems and limitations if women are confined to this role, particularly if a certain set of immutable interests and characteristics are associated with it. The Mothers in Argentina have demonstrated that the overemphasis on mothering as a public (rather than a political) identity can lead to political paralysis. As the political situation in Argentina has changed, the Mothers have found it difficult to adapt, since they see their demands as non-negotiable and themselves as above politics. Without the ability to negotiate and compromise, the political process is dead before it begins. It is unclear to what extent this kind of participation leads to empowerment, since the sense of efficacy is lost if the demands cannot be won. Nor is it clear how it changes political identities if the participation is maintained within such narrow confines. As a social movement, the women continue to do excellent work including looking for the children of the disappeared to return them to their natal families (a project fraught with difficulties), but the longer-term political impact is limited.

The breakaway organization in which Nora Cortiña participates indicates that some women did understand the nature of the political process, which, for the most part, is the art of the possible.

These women are still heavily influenced by their motherist identity, but they see other ways of furthering their demands and for improving the status and rights of mothers. This includes engaging with broader debates and participating in political structures to influence their development, rather than standing above them. I suggest that the disillusionment which must necessarily come from the fruitless demand for reappearance is more likely to feed into a sense of disempowerment than contribute to empowerment.

Perelli (1994) finds that the impact of motherist consumer organizations on women's political identity is similarly limited if women do not analyse their participation beyond their identification with their domestic role. Not all collective action is part of a process of empowerment and the development of political subjectivity. Perelli finds a particular problem with the non-negotiable stance promoted in certain motherist debates which emphasizes a certain interpretation of 'the private is political'. Clearly, there is the risk that each personal, particularistic demand becomes a right to be claimed. As Vargas (1992: 209) comments, 'the personal has the potential to become the political only when it combines itself with both consciousness and action.' Such women begin mobilizing as mothers, and remain mothers rather than political actors.

Motherhood and citizenship: the tensions

It has been apparent throughout this book that there is a tension between the collective action of women which engages with the political arena, however critically, and that which aspires to remain above or outside it. Despite the political impact of women's collective action, many *choose* to reject an overtly political identity. This removed, apolitical stance has to be understood in the context of authoritarian and corrupt political systems which have been rejected by large segments of the population. Furthermore, the political arrangements since the return to democracy in many countries have not been free of corruption and repression. It is not entirely surprising, then, if women wish to emphasize the 'female' qualities of moral superiority and apolitical collective action and remain wary of the political arena. As such, this leaves these women with less political influence in the institutional arena in the longer term.

This is reinforced by the tension between autonomy and integration found in many countries. In systems which have relied on clientelism and co-optation to maintain political stability and generate support, the desire for independence from the institutional political arena is strong. It is equally clear, however, that a strict adherence to the principle of autonomy can result in permanent exclusion. Continued apathy on the part of women, particularly some feminist organizations and 'apolitical' motherist groups, towards the institutional political arena tends to lead to disempowerment. The antipathy towards politics is explained, in part, by the culture of autonomy among opposition organizations. Finding the balance between autonomy and co-optation is important, and some women's groups have dealt with this by only supporting organizations which adhere to democratic principles of participation (Molyneux, 1998).

There are problems with the suggestion that women demonstrate greater political morality, evident in the 'ethic of care' approach and in Kaplan's (1982) emphasis on life preservation. It helps constrain women's empowerment by limiting their field of action. Many women clearly do participate politically to promote social justice, but this is not necessarily the case. Perhaps the best example of a broader approach to politics is in Argentina, where women have appeared on the political stage in large numbers quickly. Here many of the new women deputies have demonstrated a political canniness and ability to reproduce 'male' ambition and self-interest. The Peronist deputies in particular seem to have little interest in promoting 'women's interests', however defined. The expectation of a 'softer' approach to politics was apparent in the wording of the quota law, but it is too soon to tell whether there has been a change in the tone of political debate. In interview, (the then deputy) Graciela Fernández Meijide told me that she would not take on the role of Mrs Mop, cleaning up politics: she commented that she could only vouch for her own moral political conduct and refused to be responsible for others. The continuing issue of political corruption, seen in many countries, reinforces the tendency to distinguish between good and bad politics. This, in turn, equates women's politics as morally superior and removed from bad 'politics as usual'.

The inference that women are expected to be responsible for others is part of the construction of womanhood based on caring, endorsed by patriarchal institutions such as the Catholic Church. It is unclear whether citizenship, based on the notion of individuals, can incorporate a conception of an individual whose identity is to protect third persons: can motherhood be the basis for citizenship? If citizenship is based on what we have in common with one another, clearly it cannot, since it is an exclusive identity which only women can realize. Nevertheless, some of the characteristics associated with motherhood, such as care for others, can be incorporated providing the resultant form of citizenship is open to all adults. The concentration on women's socio-political role has been reinforced by the activities of social movements, many of which are concerned with social justice and eschew 'bad' party politics. Even here, however, women reflect the dominant political culture, and some treat neighbourhoods as their political fiefdoms (Craske, 1993; Jaquette, 1994c). The expectation that women will perform politically in a more honest fashion is clearly unreasonable, and possibly foolish.

The activities of women revolutionaries and the debates arising out of feminism in the region show that the concerns of women have grown far beyond narrowly defined domestic issues, although they remain more interested in domestic matters than most men. They have also pushed 'private' issues into the political arena and have expanded political debate. Consequently, a gendered perspective is emerging in the debates around effective citizenship which affects the struggle for democracy discussed throughout the book. Women have challenged the narrow terms of political citizenship with slogans such as 'democracy in the country and the home'. Women in Nicaragua and Cuba have challenged the antipathy towards feminism within revolutionary discourse and sought to make the systems more open to women citizens.

Women have clearly demonstrated their capacity for political participation without copying traditional male patterns of political involvement. Because women have been excluded from politics by both authoritarian governments and dominant gender constructions, their attainment of political subjectivity has been subversive on two counts. Given that their political participation emerged largely through non-institutional structures, however, their challenge is on the wane, since at present these alternative political arenas are in decline. Perhaps the way that motherhood is construed as the fundamental biological distinction between women and men will always mean that motherhood takes on a unique social identity, distinct from profession, race or political ideology. Whatever women's motivation for political participation, their alternative interests and methods of organizing have undoubtedly influenced political structures.

Redefining politics

Given the many, and frequently rapid, changes of regime in Latin America, political participation has been continually expanding and contracting to accommodate shifting actors and issues. The impact of women on the political debate has been to challenge the boundaries between social and political issues and arenas, and to erode the distinction between the public and private. Through their participation they have forced political openings, but we have seen that these openings are often temporary, and frequently when one opening occurs there is a concomitant closure. Social movements proved to be a dynamic political force which helped undermine authoritarian regimes, and women's key role in them highlighted the antipathy towards politics as traditionally understood.

Social movements served to erode the barrier between social and political issues and spaces: this was a two-way process. The fact that these organizations were in social space allowed women to participate in greater numbers, and the fact that women were at the centre of the movements kept them in this space. The activities of revolutionary regimes also demonstrated the blurring of the distinction between political and social issues, particularly where 'women's issues' were concerned. It must be noted in both cases, however, that the situations were extreme. Under repressively authoritarian regimes, most political spaces were closed off altogether. We have seen that, with the return of electoral politics, the social movements have declined, with a particular impact on women. Similarly, in revolutionary regimes it was women's issues which were considered secondary to the real politics of national development, and thus they were the first to be sacrificed when the situation deteriorated.

Shifting the public–private divide

The erosion of the political–social distinction is mirrored in the changes in the public and private dichotomy. In Chapter 2 I suggested that a continuum rather than a divide was more helpful. In examining women's work, political participation and feminist debates, it is clear that few issues or people are confined to one sphere or the other. The informal work sector seems set to be an important part of Latin American economies, and social movements, while in decline, continue to mobilize. Both of these factors have contributed greatly to a questioning of the validity of the distinction. Cubitt and Greenslade (1997: 60) suggest that the public–private distinction is 'inappropriate in the analysis on gender in Latin America'. This is reinforced in the discussion on work, where it was demonstrated that women prefer a holistic approach which integrated rather than separated work and domestic lives. Furthermore, women's work patterns undermine the distinction by conflating domestic work with paid labour. Nevertheless, as an ideal type it informs peoples' lives and suggests appropriate types of interaction. I suggest that its importance lies in the way that people reproduce the discourse of the divide, regardless of personal circumstances (Craske, 1993).

A rigid divide, however, obscures most activities of most people, regardless of sex. It is perhaps more important to 'degender' the divide and not to map female–male onto private–public, and, furthermore, not to make one a subordinate of the other. Understanding the private as women's space denies men their role in this and underestimates women's role in public arenas. With a continuum actors and issues can shift between the two poles: the neighbourhood became more public as a site of politics but has moved back towards the private with the return of electoral politics in the region. The public can only exist with a private sphere and the private is important not just in terms of its reproductive role. In Latin America the private sphere became a bulwark against authoritarianism and a place of resistance when the military were trying to silence all opposition. A private space away from public scrutiny, however fragile, was essential to the development of an opposition.

The shifting and renegotiation of the divide is particularly evident at present with the deepening of the neoliberal project. This project is based at one level on a clear separation of public and private space, since it withdraws the state from 'private' reproductive tasks: it is, after all, a neo*liberal* project. Liberalism as a project is predicated on a separation of public and private. Current governments thus have a vested interest in redrawing the line clearly. The growth of the informal sector with neoliberal restructuring does undermine this distinction to a degree, but this paradox is being ignored for the present.

Although there have been shifts in the practice of politics and in the institutional terrain itself, the experiences of Latin American women show that political, economic and social structures are conservative institutions, resistant to change. They tend towards inertia and only respond to significant pressure or crisis. Periods of transition in a regime, themselves a result of pressure and crisis, offer important windows of opportunity for women to advance their claims before the structures re-establish themselves and become more closed to new demands.

Gender interests

The construction of gender and the concentration of women in the social and domestic arenas inform women's interests. In conceptualizing gender interests it is clear, particularly given the antagonism among women themselves, that there is no unitary understanding of gender interests.

Practical and strategic interests

Molyneux's (1985) practical and strategic distinction is helpful for understanding initial motivation and the way in which class clearly influences needs along with gender. The evidence presented in this book reinforces Molyneux's notion of practical gender interests as being a focal point for political engagement, particularly in social movements and workplace organizations. Practical issues tend to emphasize immediate, material need and, given that material need is linked to class and ethnicity, it is not surprising that social movements have concentrated on these types of demands. Furthermore, women have demonstrated that they tend to identify more easily with class and/or ethnicity than gender issues: this was apparent in the discussions on unions, social movements, revolutions and feminisms.

Despite the fact that practical gender interests defend the gender division of labour, when the deeper causes creating these gendered needs are uncovered, strategic interests become central to long-term transformation. Strategic responses may be the best way to satisfy practical interests (Molyneux, 1998). Consequently, traditional gender relations are challenged, and this leads to the questioning of natural roles for women and men. This shift from one to the other is not always the case, but I would underline that there is no clear boundary between practical and strategic issues, and that frequently issues have both practical and strategic elements to them, as does the struggle to combat them. The events in the regional feminist meetings demonstrated that, for many women participating in social movements, the development of a critique of deeply grounded sexism is not unusual. While these women do not always embrace the label 'feminist', their analysis and actions reflect feminist practices.

Women's and men's interests

The development of political activity to promote women's interests, whether practical or strategic, has challenged another barrier: the distinction between female and male interests. Generally women's interests are seen as definable in a way that men's are not: men's interests are universal interests and not constrained by gender construction. Women's increased political activity has questioned the meaning of 'women's interests'. Although emphasis is placed on the identity of life preserver, there is nothing exclusive to women about the desire to preserve life.[3] Equally, many of the issues around which women campaigned in consumer movements are of equal interest to men. A language of rights has permeated the language of interests, placing 'women's interests' within the construction of citizenship. As the terms of the political debate have changed and women, through their participation, have pushed different issues onto the political agenda, issues traditionally perceived as 'women's interests' have become more generalized.

Women are demanding recognition that their areas of competence are as legitimate and as important politically as those of men – that women's rights are citizens' rights. Women workers have appreciated how their needs are not seen as important as men's because their concerns are not seen as central to 'workers' issues'; thus by implication workers are men without child-care and domestic concerns. The transitions to democracy facilitated the shift from woman's interest to citizen's right by creating a situation where political rights generally were being negotiated. Women's practical gender interests are the ones which are most likely to be of general concern to both women *and* men, and paradoxically this becomes apparent as the strategic implications are realized. Women's practical gender issues are women's concerns because of sexist social organization, but to question whether they are women's exclusive responsibility may not happen unless women question the gender division of labour. Although the distinction between women's and men's interests will continue to wither, while there are inequalities and identifiable gender constructions there will be differences: difference, of course, is not a problem unless it is associated with subordination. For the present, because women's interests have been excluded from the political arena, they appear more subversive than many 'male interests'.

Although women have challenged the boundaries of politics, not all women with political careers in congresses and local and regional governments have confined their involvement to narrowly defined 'women's interests'. The increase in the numbers of female politicians has had an impact not just on the debates and questions raised, but, to some extent, also on the ways in which politics is conducted: as the Argentinian quota law states, the increase in women deputies is designed among other things to 'humanize' the congress, in part by introducing new working practices. This different work style is reflected in the way in which in many countries women deputies come together over common interests and to promote agendas, placing gender over party identity. In the discussions on feminism and revolutionary states, conflicts around dual militancy were highlighted – an issue men rarely encounter. There is a greater attempt to engage in cross-party dialogue among women deputies, reflecting the non-partisan nature of many 'women's issues' (and the fact that women represent such small percentages of legislatures). Women's issues do not fit easily into a left–right formulation and can lead to apparently strange bedfellows.[4]

Rarely, however, do *all* women deputies come together, and because many do it should not belie the fact that they can also act within narrow personal and/or party agendas with ruthless ambition. In Argentina, where there is now a significant number of female deputies, not all are concerned with women's issues and some prefer to keep themselves away from any identifiable 'women's caucus'. By acting together, however, and promoting certain agendas, some women politicians and activists have been able to further demands which at one time might have been considered outside politics and more issues for private negotiations within family units. The tension then is whether it is important to have women, whoever they are, in positions of power or whether the key issue is to have people who will promote women's issues whatever their sex: both are needed in the interests of democracy. Women politicians should be as varied in their interests and practices, both good and bad, as men.

The 1990s and beyond

Women have made their mark politically in ways not imagined thirty years ago, but the impact is varied. The empowerment of individuals has developed as a result of their participation and increased impact on the decision-making process. Given that gender relations are central to the structuring of power relations in society, there will always be actors who will resist change. This resistance is not just from men who might see women's gains as implying their losses, but from women who identify strongly with dominant gender constructions and find changes threatening to their limited power resources. As we have seen, the change often results in greater burdens, as women take on more income-generation activities and join grassroots community organizations without losing any of their domestic responsibilities. In contrast, as Molyneux (1998) notes, men's lives remained largely untransformed.

Politics in retreat

In the 1990s we are, as analysts, more sober in our expectations of the new Latin American democracies. In the 1980s many, myself included, were highly optimistic about the political developments in the region, particularly regarding alternative spaces and the increase in female political actors. It is clear today that the expected inclusivity of political systems has not materialized. The economic model encourages exclusion, and for many in the region their quotidian existence has not improved; nor do they look to the political arena to change it. Few people maintain high levels of political activism indefinitely. Women made a great impact in the 1970s and 1980s, and this is reflected at the national level through legal changes and developments in political rhetoric: yet further developments look unlikely at present. In the neighbourhoods many continue to engage in social movements, although frequently this is purely a reflection of collective survival strategies and community management.

The failure of social movements to maintain their influence on politics demonstrates the difficulties of effecting long-term change. The current political situation in Latin America is a delicate one: the memories of military repression are still reasonably fresh, and few would wish to jeopardize the new-found stability. It is also clear, however, that the demands which fuelled the challenges to authoritarianism are not being met by most of the civilian governments, and popular disenchantment remains a problem. Democratic governments have shown themselves to be limited in their ability to respond to citizens' demands. This relates particularly to the provision of welfare services, which are of special interest to women. Women are expected to play an increasing role as citizens but without losing their social roles. Over the course of this century expectations have grown regarding what constitutes the state's responsibilities. Latin American states illustrate the failure to respond to many of these demands, which are echoed in most other countries in the world.

The crises which have befallen Latin America over the decades have frequently been catalysts for change, and particularly for women's greater political involvement, but we must not forget that crises also act as constraints, and for many daily survival supersedes campaigning for democracy. There is also the problem of participation fatigue, particularly evident in grassroots organizations. In institutional politics, most of the women come from the same elite families as men, and for them politics is a career. This is not to say that it is easy for them to advance, but they generally have more domestic support than women participating at the grassroots, which makes their continued participation easier. Social movements are vulnerable to collapse as agendas shift and new strategies emerge. The difficulty in keeping people mobilized is also evident in revolutionary regimes, where participation in voluntary brigades wanes over time.

Political participation will probably always be a minority sport, but women will continue to increase their participation relative to men. Nevertheless, it will be some time before their influence equals that of men in Latin America. The political system responds to shifts in economic conditions, domestic political movements, global geo-political alliances and the fighting between different elite groups, not least the intervention of the military. Women have clearly demonstrated their capacity to engage with these changing political contexts to great effect, but they have also demonstrated their greater antipathy towards the political process. This antipathy is in part learnt as a result of gender constructions which place politics outside certain appropriate female behaviour, but it is also their choice to reject large parts of the political process. Women are more central to the political process in most countries, but they still encounter many obstacles. More women are in governments and congresses and have succeeded in pushing through some feminist and women-friendly agendas, but the advances are rarely as great as activists would hope. The actual practice of politics has changed little. It is still adversarial and aggressive and the timetables reflect a male work pattern. The culture of politics has changed only marginally.

Lessons from Latin America

The experiences of Latin American women would indicate that there are a number of serious constraints on their ability and inclination to participate in politics. These constraints offer lessons in a broader context. Firstly, there is an inertia within political institutions which makes the political process resistant to change. Despite the increase in all types of women's political engagement, the practice of politics has moved slowly. This slowness acts as a demobilizer in the long run, as people become disheartened. Secondly, the limited political change over the past fifteen to twenty years is reinforced by difficult economic conditions. Thirdly, although there have been developments in gender constructions which make women's political participation less remarkable, there has been a smaller shift in the lifestyles of men than those of women: consequently, women activists have extremely burdensome, if rewarding, lives. Women's issues are more often on the political agenda, but change is slow. Men still appear nervous of the changes and are defending their traditional roles, much in the same way that some women do.

Women have made an impact on the political arena in the region, and lessons can be learnt from their experience. Despite the importance of social movements, their revolutionary activity and other alternative forms of political expression, the mainstream political arena is still seen in a largely negative light. Women have made a distinction between good and bad politics, but, for the most part, politics remains bad. In most countries throughout the world, women barely make up 20 per cent of legislatures. While external constraints may explain this to some extent, women are also choosing not to participate. The costs are high and the terrain reflects an unfamiliar set of gendered practices. The Latin American case illustrates that women continue to reject this as a way of interest formation, preferring instead social organizations.

It could be argued that there are still rewards to be gained from traditional gender roles. Women may find the drudgery uninspiring, but there are many compensations. To combine their mothering role with political engagement would only add to their burdens. Many women identify positively with traditional gender roles and help reinscribe them. In this they are supported by the social, political, cultural and religious structures around them. Latin American women have demonstrated a deep antipathy towards traditional forms of politics and an attachment to their social roles. As women continue to opt out of traditional politics, the practice of citizenship remains a masculine activity and a vicious circle emerges. Given that states try to contain demands – and thus the development of citizenship – the continued antipathy of women serves their interests as well.

The Latin American case also highlights the late twentieth-century crisis regarding responsibility for social reproduction. No state has found the balance among public provision, freedom of individuals and a balanced budget. It would appear from the experiences of Cuba and Nicaragua that there are many difficulties associated with state provision of social services. High levels of state provision are not financially feasible; furthermore, intimate family units have a broader value which states cannot reproduce and might inadvertently undermine. The answer, however, does not lie in the monolithic nuclear family promoted by British and US governments. Families, whatever their form, cannot replace the state in the provision of collective goods in all areas. The Latin American case shows how the privatization of social provision limits women's ability to participate as full citizens and thus the quality of democracy. Whatever the domestic unit organization, it should not, in my view, constrain members' abilities to realize their citizenship roles.

International trends in Latin America

There are indications that similar processes seen in Northern democracies are to be found in Latin America: improved educational attainment, new work opportunities, decreasing religious influences, more gender-aware policy makers, etc. But while women are responsible for social reproduction, regardless of other responsibilities, those who wish to have a life in other arenas are left with difficult choices. In the UK, one in five women remains child-free for various reasons. Women in positions of power are much more likely than their male counterparts to be without children, which indicates that it is much more difficult for women to combine families and professions at this level. I suggest it is likely that we will see an increase in child-free women in Latin America. Given the wider gaps in income distribution in the region, however, it may be that professional women will simply succeed in having a family because paid domestic help and the cultural acceptance of this will allow them to have 'the best of both worlds'. This clearly has class implications and leaves poorer women less able to benefit from the advances in women's status; this will have age, ethnicity and geographic implications as well.

Given these considerations, women have much more to gain from greater redistributive policies and a more integrated state provision of key services. Regardless of whether the services are paid for privately through the employment of servants, or publicly through state provision, however, there needs to be a radical shift in terms of responsibility. Women being mothers should not automatically make them responsible for managing the daily servicing of the family/partner: it appears that men generally take on this role seriously only in the most extreme of situations when the result is high levels of stress. The essentializing of women as mothers militates against these shifts. Despite the significant advances women have made in political life, gender relations have developed more slowly in both the public and the private domain. We can certainly applaud the advances but we should also acknowledge the ongoing difficulties that women face in achieving the autonomy that men of their own class and ethnic groups take for granted.

Notes

Chapter 2   Women and Political Identity in Latin America

1 Only pregnancy and childbirth are actually biological.
2 Marta Lamas (1998: 18) discusses the ongoing impact in Mexico of Catholicism, which promotes 'a sexist and homophobic agenda'.
3 There are still cases where judges treat this particular crime leniently, despite *de jure* changes to the law. This reminds us of the discussions in Britain recently regarding gender and domestic killings, where it appears that women are treated more harshly by the law.
4 In the past it was not uncommon for men to have two families – an official one and a secondary one – but even here women were expected to remain faithful. Eva Perón was a product of a secondary family (Dujovne Ortiz, 1997).
5 At an anecdotal level examples of this are frequently heard. A professional single woman with her own home was upset when she and a young man both turned up to perform the same function at a public gathering which would have been prestigious for them. She allowed him to take on the role but thought he should have stood down for her out of chivalry rather than seeing their claim as equal based on the professional qualities needed. (It must be noted, however, that he may have thought his claim the greater because he was a man and it was a public engagement!)
6 The similarity of the language of the Marxist Salvador Allende and the extreme right-wing General Pinochet demonstrates this point: Miller quotes Allende as saying, 'When I say "woman", I always think of the woman-mother ... When I talk of this woman, I refer to her in her function in the nuclear family ... the child is the prolongation of the woman who in essence is born to be a mother' (Miller, 1991: 183). Pinochet's National Secretariat of Women stressed the difference

between women and men, with the emphasis on women as mothers, wives and educators (ibid.: 279, fn 77).

7 Stevens identifies the excessive constraints of mourning as particularly burdensome, since they effectively reduced women's lives to a joyless endurance test. This came into greater effect in middle age, by which time most women have experienced bereavement.

8 John Paul II, Apostolic letter *Mulieris Dignitatem* (15 August 1988), available on Vatican Home Page.

9 I am using the term 'women's groups' loosely: I do not mean to infer feminist organizations but groups comprised solely or predominantly of women. Many social movements are not gender specific but are included here.

10 For a discussion of the tensions between citizenship and motherhood from a theoretical perspective, see Pateman (1992).

11 Dichotomies remain useful 'as heuristic devices if only in order to reveal how much more complex reality is' (Molyneux, 1998: 234).

12 Clearly, Israel's conscription rules challenge this, but even here women and men are given different tasks, which generally keeps women from the front line.

13 For further discussion in theorizing the development of social movements and the impact on democratic development, see Foweraker (1995; 1997).

14 The many legal changes which resulted to a large degree from women's participation in the struggle for democracy are outlined in Chapter 4.

15 Freire was an educator who believed in a critical pedagogy which 'enabled the oppressed to identify the sources of their oppression' (Alvarez, 1990: 62).

Chapter 3 Setting the Scene

1 This section gives a very brief account of Latin American political structures to highlight the main developments. For further discussion, good introductory accounts are Skidmore and Smith (1997), Keen (1996) and Cubitt (1995). For an economic history of the region, see Bulmer-Thomas (1994) or Sheahan (1987). There are also a number of excellent country-specific studies.

2 The term 'bureaucratic authoritarianism' (BA) was coined by Guillermo O'Donnell in 1973 to describe the new military regimes in Argentina and Brazil in the 1960s, but came to be used generally as a label for the military states of the 1960s and 1970s. I prefer to use National Security States, since BA is a (much criticized) model of political economy and not all states here conform to it: for further discussion, see Cammack and O'Brien (1985).

3 Although it must be noted that Mexico's slow transition from one-party rule continues alongside regular, if not always free, elections.

Furthermore, Peru's president, Alberto Fujimori, suspended congress in 1992 in an executive coup (*auto-golpe*), although he was re-elected president in 1995.

4 For further discussion of corporatism in Latin America and its relationship with authoritarianism, see Malloy (1977).

5 Appeals are made to *el pueblo* (the people), which underlines the idea of community, unlike voters or citizens; see Laclau (1987) for a discussion of emotional appeals to *el pueblo*.

6 Officialist unions are those endorsed by the state or with strong links to it.

7 For an analysis of parties and party systems in the region, see Mainwaring and Scully (1995).

8 Virtual unknowns have won the presidency in two countries: Fernando Collor de Mello took office as Brazil's president in 1990, and Alberto Fujimori won the Peruvian presidency in 1990 against another non-party man, the writer Mario Vargas Llosa. Unfortunately the experiences have been no more positive for democracy: Collor was impeached by congress for corruption; Fujimori suspended congress and the military continues to play an important role in the country's politics. It could be argued in the Brazilian case that the impeachment represented progress, since Collor was dealt with through due process of the law rather than a military coup.

9 See Smith (1992) for a discussion of the links between economic and political liberalization.

10 This datum excludes Cuba and Guatemala. Of the other countries, only Brazil, El Salvador and Uruguay registered less than 89 per cent nominal Catholics, with 70, 75 and 66 per cent respectively (CIA Factbook: http://www.odci.gov/cia/publications/factbook/).

11 During my fieldwork in Argentina, I was told repeatedly that the Catholic Church was regaining prestige and influence after its low profile in the early years of democratic transition. This is of particular importance to women, since it is a conservative church with very traditional views on gender relations.

12 The recorded life expectancy figures differ slightly in Valdés and Gomáriz (1995: 116) but the ordering is the same.

13 Latin American women experience a problem with obtaining information on contraceptives and in the narrowness in choices. An Argentinian health-care activist, Dr Mabel Bianco, commented that the pill remains the most commonly used method: condoms are considered 'unmanly' and the IUD and cap are difficult to obtain (interview, 19 July 1995).

14 Interview, 25 July 1995. Dr Moreno's colleague Mabel Bianco (previously in the Sub-secretariat for Women) commented that in the past midwives were able to carry out illegal, but safe, abortions. Recently, however, obstetrics was moved to the nursing degree, which takes six

years to carry out instead of three, so there are fewer midwives able to perform this service (interview, 19 July 1995).

15 The definition of what constitutes a household is not universally agreed: some consider it a home, others the hearth, others the pooling of resources.

16 'Although women comprise fifty percent of the world's adult population and represent one third of the official labour force, they perform almost two thirds of all working hours yet receive one-tenth of the world's income' (Tiano, 1984: 11, citing UN statistics).

17 The export-oriented industrialization based on the experience of the South-East Asian 'Tiger' economies was thought to be a model in Latin America. In those Latin American countries where this model was established – Mexico, Central America and the Caribbean – there were elements of this, but it did not reflect the work experience of the majority of Latin American women (see McClenaghan, 1997).

18 García and de Oliveira (1997) give different typologies of women engaged in extra-domestic work.

Chapter 4 Formal Political Representation

1 For a discussion of Eva's contribution to Peronism, see Navarro (1982). There are numerous books on her extraordinary life and she still elicits equal measures of devotion and antipathy among Argentines.

2 Elections in both Paraguay and Mexico have been characterized by fraud for much of this period, although both countries have registered significant improvements over the last decade. Paraguay was effectively a dictatorship under General Stroessner.

3 A further ten countries have the position of vice-president.

4 By making this observation, however, I do not wish to suggest that these are not important ministries; indeed, they are on a par with finance, defence and foreign affairs. The point is to highlight the ghettoization of women and the difficulty in transgressing dominant constructions of gender which are reinforced by the state.

5 The wife of the governor of the province of Buenos Aires, Hilda González de Duhalde, has established a Liga Femenina to generate links between organized women in low-income neighbourhoods and the provincial government. Ostensibly apolitical, the rhetoric she employs is very similar to Evita's, as is the name of the organization. Coincidentally, Governor Duhalde is expected to be the Peronists' presidential candidate in 1999. For a greater discussion of Sra de Duhalde's views, see Chapter 8.

6 The DIF is Desarrollo Integral de la Familia (Integral Family Development), which is a welfarist organization aimed at supporting poorer families. It often serves to add another instrument of clientelism in the Mexican political system.

7 It should be noted that the time frame of analysis is not uniform across the countries, since it takes into account only periods of electoral rule.

8 Globally, the trend to have lower female representation in the upper house is more common, although it appears that the upper house has an inverse relationship with the lower: that is, in countries with high numbers of women deputies (or equivalent), women make up a smaller proportion of senators. In countries with low female representation in the lower house, the proportion of female senators can be high, but there is no rule (see Interparliamentary Union data on the Internet: <www.ipu.org/wmn-e/classif.htm>).

9 This was the case of the independent organization I studied in Guadalajara (Craske, 1993; cf. Stephen, 1989).

10 Archenti and Gómez (1994) have shown that, in Argentina, women are increasingly involved in government commissions not associated with 'women's issues'; however, Graciela Fernández Meijide told me in interview that she had not succeeded in participating in the economic commission she requested (August 1995). This could reflect the weak position of the party at the time rather than the fact that she is a woman.

11 Fanny Pollarolo of the Chilean Socialist Party suggests that the problem of double militancy is worse for those on the right, since they are generally less sympathetic to women's issues. Furthermore, this situation is worsening with the backlash (interview, 27 August 1995).

12 This is a change in the legal rights over children, which had traditionally rested with the fathers. This has particular salience when it is remembered that the disappeared were not officially dead: consequently, mothers left alone with children in these circumstances could not travel abroad with them since they did not have the father's permission.

13 One activist, Lucrecia Oller, suggested that President Menem had made an agreement with the Pope: Menem would avoid liberalization on sexual matters if Pope John Paul II refrained from criticizing the government for poverty levels (interview, 8 August 1995).

14 Between 1996 and 1998 another eight countries introduced quota laws: Brazil, Bolivia, Costa Rica, the Dominican Republic, Ecuador, Panama, Peru and Venezuela. However, the impact in these other countries will be less marked because, with the exception of Bolivia, they use open-list systems. In the Bolivian case the law applies only to those seats elected from proportional representation lists, which account for fewer than half of the deputies. In the Panamanian case the quotas are for intra-party primaries to select candidates. While the laws will have a positive impact on the representation of women in the congresses, it will not be as noticeable as in Argentina. Mark Jones suggests that male deputies understood there was little threat to their own positions and this is why the laws were passed relatively easily (personal communication, August 1998).

15 Interview, 7 August 1995.
16 Women cannot be placed at the bottom of the list: in most cases they are placed third (then sixth, then ninth, etc.), and rarely come second unless there are only two seats to be renewed and the parties are required by the law to have at least one woman.
17 Interview with Riet Delsing, 4 September 1995.
18 Interview, 22 August 1995.
19 Yelicic, interviewed 28 July 1995. Estenssoro launched a new magazine for women in 1995 which was aimed at thirtysomething professionals who, like herself, might not consider themselves feminists, but who understand problems of discrimination (interview, 10 August 1995). This emphasis on 'fame' is often linked to family connections. Women with 'historic' surnames are noticeable in many countries. In Chile, the Socialist Party member and temporary Vice-President for Women's Affairs, María Angélica Ibáñez, commented that, while this is a problem, it must be remembered that there are plenty of mediocre men who have arrived this way! (interview, 7 September 1995).
20 Interview, 9 August 1995.
21 It must be remembered that trade unions in Argentina have been key political players and associated most with the Peronist party.
22 Interview, 9 August 1995.
23 Interview, 28 July 1995.
24 Under this rubric I include state-sponsored ministries, secretariats, departments, federations and institutes which are designed to improve the status of women. That having been said, these organizations have different levels of power depending on their legal status. It must be remembered that there are also women's commissions within city governments, such as the Consejo Asesor de la Mujer (Women's Advisory Council) in Buenos Aires established by Clori Yelicic.
25 For further analysis of the emergence of the CNDM, see Alvarez (1990).
26 The first ministry in the post-military era was set up by the Alfonsín government. The Undersecretariat for Women was under the auspices of the Ministry of Social Welfare and in the Secretariat of Children and Family – a traditional place for women's issues, as Feijoó points out (1994: 69). In contrast, in Chile SERNAM was established by an act of law, which means it cannot be disbanded easily (Paulina Veloso, sub-director, interview, 30 August 1995).
27 Interview, 17 August 1995.
28 Interview, 30 August 1995.
29 Paulina Veloso, interviewed 30 August 1995.
30 For a discussion of the FMC and the revolution generally, see Chapter 7.
31 The political scientist Nélida Archenti suggested that there was a surge in membership of organizations in the immediate aftermath of

the transition to electoral politics and that women affiliated to parties in larger numbers than men (interview, 7 August 1995).

32 Interview, 28 July 1995.

33 Interview, 19 July 1995.

34 Data from the Mexican Embassy, London.

35 Interview, 29 August 1995.

36 Interview, 7 September 1995.

37 Interview, 31 August 1995 (author's translation).

38 Interview with Ibáñez, 7 September 1995.

39 1951 was the first opportunity for women to vote in national elections (the franchise having been won in 1947).

40 This was a charitable foundation which allowed Eva a great source of patronage and which was hugely successful in demonstrating her commitment to the poor. She administered it rigorously and oversaw most of the projects and petitions herself. The foundation was not publicly accountable.

41 Gloria Bonder commented during an interview (18 July 1995) that the women were unusual for their humble backgrounds and that they were not afraid of courting public power and in using their femininity to achieve it. She also commented that as a group they were easy to identify for their dress style, which contrasted greatly with that of the socialist woman politician, who was austere and moralistic.

42 Interview, 17 August 1995.

43 Clearly men operate in the private domain, but their identities tend to rest to a greater degree on their professional status.

44 Interview, 31 August 1995.

45 See Stetson and Mazur (1995a) for a discussion of state feminism: this is also discussed in Chapter 8.

46 Valdés and Gomáriz (1995: 186–7) outline those ministries which have separate women's programmes: they focus on education, public health, agriculture, labour and social welfare, justice, foreign affairs and the interior. It may seem strange that economic affairs and the treasury do not feature.

47 The authors also note that there were no women bureaucrats as 'political personnel' and few 'of particular confidence' (Da Silveira et al., 1991: 90–92).

48 Lawyer, interviewed 22 August 1995.

49 Interview, 18 July 1995.

50 Interview, 31 July 1995

51 Interview, 31 August 1995 (author's translation).

Chapter 5   The Impact of Work on Political Identity

1 Interview, 7 August 1995.

2 Such activities include small-scale food production, ironing, needlework and child-minding.

3 *Maquiladoras* are assembly plants of generally US-owned corporations. Before the establishment of the North American Free Trade Agreement (NAFTA), US companies were able to take advantage of significantly cheaper Mexican labour, but avoided paying tariffs when the products entered the country because the components had largely been manufactured in the USA. It remains to be seen what effect the complete removal of tariffs from US–Mexican trade over the next decade will have on the *maquiladoras*.

4 Clearly the full impact of the economic crisis in South-East Asia has yet to be felt.

5 A study in Uruguay considered the status of women workers: 65 per cent were in the lowest category and none at all in the highest (Fisher, 1993: 65).

6 Interview, 31 July 1995. At the time of the fieldwork, many commented that the Argentine finance minister Domingo Cavallo blamed women for (male) unemployment and the crisis of the state (since it now has to provide services previously assumed by women).

7 Elizabeth Lawrence (1994) makes this point regarding women in Northern democracies, but I consider it an important point to be raised here. I also thank Judith Clifton for pointing out that in some industries in Latin America union membership is obligatory.

8 Under the present Peronist president, Carlos Menem, official unemployment has reached a record high of nearly 20 per cent which has led to significant labour unrest, particularly in the industrial heartland. Nevertheless, the Confederación General de Trabajadores (CGT) preferred the idea of the Peronist Hilda de Duhalde as governor of Buenos Aires Province rather than FREPASO's Graciela Fernández Meijide (*Clarín*, 9 March 1997). Duhalde is the wife of the current Peronist governor of Buenos Aires, while Fernández Meijide became involved in institutional politics by way of human rights campaigning.

9 Clientelism refers to patron–client relationships of exchange with asymmetrical power relations: see Chapter 3.

10 Interview with María Angélica Ibáñez of the Socialist Party and Centro de Estudios Sociales, 7 September 1995.

11 Although they also point out that women primary school teachers were engaged in highly confrontational mobilizations with the police in 1972 (Amado and Checa, 1990: 24).

12 Carrillo (1990: 225) finds similar attitudes in Mexico, where many believe that involvement in unions will lead to dismissal.

13 See Navarro (1985) and Henault (1994) on Argentina, Bareiro et al. (1993) on Paraguay and Scott (1994) on Peru.

14 Interview, 17 July 1995.

15 Interview, 16 August 1995.

16 Interview with Norma Rial, 17 July 1995.

17 See Foweraker (1993) for a comprehensive account of the struggles

within the SNTE during the 1980s, including the role played by women and indigenous communities: see also Cook (1996).

18 Compare with Amado and Checa's discussion of the teachers' union in Argentina (1990). Here members comment on how antagonistic activists were to feminist discourse.

19 In the case of the Brazilian and Mexican domestic workers' organizations, the articles were written by those involved rather than by independent analysts.

20 For a discussion of women assembly plant workers on a global scale and gender relations in the workplace, see Pearson (1992). See Wilson (1993) for a discussion of the gender division of labour in sweatshops.

21 These strategies are similar to those used by social movements discussed in the next chapter.

22 Cf. Perelli's (1994) discussion on non-workplace collective action in Uruguay.

23 Much has been written about the male character of liberal citizenship (see Phillips, 1991).

Chapter 6   Social Movements

1 Volk (1997: 8) understands civil society as 'that civic space which lies outside the direct control of the state and the market. Civil society is more than just the articulation of the space between "public" and "private" spheres in modern society.'

2 The range of social movements which have emerged in the 1970s and 1980s is astounding and is reflected both in the general literature and in studies with a more specifically gender perspective: included in the latter category are Alvarez (1990); Miller (1991); Fisher (1993); Radcliffe and Westwood (1993); and Jaquette (1994a).

3 Waylen (1996a) has a useful discussion of authoritarian regimes and gender. Pinochet was particularly aware of the potential of women as political actors, since El Poder Femenino (Women's Power: see Chapter 7 for further discussion) had been involved in encouraging the military coup which deposed the elected president Salvador Allende. Pinochet was quick to demobilize the women after the coup and channelled their energies through the official National Secretariat of Women, headed by his wife (Chuchryk, 1994: 73). Feminists were seen as subversive from the outset.

4 This section focuses on women as human rights activists, rather than giving an analysis of women's rights as human rights. This is obviously an important debate but outside the limitations if this book: see Jelin (1996) for further discussion.

5 The term *desaparecidos* was coined to describe the events in Guatemala in the 1960s when members of the Communist Party were 'disappeared' – a tactic that was soon to become widespread.

6 Interview with members of the APDH, 21 July 1995 (Susana Alicia Finkelstein, Mirta Henault; Bíbi Vogel; Susana Pérez Gallart; Ana María Norvick; Silvia Coppola). It must be noted, however, that in conversation Nora Cortiña stressed that economic issues were also a matter of human rights and that the Mothers (of Línea Fundadora) wanted to show solidarity with those in poorer neighbourhoods (interview, 27 July 1995).

7 The non-negotiable stand and insistence on an apolitical identity later led to a schism in the movement and the division into two groups: Línea Fundadora and the Mothers. The former decided that the demand to have the disappeared returned alive was impossible and that the group would be marginalized if it did not negotiate and deal with the incoming civilian authorities. They have chosen a more pragmatic, and possibly more traditionally political, stance in response to shifting political circumstances.

8 Ironically, in Argentina impending motherhood put many women at particular risk. Pregnant women were disappeared and killed after they had given birth, and their children were adopted by supporters of the regime. The Grandmothers of the Plaza de Mayo aim to find these children.

9 These women came to international prominence when a Dutch film crew attending the football World Cup in Argentina in 1978 chose to film the Mothers rather than the opening ceremony. Ironically the authorities were trying to focus attention on the symbolism of white doves at the ceremony (Bouvard, 1994).

10 Obviously many movements campaigned around both issues.

11 Members of the Taller Permanente de la Mujer (feminist support organization) stressed that they preferred to maintain autonomy from political parties to allow them greater freedom of movement: they don't want to be tied by party manifestos (interview with Piera Oria and Zulema Palma, 26 July 1995).

12 The important links between feminist organizations and social movements are discussed in Chapter 8.

13 In Chile the Vicariate of Santiago played a key role in denouncing human rights abuses: see Lowden (1993).

14 Abuses have been particularly brutal in El Salvador: on 16 November 1989 six Jesuits, their housekeeper and her daughter were brutally murdered and their bodies mutilated at the Universidad Centroamericana (UCA); in December 1980 a group of three nuns and a laywoman, all US citizens, were raped and murdered by government-backed death squads; and Archbishop Oscar Arnulfo Romero was murdered at the altar of the chapel of the Divine Providence Hospital, San Salvador, on 24 March 1980. As recently as 26 April 1998, Auxiliary Archbishop Juan Gerardi was brutally murdered in Guatemala. Only days previously he had presided over the release of the report on human rights abuses. This

report laid the blame for abuses carried out over thirty years firmly at the feet of the army.

15 Although it must be remembered that not all parish groups were progressive and encouraging of political activity (Napolitano, 1998).

16 Alvarez (1990), in her account of the 'People's Church' in Brazil, shows how the liberation theologians embraced only some of the new feminist debates, leaving some difficult issues at the margins.

17 For a discussion of the UN's support of women, see Pietilä and Vickers (1994).

18 Nora Cortiña of the breakaway Línea Fundadora explained how involvement with human rights organizations led her to question the accepted role of women in society and to embrace a much more openly feminist discourse (interview, August 1995).

19 The problem in part is the style of public speaking, especially in terms of assertiveness and aggressiveness: this is also the case in trade unions (Fisher, 1993).

20 There are assumptions about the positive impact of community action, but, as I showed in Mexico, some organizations were designed to depoliticize issues (Craske, 1993).

Chapter 7   Revolutionary Empowerment?

1 For a discussion of Bolivia, see Ardaya Salinas (1994) and Villarroel Smeall (1994); for Mexico, see Soto (1990), Deutsch (1991) and Bushe and Mumme (1994).

2 Margaret Randall (1994) comments on the way individual 'exceptions' hide many unknown women who are never celebrated but are just as important. Similarly, in Mexico, Deutsch (1991: 263) argues that 'the writers of *corridos* (songs) converted nameless legions of courageous, tough female combatants and *soldaderas* into submissive, feminine romantic figures like "La Adelita"'.

3 Augusto César Sandino became a national martyr after his murder: he was ambushed and shot while leaving a presidential dinner, following 'successful negotiations' between the rebels and the government, on 21 February 1934 (Smith, 1993: 99).

4 Dora María Téllez also headed FSLN (Frente Sandinista de Liberación Nacional) forces on the Western Front and supervised the taking of the National Palace in 1978, and Mónica Baltodano headed the forces that took Granada (Fernández Poncela, 1997).

5 Miller (1991: 145) comments that, of all the revolutionary movements that emerged in the 1960s, only the Colombian one had a specific platform on the rights of women: 'On a basis of equality with men, women will take part in the economic, political, and social activities of the country.' The Mexican Ejército Zapatista de Liberación Nacional

(EZLN), which made an audacious attack against the Mexican state on 1 January 1994, made policy statements on women's role in society from the start.

6 Rectification refers to the period from 1989 when the Soviet bloc collapsed and Cuba was confronted with the need for restructuring. It distinguishes the country from any ties with *glasnost* and *perestroika*, and does not allow for any notion of radical political restructuring. Castro gave many speeches indicating his antipathy towards *glasnost* and *perestroika*.

7 Nominal membership of the FMC has increased from 74 per cent in 1974 to 82.3 per cent in 1994, with housewives making up the largest group (Molyneux, 1996: 23 fn 62).

8 As Molyneux notes (1996: 31), 'employment was, in both ideological and practical terms, the basis of membership in the socialist community.' Thus the implications of women withdrawing themselves from the paid-labour force are greater than in other countries.

9 This is discussed at greater length in the following chapter: see also Stetson and Mazur (1995a).

10 32.9 per cent of state employees are women (Véliz and Aguilar, 1992: 43). One must remember to contrast Cuba with countries at a similar stage of socio-economic development in 1959 and not with industrialized societies such as Argentina or Chile.

11 US involvement in Nicaragua was complex as was later demonstrated by the Iran–Contra affair, which disgraced many among the US political and military establishment.

12 In 1972 the capital, Managua, suffered a massive earthquake which razed large parts of the city. The money from the international relief effort was not used to rebuild the city and much of it was channelled into private bank accounts of Somoza and his associates.

13 Luisa Amanda Espinosa was the first female FSLN member to be killed by the Somoza National Guard.

14 Compare this with Eva and Juan Perón's comments in Chapter 4.

15 There had always been a cool relationship between the Catholic hierarchy and the FSLN: the then archbishop, Miguel Obando y Bravo, was particularly antipathetic towards the government. A number of clergy at the grassroots, however, had been active both in the struggle to overthrow Somoza and in the construction of the new Nicaragua.

16 Women occupied 36 per cent of senior government posts, and between 27 and 40 per cent of judicial posts: in the latter group they were better represented in lower ranking positions (Fernández Poncela, 1997: 41).

17 Kandiyoti (1988) discusses how women may defend patriarchal systems, since, along with the disadvantages, there are also established norms which give women important roles in society.

Chapter 8 Feminisms in Latin America

1 For introductions to feminist thought, see Tong (1989) and Bryson (1992).
2 During my fieldwork in Argentina, I was told by a number of people that the Argentines are extremely contentious and find collective action constraining: it generally ends in splits and schisms. The heavy use of psycho-therapists was given as evidence for this focus on the self: Buenos Aires is reputed to have more therapists per capita than New York. Obviously it would be very difficult to verify this view, but the idea of a nation of people antipathetic towards collective action was a strong one, and in sharp contrast to Chile, where so many groups and organizations exist.
3 It is worth remembering that, in Britain in the 1970s, married women could not sign a credit agreement, even if they earned more money than their husbands! It is sometimes easy to forget how much has been gained in a relatively short period of time for women in virtually all countries.
4 All quotes from an interview, 4 August 1995.
5 The sociologist María del Carmen Feijoó argues that Duhalde's language succeeds in speaking to people where feminism does not (interview, 7 August 1995). She has tapped into the most 'populist' of feminism's demands.
6 For various discussions of the women's movement in Chile, see Chuchryk (1994), Frohmann and Valdés (1993), Matear (1995; 1997) and Waylen (various).
7 At the time of fieldwork (1995) the nine deputies were Isabel Allende and Fanny Pollarolo of the Socialist Party, María Antonieta Saa, Rony Rebolledo and Martita Woerner of the Party for Democracy, Mariana Aylwin for the Christian Democrats, Mónica Prochelle and María Angélica Cristi for the right-wing Renovación Nacional, and the independent Evelyn Matthei.
8 Interview, 27 August 1995.
9 The academic Silvina Ramos commented to me that, on a discussion panel of several female academics and public figures, she was the only one who 'came out' as a feminist. I was also told by several commentators, including the political scientist Nélida Archenti and the author Gabriela Cerrutti, that most Argentine women don't think about feminism until they are in their thirties and encounter the glass ceiling and then other constraints are felt more keenly.
10 Interview, 7 August 1995.
11 The distinction should not be understood too rigidly but serves as a reminder that the Latin American feminists were not all self-regarding bourgeois 'ladies', but people who understood the complexities of the issues (Sternbach et al., 1992).

12 The Opus Dei University in Buenos Aires was going to establish a women's studies programme, but one can only wonder at the content of such a course with Opus Dei backing.

13 This theme is repeated: see Sternbach et al. (1992) and the various articles in Jaquette (1994a), especially Chuchryk.

14 Interview, 9 August 1995.

15 In Buenos Aires the women's group the Taller Permanente de la Mujer (Women's Permanent Workshop) runs many projects in support of women with different needs, much of it legal and health-care advice with free consultations. They have been accused of *asistencialismo* (welfarism), particularly by people they consider 'post-modern feminists', but they respond that they cannot turn away the women seeking help, and they do suggest alternatives, including pressuring authorities, where possible. They acknowledge that they are in a difficult position, with the state not complying with its obligations and relying increasingly on private NGOs such as the Taller to make up the shortfall: they still feel they cannot sit back and do nothing (interview with Zulema Palma and Piera Oria, activists in the Taller, 26 July 1995). The reduction in the state, as promoted by neoliberals, has many implications for service provision (again, we see similar problems in Europe).

16 She has returned to education and is particularly interested in gender perspectives in her studies. Interview, August 1995.

17 In Fisher's (1993: 68) study on Uruguay's unions, the women organized a session for themselves and some men helped out in the kitchen and creche. One activist, Carmen, tells how one male unionist commented, 'I'm moved, this is something wonderful, we've all got to learn from this.' But this is a rare example from the literature.

18 Gloria Bonder, who had worked in the ministry, commented that the backlash against the term had been led by the re-emergent Catholic Church, which was increasingly emphasizing 'natural' family roles for women and suggesting that women's failure to fulfil these roles had led to an increase in family breakdown, homosexuality, unemployment and any other social 'problems'. These explanations had gained ground with the pressures resulting from record unemployment (approximately 20 per cent) (interview, 18 July 1995).

19 An excellent analysis of the meetings (not including that in Costa del Sol) is given in Sternbach et al. (1992), from which the information here is taken unless otherwise indicated: see also Miller (1991), Chapter 7.

20 Following Sternbach at al. (1992), I will use the term 'veterans' for those women who prioritize feminist organization in their political life to distinguish them from those who are primarily party activists or who became politically involved through social movements. This is not to say that their feminism is more 'authentic', but simply a way of differentiating the actors for the purposes of the discussion.

21 As Vargas (1992) notes, the numbers really are impressive when it is remembered that the majority pay their own travel costs, which are considerable despite strategies to limit them as much as possible.
22 Paulina Veloso has always been sympathetic to women's movements although not an activist herself. Her own experience was in human rights and labour legislation (she is a lawyer), and although she did not seek a position at SERNAM she has enjoyed the experience. Her only concern is her loss of personal prestige and the lesser weight given her intellectual arguments since being there. She commented that in future she would take a more gendered approach with her to another position (interview, 30 August 1995).
23 This was indicated by Pope John Paul II's letter to the world's women before the Fourth Conference on Women in Beijing.
24 Interview, 27 July 1995.

Chapter 9　　Conclusions

1 It is unclear that the dominance of the neoliberal project will continue, but for the present there appear to be few alternatives being promoted by governments and opposition parties.
2 This is not always reflected in official documents such as censuses, which still refer to heads of household.
3 I do not wish to underestimate the degree to which men outnumber women as perpetrators of violence; indeed in Argentina it is said that no women were recorded as participating in torturing victims during the Dirty War (interview, Gabriela Cerrutti, 27 July 1995). Nevertheless, men also campaigned against human rights abuses and confronted the repressive regimes in many ways.
4 Perhaps an extreme example of this was during the 1994 UN Population Conference, when some feminists allied themselves with both some Islamicists and the Pope in certain debates on birth rates and the environment.

References

Alvarez, S. (1990) *Engendering Democracy in Brazil*. Princeton, NJ: Princeton University Press.

Alvarez, S. (1994) 'The (Trans)formation of feminism(s) and gender politics in democratizing Brazil', in J. Jaquette (ed.), *The Women's Movement in Latin America: participation and democracy*. Boulder, CO: Westview Press, pp. 13–64.

Amado, A. M. and Checa, A. (1990) *Participación sindical feminina en la Argentina: sindicato docente, un estudio de caso*. Buenos Aires: Instituto Latinoamericano de Estudios Transnacionales (ILET).

Anderfuhren, M. (1994) 'The Union of Women Domestic Employees, Recife, Brazil', in M. H. Martens and S. Mitter (eds), *Women in Trade Unions: organizing the unorganized*. Geneva: International Labour Office, pp. 17–32.

Archenti, N. and Gómez, P. L. (1994) 'Las legisladores Argentinas: su quehacer en la transición democrática 1983–1991', in *América Latina Hoy*, no. 9 (segunda epoca), pp. 61–9.

Ardaya Salinas, G. (1994) 'Women and politics: gender relations in Bolivian political organizations and labor unions', in B. Nelson and N. Chowdhury (eds), *Women and Politics Worldwide*. New Haven, CT: Yale University Press, pp. 114–26.

Arellano López, S. and Petras, J. (1994) 'NGOs and poverty alleviation in Bolivia', in *Development and Change*, 25, pp. 555–68.

Azicri, M. (1979) 'Women's development through revolutionary mobilisation: a study of the Federation of Cuban Women', in *International Journal of Women's Studies*, 2/1, pp. 27–50.

Bareiro, L., Soto, C. and Monte, M. (1993) *Alquimistas: documentos para otra historia de las mujeres*. Asunción: Centro de Documentación y Estudios.

Barrig, M. (1994) 'The difficult equilibrium between bread and roses: women's organizations and democracy in Peru', in J. Jaquette (ed.), *The Women's Movement in Latin America: participation and democracy*. Boulder, CO: Westview Press, pp. 151–76.

Bartra, E. (1994) 'The struggle for life, or pulling off the mask of infamy', in B. Nelson and N. Chowdhury (eds), *Women and Politics Worldwide*. New Haven, CT: Yale University Press, pp. 448–60.

Beckwith, K. (1986) *American Women and Political Participation: the impact of work, generation and feminism*. New York: Greenwood Press.

Benería, L. and Roldán, M. (1987) *The Crossroads on Class and Gender*. Chicago: University of Chicago Press.

Benjamin, M. and Mendonça, M. (1997) *Benedita da Silva: an Afro-Brazilian woman's story of politics and love*. Oakland, CA: Food First Books.

Bianchi, S. (1993) 'Las mujeres en el Peronismo (Argentina, 1945–55)', in G. Duby and M. Perrot (eds), *Historia de las mujeres*, vol. V: El siglo XX. Madrid: Taurus, pp. 696–707.

Bourque, S. (1989) 'Gender and the state: perspectives from Latin America', in S. E. Charlton, J. Everett and K. Staudt (eds), *Women, the State and Development*. Albany: State of New York University Press, pp. 114–29.

Bouvard, M. G. (1994) *Revolutionizing Motherhood: the Mothers of the Plaza de Mayo*. Wilmington, DE: Scholarly Resources.

Brodie, J. (1994) 'Shifting the boundaries: gender and the politics of restructuring', in I. Bakker (ed.), *The Strategic Silence: gender and economic policy*. London: Zed Press–North/South Institute, pp. 46–60.

Bruera, S. and González, M. (1993) 'Participación municipal de las mujeres', in *El espacio posible: mujeres en el poder local*, Ediciones de las mujeres, no. 19, pp. 133–51. Santiago: Isis International.

Bryson, V. (1992) *Feminist Political Theory: an introduction*. New York: Paragon House.

Bulmer-Thomas, V. (1994) *The Economic History of Latin America since Independence*. Cambridge: Cambridge University Press.

Bush, D. M. and Mumme S. P. (1994) 'Gender and the Mexican Revolution: the intersection of family, state and church', in M. A. Tétreault (ed.), *Women and Revolution in Africa, Asia and the New World*. Columbia: University of South Carolina Press, pp. 343–75.

Bystydzienski, J. (1992) 'Introduction', in J. Bystydzienski (ed.), *Women Transforming Politics: worldwide strategies for empowerment*. Bloomington: Indiana University Press, pp. 1–8.

Cammack, P. (1994) 'Democratization and citizenship in Latin America', in G. Parry and M. Moran (eds), *Democracy and Democratization*. London: Routledge, pp. 174–95.

Cammack, P. and O'Brien, P. (eds) (1985) *Generals in Retreat: the crisis of military rule in Latin America*. Manchester: Manchester University Press.

Camp, R. (1995) *Politics in Mexico*. Oxford: Oxford University Press.

Carrillo, T. (1990) 'Women and independent unionism in the garment industry', in J. Foweraker and A. Craig (eds), *Popular Movements and Political Change in Mexico*. Boulder, CO: Lynne Reinner, pp. 213–33.

Chaney, E. (1973) 'Women in Latin American politics: the case of Peru and

Chile', in A. Pescatello (ed.), *Female and Male in Latin America*. Pittsburgh: University of Pittsburgh Press, pp. 104–39.

Chant, S. (1991) *Women and Survival in Mexican Cities*. Manchester: Manchester University Press.

Chant, S. (1993) 'Women's work and household change in the 1980s', in N. Harvey (ed.), *Mexico: the dilemmas of transition*. London: British Academic Press, pp. 318–54.

Chant, S. (1994) 'Women and poverty in urban Latin America: Mexican and Costa Rican experiences', in F. Meer (ed.), *Poverty in the 1990s: the responses of urban women*. Paris: UNESCO/International Social Science Council.

Chinchilla, N. S. (1994) 'Feminism, revolution and democratic transition in Nicaragua', in J. Jaquette (ed.), *The Women's Movement in Latin America: participation and democracy*. Boulder, CO: Westview Press, pp. 177–98.

Chuchryk, P. (1994) 'From dictatorship to democracy: the women's movement in Chile', in J. Jaquette (ed.), *The Women's Movement in Latin America: participation and democracy*. Boulder, CO: Westview Press, pp. 65–108.

Cook, M. L. (1996) *Organizing Dissent: unions, the state and the democratic teachers' movement in Mexico*. University Park, PA: Pennsylvania State University Press.

Corcoran Nantes, Y. (1993) 'Female consciousness or feminist consciousness?: women's consciousness raising in community-based struggles in Brazil', in S. Radcliffe and S. Westwood (eds), *'Viva': women and popular protest in Latin America*. London: Routledge, pp. 136–55.

Cortina, R. (1990) 'Gender and power in the teacher's union of Mexico', in *Estudios Mexicanos/Mexican Studies*, 6/2, pp. 241–62.

Craske, N. (1993) 'Women's participation in Mexican urban politics: the case of Guadalajara's low-income neighbourhoods', unpublished Ph.D. thesis, Department of Government, University of Essex.

Craske, N. (1998) 'Remasculinisation and the neoliberal state in Latin America', in G. Waylen and V. Randall (eds), *Gender, Politics and the State*. London: Routledge, pp. 100–20.

Cubitt, T. (1995) *Latin American Society*, 2nd edn. Harlow: Longman.

Cubitt, T. and Greenslade, H. (1997) 'Public and Private Spheres: the end of dichotomy', in E. Dore (ed.), *Gender Politics in Latin America*. New York: Monthly Review Press, pp. 36–51.

Da Silveira, I., Hermida, M. and Nazarenko, N. (1991) 'Presencia de la mujer en la administración pública', in G. Sapriza (ed.), *Mujer y poder: en los márgenes de la democracia uruguaya*. Montevideo: GRECMU, pp. 79–107.

Daines, V. and Seddon, D. (1994) 'Fighting for survival: women's responses to austerity programs', in J. Walton and D. Seddon (eds), *Free Markets and Food Riots: the politics of global adjustment*. Oxford: Blackwell, pp. 57–96.

Delgado González, M. (1994) 'Workers' education for women members of rural workers' organizations in Central America and the Dominican Republic', in M. H. Martens and S. Mitter (eds), *Women in Trade Unions: organizing the unorganized*. Geneva: International Labour Office, pp. 115–29.

Delmar, R. (1986) 'What is feminism?', in J. Mitchell and A. Oakley (eds), *What is Feminism?* Oxford: Blackwell, pp. 8–32.

Deutsch, S. M. (1991) 'Gender and sociopolitical change in twentieth-century Latin America', in *Hispanic American Historical Review*, 71/2, pp. 251–306.

Deutsch, S. M. (1997) 'What difference does gender make? The extreme right in the ABC countries in an era of fascism', in *Estudios Interdisciplinarios de América Latina y el Caribe*, 8/2, pp. 5–21.

Dietz, M. (1989) 'Context is all: feminism and theories of citizenship', in J. Conway, S. Bourque and J. Scott (eds), *Learning about Women: gender, politics and power*. Ann Arbor: University of Michigan Press, pp. 1–24.

Dujovne Ortiz, A. (1997) *Eva Perón: a biography*, trans. S. Fields. London: Warner Books.

Feijoó, M. C. (1994) 'From family ties to political action: women's experiences in Argentina', in B. Nelson and N. Chowdhury (eds), *Women and Politics Worldwide*. New Haven, CT: Yale University Press, pp. 59–72.

Feijoó, M. C. and Gogna, M. (1990) 'Women in the transition to democracy', in E. Jelin (ed.), *Women and Social Change in Latin America*. London: Zed Press/UNRISD, pp. 79–114.

Feijoó, M. C. and Nari, M. M. A. (1994) 'Women and democracy in Argentina', in J. Jaquette (ed.), *The Women's Movement in Latin America: participation and democracy*. Boulder, CO: Westview Press, pp. 109–30.

Fernández Poncela, A. M. (1995) 'Participación social y política de las mujeres en México: un estado de la cuestión', in A. M. Fernández Poncela (ed.), *Las mujeres en México: participación política al final del milenio*. Mexico City: El Colegio de México, pp. 28–84.

Fernández Poncela, A. M. (1997) 'Nicaraguan women: legal, political and social spaces', in E. Dore (ed.), *Gender Politics in Latin America*. New York: Monthly Review Press, pp. 36–51.

Fisher, J. (1993) *Out of the Shadows: women, resistance and politics in South America*. London: LAB.

Foweraker, J. (1989) *Making Democracy in Spain*. Cambridge: Cambridge University Press.

Foweraker, J. (1993) *Popular Mobilization in Mexico*. New York: Cambridge University Press.

Foweraker, J. (1995) *Theorizing Social Movements*. London: Pluto Press.

Foweraker, J. (1997) *Citizenship Rights and Social Movements: a comparative and statistical analysis*. Oxford: Oxford University Press.

Frohmann, A. and Valdés, T. (1993) '*Democracy in the Country and in the*

Home': the women's movement in Chile. Santiago: FLACSO Serie Estudios Sociales.

Gabriel, C. and Macdonald, L. (1994) 'NAFTA, Women and Organizing in Canada and Mexico: forging a "feminist internationality"', in *Millennium: Journal of International Studies*, 23/3, pp. 535–62.

García, B. and de Oliveira, O. (1997) 'Motherhood and extradomestic work in urban Mexico', in *Bulletin of Latin American Research*, 16/3, pp. 367–84.

Gershuny, J. and Berthoud, R. (1997) 'New partnership? Men and women in the 1990s', ESRC Research Centre on Micro-social Change, University of Essex, mimeo.

González Suárez, M. (1994) 'With patience and without blood: the political struggles of Costa Rican women', in B. Nelson and N. Chowdhury (eds), *Women and Politics Worldwide*. New Haven, CT: Yale University Press, pp. 174–88.

Graham, C. (1994) *Safety Nets, Politics and the Poor: transitions to market economies*. Washington, DC: Brookings Institution.

Hellman, J. A. (1997) 'Social movements: revolution, reform and reaction' in *NACLA: Report on the Americas*, 30/6, pp. 13–18.

Henault, M. (1994) 'Gremialismo y participación femenina', in D. Maffía and C. Kuschnir (eds), *Capacitación política para mujeres: género y cambio social en la Argentina actual*. Buenos Aires: Feminaria, pp. 189–203.

IDB (Inter-American Development Bank) (1995) *Women in the Americas: bridging the gender gap*. Washington, DC: Inter-American Development Bank.

Inter-Parliamentary Union (1997) 'Women in national parliaments', <http://www.ipu.org/>

Jaquette, J. (ed.) (1994a) *The Women's Movement in Latin America: participation and democracy*. Boulder, CO: Westview Press.

Jaquette, J. (1994b) 'Introduction: from transition to participation – women's movements and democratic politics', in J. Jaquette (ed.), *The Women's Movement in Latin America: participation and democracy*. Boulder, CO: Westview Press, pp. 1–12.

Jaquette, J. (1994c) 'Conclusion: women's political participation and prospects for democracy', in J. Jaquette (ed.), *The Women's Movement in Latin America: participation and democracy*. Boulder, CO: Westview Press, pp. 223–38.

Jelin, E. (1996) 'Women, Gender and Human Rights', in E. Jelin and E. Hershberg (eds), *Constructing Democracy: human rights, citizenship and society in Latin America*. Boulder, CO: Westview Press, pp. 101–20.

Jelin, E. (1997) 'Engendering human rights', in E. Dore (ed.), *Gender Politics in Latin America: debates in theory and practice*. New York: Monthly Review Press, pp. 65–83.

Joffre Lazarini, R. and Martínez, O. (1994) 'Unions and domestic workers in Mexico City', in M. H. Martens and S. Mitter (eds), *Women in Trade*

Unions: organizing the unorganized. Geneva: International Labour Office, pp. 33–44.

Jones, M. (1996) 'Increasing women's representation via gender quotas: the Argentine *Ley de cupos*' in *Women and Politics*, 16/4, pp. 75–96.

Kampwith, K. (1996) 'The Mother of the Nicaraguans: doña Violeta and the UNO's gender agenda', in *Latin American Perspectives*, 23/1, pp. 67–86.

Kandiyoti, D. (1988) 'Bargaining with patriarchy?', in *Gender and Society*, 2/3, pp. 274–90.

Kaplan, T. (1982) 'Female consciousness and collective action: the case of Barcelona 1910–1918', in *Signs: Journal of Women in Culture and Society*, 7/3, pp. 545–66.

Keen, B. (1996) *A History of Latin America: independence to the present*, 2, 5th edn. Boston: Houghton Mifflin.

Laclau, E. (1987) 'Peronism in historical and comparative perspective', in E. Archetti, P. Cammack and B. Roberts (eds), *Sociology of Developing Societies: Latin America*. London: Macmillan, pp 137–46.

Lamas, M. (1998) 'Scenes from a Mexican battlefield', in *NACLA: Report on the Americas*, 31/4, pp. 17–21.

Lawrence, E. (1994) *Gender and Trade Unions*. London: Taylor & Francis.

Lowden, P. (1993) 'The Ecumenical Committee for Peace in Chile (1973–75): the foundation of moral opposition to authoritarian rule in Chile', in *Bulletin of Latin American Research*, 12/2, pp. 189–205.

Lutjens, S. L. (1994) 'Remaking the public sphere: women and revolution in Cuba', in M. A. Tétreault (ed.), *Women and Revolution in Africa, Asia and the New World*. Columbia: University of South Carolina Press, pp. 366–93.

Macaulay, F. (1996) '"Governing for everyone": the workers' party administration in São Paulo, 1989–1992', in *Bulletin of Latin American Research*, 15/2, pp. 211–30.

McClenaghan, S. (1997) 'Women, work and empowerment: romanticizing the reality', in E. Dore (ed.), *Gender Politics in Latin America*. New York: Monthly Review Press, pp. 19–35.

Machado, L. M. V. (1993) '"We learned to think politically": the influence of the Catholic Church and the feminist movement on the emergence of the health movment of the Jardim Nordeste area in São Paulo, Brazil', in S. Radcliffe and S. Westwood (eds), *'Viva': women and popular protest in Latin America*. London: Routledge, pp. 88–111.

McLellan, D. (1977) *Karl Marx: selected writings*. Oxford: Oxford University Press.

Mainwaring, S. and Scully, T. R. (eds) (1995) *Building Democratic Institutions: party systems in Latin America*. Stanford, CA: Stanford University Press.

Malloy, J. (ed.) (1977) *Authoritarianism and Corporatism in Latin America*. Pittsburgh: University of Pittsburgh Press.

Martens, M. H. (1994) 'Lessons for organizing the unorganized', in M. H. Martens and S. Mitter (eds), *Women in Trade Unions: organizing the unorganized*. Geneva: International Labour Office, pp. 199–202.

Martin, J. (1990) 'Motherhood and power: the production of a women's culture of politics in a Mexican community', in *American Ethnologist*, 17/3, pp. 470–90.

Marx, J. (1994) 'Mujeres, participación política y poder', in D. Maffía and C. Kuschnir (eds), *Capacitación política para mujeres: género y cambio social en la Argentina actual*. Buenos Aires: Feminaria, pp. 123–35.

Massolo, A. (n.d.) 'Caceroleras y acción de mujeres', in *Topodrillo*, no. 21, pp. 34–7.

Massolo, A. and Schteingart, M. (eds) (1987) *Participación social, reconstrucción y mujer: el sismo de 1985*. Documentos de Trabajo #1, Mexico City: PIEM/El Colegio de México/Unicef.

Matear, A. (1995) 'The Servicio Nacional de la Mujer (SERNAM): women and the process of democratic transition in Chile 1990–94', in D. Hojman (ed.), *Neoliberalism with a Human Face? The politics and economics of the Chilean model*. Institute of Latin American Studies, University of Liverpool, Monograph Series no. 20, pp. 93–117.

Matear, A. (1997) 'Gender and the state in rural Chile', in *Bulletin of Latin American Research*, 16/1, pp. 97–105.

Mattelart, M. (1980) 'Chile: the feminine version of the coup d'état', in J. Nash and H. I. Safa (eds), *Sex and Class in Latin America*. South Hadley, MA: J. F. Bergin, pp. 279–301.

Mazur, A. and Stetson, D. M. (1995) 'Conclusions: the case for state feminism', in A. Mazur and D. M. Stetson (eds), *Comparative State Feminism*. Thousand Oaks, CA: Sage, pp. 272–91.

Miller, F. (1991) *Latin American Women and the Search for Social Justice*. Hanover, NH, and London: University of New England Press.

Mitter, S. (1994) 'A comparative survey', in M. H. Martens and S. Mitter (eds), *Women in Trade Unions: organizing the unorganized*. Geneva: International Labour Office, pp. 3–14.

Mohr Peterson, J. (1990) 'Gender subjectivity and popular urban movements in Mexico', paper presented at the seminar *Fronteras, Puentes y Barreras*, mimeo.

Molyneux, M. (1985) 'Mobilization without emancipation? Women's interests, the state and revolution in Nicaragua', in *Feminist Studies*, 11/2, pp. 227–54.

Molyneux, M. (1996) *State, Gender and Institutional Change in Cuba's 'Special Period': the Federación de Mujeres Cubanas*. London: Institute of Latin American Studies, Research Paper #43.

Molyneux, M. (1998) 'Analysing women's movements', in *Development and Change*, 29/2, pp. 219–45.

Moore, H. (1988) *Feminism and Anthropology*. Cambridge: Polity Press.

Munck, G. (1990) 'Identity and ambiguity in democratic struggles', in

J. Foweraker and A. Craig (eds), *Popular Movements and Political Change in Mexico*. Boulder, CO: Lynne Reinner, pp. 23–42.

Napolitano, V. (1998) 'Between "traditional" and "new" Catholic Church religious discourses in urban western Mexico', in *Bulletin of Latin American Research*, 17/3.

Navarro, M. (1982) 'Evita's charismatic leadership', in M. Coniff (ed.), *Latin American Populism in Comparative Perspective*. Albuqueque, University of New Mexico Press, pp. 47–66.

Navarro, M. (1985) 'Hidden, silent and anonymous: women workers in the Argentine trade union movement', in N. Soldon (ed.), *The World of Women's Trade Unionism*. Wesport, CT: Greenwood Press, pp. 165–98.

Nazzari, M. (1983) 'The "woman question" in Cuba: an analysis of material constraints on its solution', in *Signs: Journal of Women in Culture and Society*, 9/21, pp. 246–63.

Pateman, C. (1992) 'Equality, difference, subordination: the politics of motherhood and women's citizenship', in G. Bock and S. James (eds), *Beyond Equality and Difference: citizenship, feminist politics and female subjectivity*. London: Routledge, pp. 17–31.

Pearson, R. (1991) 'Male bias and women's work in Mexico's border industries', in D. Elson (ed.), *Male Bias in the Development Process*. Manchester: Manchester University Press, pp. 133–63.

Pearson, R. (1992) 'Gender issues in industrialization', in T. Hewitt, H. Johnson and D. Wield (eds), *Industrialization and Development*. Oxford: Open University Press and Oxford University Press, pp. 222–47.

Peña, D. (1987) '*Tortuosidad*: shop floor struggles of female *maquiladora* workers', in V. Ruiz and S. Tiano (eds), *Women on the US–Mexican Border: responses to change*. Boston: Allen & Unwin, pp. 129–54.

Perelli, C. (1994) 'The uses of conservatism: women's democratic politics in Uruguay', in J. Jaquette (ed.), *The Women's Movement in Latin America: participation and democracy*. Boulder, CO: Westview Press, pp. 131–50.

Phillips, A. (1991) *Engendering Democracy*. Cambridge: Polity Press.

Pietilä, H. and Vickers, J. (1994) *Making Women Matter: the role of the United Nations*. London: Zed Press.

Pinto, M. B. F. (1993) 'Ejecutivo local en femenino', in *El espacio posible: mujeres en el poder local*, Ediciones de las Mujeres, no. 19, pp. 67–96. Santiago: Isis International.

Poole, D. and Rénique, G. (1992) *Peru: time of fear*. London: Latin American Bureau.

Prates, S. (1989) 'Organizations for domestic workers in Montevideo: reinforcing marginality?', in E. Chaney and M. García Castro (eds), *Muchachas No More: household workers in Latin America and the Caribbean*. Philadelphia: Temple University Press, pp. 271–90.

Pringle, R. and Watson, S. (1992) '"Women's interests" and the poststructuralist state', in M. Barrett and A. Phillips (eds), *Destabilizing Theory: contemporary feminist debates*. Cambridge: Polity Press, pp. 53–73.

Psacharopoulos, G. and Tzannatos, Z. (1992) *Women's Employment and Pay in Latin America: overview and methodology*. Washington, DC: World Bank.

Radcliffe, S. (1993) '"People have to rise up – like the great women fighters": the state and peasant women in Peru', in S. Radcliffe and S. Westwood (eds), *'Viva': women and popular protest in Latin America*. London: Routledge.

Radcliffe, S. and Westwood, S. (eds) (1993) *'Viva': women and popular protest in Latin America*. London: Routledge.

Rai, S. (1996) 'Women and the state in the Third World', in H. Afshar (ed.), *Women and Politics in the Third World*. London: Routledge, pp. 25–39.

Ramos Escandón, C. (1994) 'Women's movement, feminism and Mexican politics', in J. Jaquette (ed.), *The Women's Movement in Latin America: participation and democracy*. Boulder, CO: Westview Press, pp. 199–222.

Randall, M. (1981) *Women in Cuba: twenty years later*. Brooklyn, NY: Smyrna Press.

Randall, M. (1994) *Sandino's Daughters Revisited: feminism in Nicaragua*. New Brunswick, NJ: Rutgers University Press.

Randall, V. (1987) *Women and Politics: an international perspective*, 2nd edn. London: Macmillan.

Rigat-Pflaum, M. (1991) *Sindicatos: ¿un espacio para hombres y mujeres?* Buenos Aires: FESUR.

Roberts, K. (1995) 'Neoliberalism and the transformation of populism in Latin America: the Peruvian case', in *World Politics*, 48/1, pp. 82–116.

Rodríguez, L. (1994) 'Barrio women: between the urban and feminist movement', in *Latin American Perspectives*, 21/3, pp. 32–48.

Rodríguez, V. E. (ed.) (1995) *Memoria of the Bi-National Conference: Women in Contemporary Mexican Politics*. Austin: Mexican Centre of ILAS, University of Texas.

Roldán, M. (1993) 'Industrial restructuring, deregulation and new JIT labour processes in Argentina: towards a gender-aware perspective?', in *IDS Bulletin*, 24/2, pp. 42–52.

Roxborough, I. (1987) 'Populism and class conflict', in E. Archetti, P. Cammack and B. Roberts (eds), *Sociology of 'Developing Societies': Latin America*. London: Macmillan, pp. 119–24.

Safa, H. (1995) 'Economic restructuring and gender subordination', in *Latin American Perspectives*, 22/2, pp. 32–50.

Schild, V. (1994) 'Recasting "popular" movements: gender and political learning in neighborhood organizations in Chile', in *Latin American Perspectives*, 21/2, pp. 59–80.

Schirmer, J. (1993) 'The seeking of truth and the gendering of consciousness: the Comadres of El Salvador and the Conavigua widows of Guatemala', in S. Radcliffe and S. Westwood (eds), *'Viva': women and popular protest in Latin America*. London: Routledge, pp. 30–64.

Scott, A. M. (1994) *Divisions and Solidarities: gender, class and employment in Latin America*. London: Routledge.

Scott, J. C. (1985) *Weapons of the Weak: everyday forms of peasant resistance.* New Haven, CT: Yale University Press.

Sheahan, J. (1987) *Patterns of Development in Latin America: poverty, repression and economic strategy.* Princeton, NJ: Princeton University Press.

Skidmore, T. and Smith, P. (1997) *Modern Latin America*, 4th edn. Oxford: Oxford University Press.

Smith, H. (1993) *Nicaragua: self-determination and survival.* London: Pluto Press.

Smith, P. (1992) 'The political impact of free trade on Mexico', in *Journal of Interamerican Studies and World Affairs*, 34/1, pp. 1–25.

Soto, S. (1990) *Emergence of the Modern Mexican Woman: her participation in the revolution and struggle for equality 1910–1940.* Denver, CO: Arden Press.

Sparr, P. (ed.) (1994a) *Mortgaging Women's Lives.* London: Zed Press.

Sparr, P. (1994b) 'What is structural adjustment?', in P. Sparr (ed.), *Mortgaging Women's Lives.* London: Zed Press.

Staudt, K. (1987) 'Programming women's empowerment: a case from northern Mexico', in V. Ruiz and S. Tiano (eds), *Women on the US–Mexican Border: responses to change.* Boston: Allen & Unwin, pp. 155–73.

Stephen, L. (1989) 'Popular feminism in Mexico', in *Zeta* (Baja California), mimeo.

Sternbach, N. S., Navarro Aranguren, M., Chuchryk, P. and Alvarez, S. (1992) 'Feminisms in Latin America: from Bogotá to San Bernardo', in A. Escobar and S. Alvarez (eds), *The Making of Social Movements in Latin America.* Boulder, CO: Westview Press, pp. 207–39.

Stetson, D. M. and Mazur, A. (eds) (1995a) *Comparative State Feminism.* Thousand Oaks, CA: Sage.

Stetson, D. M. and Mazur, A. (1995b) 'Introduction', in D. M. Stetson and A. Mazur (eds), *Comparative State Feminism.* Thousand Oaks, CA: Sage, pp. 1–21.

Stevens, E. (1973) '*Marianismo*: the other face of *machismo* in Latin America', in A. Pescatello (ed.), *Female and Male in Latin America.* Pittsburgh: University of Pittsburgh Press, pp. 89–101.

Stubbs, J. (1994) 'Revolutionizing women, family and power', in B. Nelson and N. Chowdhury (eds), *Women and Politics Worldwide.* New Haven, CT: Yale University Press, pp. 189–207.

Supplee, J. (1994) 'Women and the counter-revolutions in Chile', in M. A. Tétreault (ed.), *Women and Revolution in Africa, Asia, and the New World.* Columbia: University of South Carolina Press, pp. 394–414.

Tabak, F. (1994) 'Women and the struggle for democracy and equal rights in Brazil', in B. Nelson and N. Chowdhury (eds), *Women and Politics Worldwide.* New Haven, CT: Yale University Press, pp. 127–41.

Taylor, L. (1996) 'Civilising civil society: distracting popular politics from politics itself' in I. Hampshire-Monk and J. Stanyer (eds), *Contemporary*

Political Studies 1996, vol. 2, Proceedings of the Annual Conference of the PSA, Glasgow, pp. 778–85.

Tiano, S. (1984) 'The public–private dichotomy: theoretical perspectives on "women in development"', in *Social Science Journal*, 21/4, pp. 11–28.

Tirado, S. (1994) 'Weaving dreams, constructing realities: the 19 September National Union of Garment Workers in Mexico', in S. Rowbotham and S. Mitter (eds), *Dignity and Daily Bread*. London: Routledge, pp. 100–13.

Tong, R. (1989) *Feminist Thought: a comprehensive introduction*. London: Routledge.

UN (United Nations) (1995) *The World's Women 1995: trends and statistics*. New York: United Nations.

Valdés, T. and Gomáriz, E. (1995) *Latin American Women: compared figures*. Santiago: FLACSO and Instituto de la Mujer (Madrid).

Vargas, V. (1992) 'The feminist movement in Latin America: between hope and disenchantment', in *Development and Change*, 23/3, pp. 195–214.

Varley, A. (1996) 'Women-heading households: some more equal than others?', in *World Development*, 24/3, pp. 505–20.

Véliz, E. and Aguilar, C. (1992) *Mujeres Latinoamericanas en cifras: Cuba*. Santiago: FLACSO/Instituto de la Mujer (Madrid).

Villarroel Smeall G. (1994) 'Women, Adamocracy, and the Bolivian social revolution', in M. A. Tétreault (ed.), *Women and Revolution in Africa, Asia and the New World*. Columbia: University of South Carolina Press, pp. 319–42.

Volk, S. (1997) 'Democracy versus democracy', in *NACLA: Report on the Americas*, 30/4, pp. 6–12.

Waylen, G. (1993) 'Women's movements and democratisation in Latin America', in *Third World Quarterly*, 14/3, pp. 573–87.

Waylen, G. (1996a) *Gender in Third World Politics*. Buckingham: Open University Press.

Waylen, G. (1996b) 'Analysing women in politics of the Third World', in H. Afshar (ed.), *Women and Politics in the Third World*. London: Routledge, pp. 7–24.

Waylen G. (1996c) 'Gender and democratic consolidation', paper presented at the Annual Meeting of the American Political Science Association, San Francisco.

Wilson, F. (1993) 'Workshops as domestic domains: reflections on small-scale industry in Mexico', in *World Development*, 21/1, pp. 67–80.

Index

DEMCO